Wise Social Studies Teaching in an Age of High-Stakes Testing

Essays on Classroom Practices and Possibilities

A volume in
Research in Curriculum and Instruction
O.L. Davis, Jr., *Series Editor*

Research in Curriculum and Instruction

O.L. Davis, Jr., *Series Editor*

2005 *Wise Social Studies Teaching in an Age of High Stakes Testing*
Edited by Elizabeth Anne Yeager and O.L. Davis, Jr.

2005 *Deep Change: Cases and Commentary on Schools and Programs of Successful Reform in High Stakes States*
Edited by Gerald Ponder and David Strahan

2005 *Exposing a Culture of Neglect: Herschel T. Manuel and Mexican American Schooling*
By Matthew D. Davis

2004 *Explorations in Curriculum History Research*
Edited by Lynn M. Burlbaw and Sherry L. Field

2003 *Narrative Inquiries of School Reform: Storied Lives, Storied Landscapes, Storied Metaphors*
By Cheryl J. Craig

Wise Social Studies Teaching in an Age of High-Stakes Testing

Essays on Classroom Practices and Possibilities

Edited by

Elizabeth Anne Yeager
University of Florida

and

O.L. Davis, Jr.
The University of Texas at Austin

INFORMATION AGE
PUBLISHING

Greenwich, Connecticut 06830 • www.infoagepub.com

Library of Congress Cataloging-in-Publication Data

Wise social studies teaching in an age of high-stakes testing : essays on classroom practices and possibilities / edited by Elizabeth Anne Yeager, O. L. Davis, Jr.
   p. cm. – (Research in curriculum and instruction)
 Includes bibliographical references and index.
 ISBN 1-59311-372-2 (pbk.) – ISBN 1-59311-373-0 (hardcover)
 1. Social sciences–Study and teaching (Elementary)–United States. 2. Social sciences–Study and teaching (Secondary)–United States. 3. Effective teaching–United States. I. Yeager, Elizabeth Anne, 1960- II. Davis, O. L. (Ozro Luke), 1928- III. Series.
 LB1584.W54 2005
 300'.71–dc22
                                                2005013179

Copyright © 2005 Information Age Publishing Inc.

All rights reserved. No part of this publication may be reproduced, stored in a retrieval system, or transmitted, in any form or by any means, electronic, mechanical, photocopying, microfilming, recording or otherwise, without written permission from the publisher.

Printed in the United States of America

CONTENTS

Foreword
    O.L. Davis, Jr.   *vii*

1. Introduction: The "Wisdom of Practice" in the Challenging Context of Standards and High-Stakes Testing
    Elizabeth Anne Yeager   *1*

2. "I'm Not Saying These Are Going To Be Easy": Wise Practice in an Urban Elementary School
    Keith C. Barton   *11*

3. How She Stopped Worrying and Learned to Love the Test...Sort Of
    Andrea S. Libresco   *33*

4. Voices of Florida Elementary School Teachers: Their Conceptions of Wise Social Studies Practice
    Diane Yendol-Hoppey, Jennifer Jacobs, and Keith Tilford   *51*

5. A Good Teacher in Texas: Conversations about Wisdom in Middle School Social Studies Practice
    Mary Lee Webeck, Cinthia S. Salinas, and Sherry L. Field   *69*

6. The Impact of Accountability Reform on the "Wise Practice" of Secondary History Teachers: The Virginia Experience
    Stephanie D. van Hover and Walter F. Heinecke   *89*

7. More Journey Than End: A Case Study of Ambitious Teaching
    S.G. Grant   *117*

8. Wise Practice in an Innovative Public School
    Diana Hess   *131*

9. Wise Practice in High School Social Studies: The Case of Joe Gotchy
Bruce Larson   *153*

10. Engaging Pedagogy in an Advanced Placement European History Classroom
John K. Lee   *165*

11. A Journey Toward Wiser Practice in the Teaching of American History
Timothy Kelly and Bruce VanSledright   *183*

About the Authors   *203*

FOREWORD

Many contemporary educational reformers, especially politicians, bureaucrats, and too many school administrators, insist that certain dimensions of teaching are better than all others. These "best practices," they believe, are universal, consistently applicable, and effective with all students in all schools. This belief is based on neither clear-cut research nor reflected experience. In essence, it is only a hunch (sometimes an hypothesis) clothed in ideology. "Best practices" has become, moreover, a triumphant slogan.

These true-believing reformers admit only one problem with their belief in best practices. For teaching in general as well as in specific curriculum fields, none of these best practices have yet been identified. This problem, they insist, is both trivial and temporary. These advocates, clinging tightly to the NCLB-related federal mandates, believe that the problem can and will be solved in due course through the use of research designs proven valuable in fields like medicine, but not commonly used in education.

Indeed, these beliefs currently highlight substantial research efforts currently underway in the teaching of reading. On the basis of a vigorously contested decision that almost all 20th-century research in reading was hopelessly inadequate, federal policymakers and bureaucrats have selected one set of teaching procedures as best practices in the teaching of reading. Only these phonics-based practices receive available federal research funds for studies of teaching. Thus, research on best practices in the teaching of reading appears, contrary to the announced logic of best practices, to precede rather than follow decisions that such practices should be employed in all the schools of the nation. Simply, ideological advocacy of predetermined practices has converted the asserted research endeavor into shameful efforts of legitimation. This situation, viewed within the frameworks of public educational policy as well as in scientific inquiry and the improvement of teaching practices, is serious and troubling. Politics, however, routinely trumps reason. Continuation of this fundamentally flawed research emphasis and empty rhetorical advocacy likely will continue into an indefinite future.

Perhaps, on the other hand, this unmerited and rigid federal grip on reading instruction offers especially fruitful opportunities to improve teaching in other school subjects such as history. Elizabeth Anne Yeager and I, along with authors of the chapters included in this book, believe that such opportunities surely exist . . . at least for a time. Moreover, we believe that quite a number of teachers and researchers also recognize these prospects and desire to focus their efforts along more richly productive lines. Choosing a road much less traveled but more logically clear, we make available in this volume a number of descriptions and interpretations of what we call "wise practices" in the teaching of history in American elementary and secondary schools.

Teaching practice is wise, in large part, because *it is not generalizeable* across students in class groups of different schools and in different circumstances. As such, it is the polar opposite of the attributes of best practices. Wise practice *attends to particularities* . . . for example, the instruction of Eric Mendoza and others in his fifth grade who are studying aspects of the industrial revolution in their American history class taught by Miss Spearman during the fourth period of the day on March 9, 2005, in Annie Purl Elementary School in Georgetown, Texas, during the second presidential administration of George W. Bush. In this very important respect, wise teaching relates conspicuously to Joseph Schwab's understanding of the practical in curriculum inquiry. Wise practices constitute the enacted decisions derived from deliberation about practical matters, ones that are *not* problems to be solved, but, rather, ones having to do with issues for which decisions must be made.

This characterization of wise and best practices, however appropriate, is also too categorical. Some, maybe many, practices identified as best through research and/or experience reasonably may be chosen by teachers to use in the conduct of the particulars of their wise teaching. Similarly, researchers and others may identify quite a number of practices employed by wise teachers as best practices. The points of difference between these two general aspects of practice, however, must not be obscured by an insistence that their similarities are practically and conceptually more important than their differences. These two types of practice differ significantly for two very different reasons.

Probably most importantly, wise practices are *embedded within* teachers' knowledge of the subject matter of the course/subject being taught. Another way of phrasing this circumstance is that wise practices are embedded within the subject that feeds from the intellectual discipline or practical art to which it is related. In this regard, "wise" practices *cannot be* "best" practices. Simply, wise practices in the teaching of a particular history lesson reasonably may *not* be wise when employed in other history lessons. As well, wise practices in the teaching of history reasonably are *not* wise in the teaching of other subjects (e.g., literature, chemistry). This idea, further, does *not* suggest that elementary and secondary school teachers of history use their university professors' lectures as a model for their development and use of their own wise practices. Similarly, the current popularity of DBQs (document-based questions) only *may be* a dimension of wise teaching practice in elementary and secondary history offerings. The best of these exercises are absent a number of essential elements that would make them even vaguely congruent with historians' examination and evaluation of documents and their composition of a meaningful narrative in which the document(s) provide substantial legitimacy to proffered claims. The development and use of wise teaching practices in history, particularly for elementary and secondary teachers, depends on teachers' continuing, mindful translation of their substantial content knowledge of history into pedagogical content knowledge.

Another fundamental difference between wise practices and best practices appears to be transparent. Teachers *control* both their *decisions* to employ and their *use* of wise practices. That is, they ponder, select, employ, and reflect on their practices. In powerful contrast, teachers *do not control* their use of best practices.

Indeed, underlying the whirlwind of advocacy of best practices is the conviction that every "best practice" is *better* than any other possible practice in the teaching of all students in all courses in all schools under all circumstances. On the basis of this illogical belief, the advocacy has established a mindless orthodoxy of essential events within the bureaucracies of American schooling. This theoretical ordering, on the other hand, fails to account for political meddling, as in the case of federalized decisions to stress exclusively phonics-based reading programs. The orthodoxy of research and implementation, nevertheless, remains. First, "best practices" must be identified. Second, bureaucratic mavens (e.g., U.S. Department of Education and state agency officials) mandate that teachers employ these "best practices" in their teaching. Third, other authorities (e.g., state agency bureaucrats, senior school administrators) must invent means by which teachers will be rewarded for their use of these practices and punished if they do not use them. This practical distinction between wise practices and best practices is stark, brutal, and harsh.

At least two more general caveats about wise practices must be recognized. Each merits elaborated discussion.

One, to call some practices as wise absolutely is not to label them as *good*. Neither should other practices, even best practices, be identified as *bad*. Use of the adjectives *good* and *bad* commonly mean that value or worth (of an indeterminate nature) is asserted as a general attribute.

Thus, for example, "discussion is a good teaching practice in the teaching of history" asserts that all discussion in all teaching situations in history and for all purposes, to mention only three aspects of the practical, always has positive value. Another example is "lecturing (teacher talk to students) is a bad teaching practice in history." Experienced teachers and observers understand both of these claims to be vacuous. Similarly, some practices used by wise teachers that likely will make but a few "top ten" lists are not necessarily "off limits" for use. Common sense supports these observations. Surely, as individuals read the portrayals of wise teaching in this volume's chapters, they will note some that they believe are very productive and others that they find objectionable. Also, readers may detect errors of historical fact and interpretation in teacher quotations even as they may forget (or deride as flaws in teacher knowledge) about the ordinary dailiness and the extraordinary rapidity of classroom interactions. Still, the practices that are portrayed here were not scripted nor should they be judged either good or bad. As good as these reports are, we readers do not know enough to make such judgments. Decidedly more importantly, we cannot talk with the teacher about the issue in question, the reasoning that prompted the decision to use a particular practice, the phrasing of assertions and questions, and his or her reflection about those decisions. The criteria of worth, consequently, must be about *appropriateness and intentionality as understood by the teacher* who has decided, on the basis of serious deliberation, that the specific practice(s) should be used in the particular(s) of the specific teaching situation. Furthermore, in teaching wisely, "anything goes" is neither acceptable nor responsible. Teachers' employment of wise practices carries the obligation, if asked, to explain and justify the decisions that they have made.

Two, teachers' once-wise practices can degenerate into only personally preferred practices. Such a situation robs the possible distinction of wise from the practices that teachers use in the varying particulars that they encounter in their teaching. In fact, teachers' personally preferred and routinely used practices are strong candidates to become another kind of "best practices." These practices are ones that individual teachers may come to believe are "effective" or "good" or "useful" for them, but perhaps not for other teachers' use in their teaching. This prospect—in our culture that exalts the "best" of things, from soaps and suits and surgeries to music and mothers and machines—is as deceptively reasonable as it is logically and educationally unacceptable. Still, the power of teachers' personal preferences in the construction and abandonment of their wise teaching practices must be acknowledged.

In light of this rationale, perhaps a more prominent emphasis of this book should have been "toward *wiser* practices" in the teaching of history. That meaning captures much of the intent of this book's researchers and editors. Nevertheless, we believe that the book's current title and emphasis represent the state of current knowledge and research. We also understand that a possible future collection of essays will feature the ongoing search for *wiser* practices.

As editor of this Research in Curriculum and Instruction series, I believe that this volume offers much of value to the educational enterprise, not solely to the teaching of history in schools. I am confident, in particular, that history teachers, teacher educators, and researchers will find the book's essays to be informative, stimulating, and, possibly, provocative. That this collected research fosters reflection and inquiry, as well as theoretical development and argumentation, would be generous praise. Especially, I hope that this effort will prompt teachers and scholars in other curriculum fields to wonder about, to explore, and to describe and interpret wise teaching practices in their own areas. Such work can only add richness and higher quality to the pursuits undertaken here.

Welcome to the consideration of and the continuing search for both wise and wiser teaching practices in history.

—O. L. Davis, Jr.
Catherine Mae Parker Centennial
Professor of Curriculum and Instruction,
The University of Texas at Austin

CHAPTER 1

INTRODUCTION

The "Wisdom of Practice" in the Challenging Context of Standards and High-Stakes Testing

Elizabeth Anne Yeager

Teaching in public schools today, in the context of the "shell game" that is high-stakes testing, must be completely frustrating: alternately pressured and frenetic, unimaginative and stifling. If we are not asking why anyone would want to teach in this climate, the curious among us must be asking how and what anyone *could* teach in it. That is, if teachers want to practice what they have learned about pedagogy that fosters both student achievement and student engagement, how and where do they do it? In the field of social studies, in particular, what are good teachers to do? What are their options if social studies is tested, especially if the assessment is narrowly conceived? Equally important, what are the options if social studies is *not* on the test because it is not considered essential to the curriculum?

Researchers have begun to accumulate data documenting the impact of the recent emphasis on state-mandated curriculum standards and high-stakes testing on student learning, teacher identity, professional development, and, most important, on effective and meaningful instruction, including in social studies (e.g., Amrein & Berliner, 2002; Black & Valenzuela, 2004; Bustos-Flores & Riojas-Clark, 2003; Corbett and Wilson, 1991; Grant, 1997a, 1997b, 2001a, 2001b; Grant et al., 2001, 2002a, 2002b; Hoffmann et al., 2001; Koretz, 2002; McNeil, 2000; Ohanian, 1999; Shepard, 2000; Smith, 1991; Valenzuela, 2002; Wright, 2002). Indeed, some of these reports paint a distressing picture of where schools are headed as they become trapped in a steady stream of educational mandates.

Given this climate in U.S. public schools, the challenges and possibilities of teaching social studies within the context of mandatory state standards and high-stakes testing are worth exploring. Certainly, each contributor to this book believes that social studies is a potentially powerful, engaging, and relevant curriculum area for a variety of students in myriad school settings, not just for students who are already motivated and interested in learning more about the world around them. Each also believes that more research, including case studies, should focus specifically on effective practice in settings where mandatory curriculum standards and assessments influence what happens (or does not happen) with the teaching of social studies.

The chapters in this volume illustrate how teachers are bringing creativity, higher-order thinking, and meaningful learning activities into particular school settings despite pressures of standards and testing. We chose the word *wise* for the title of this book, and we use it frequently to describe the pedagogical practices we have identified. The words *powerful* and *ambitious* are used as well. The larger point, as Keith C. Barton makes in his chapter, is that there is no necessary connection between content standards and high-stakes tests on the one hand, and low-level, rote instruction on the other. He reminds us, as Thornton (1991) and Wiggins (1987) previously have argued, that "teachers play a crucial role in mediating educational policy, and their intentions and interpretations have at least as much influence on classroom practice as does the content of standards and high-stakes tests." Barton also asserts that "this makes it all the more crucial to identify the wisdom of practice that enables teachers... to engage students in powerful educational experiences."

Mary Lee Webeck, Cinthia S. Salinas, and Sherry L. Field ask in their chapter, "How is it that teachers make choices about their practice in light of the standards and high-stakes testing climate in contemporary schools? How do teachers, practicing wisely, create spaces in which to balance curriculum enactment with the stresses many teachers feel in response to mandated testing?" Such inquiry is an important focus at a time when teaching "may be perceived to have drifted away from the notion of quality and contextualized learning and toward test-based teaching and learning."

Davis (1997) has pointed out that specific characteristics of wise practice are likely to differ from one context to another, and that they are always situated thoroughly in their context. As S. G. Grant states in his chapter, "A view of the multiple and interacting influences on teachers' work cautions against separating teachers and their practices from the contexts in which they work." Davis also argues, "Recognizable and ordinary individuals use [their practices] in real, specific circumstances. And consequently, when other professionals learn about these wise practices, they acknowledge the reports' enhanced authenticity and credibility."

Nonetheless, some researchers have noted the lack of a rich "history of practice" in teaching and in the teaching of social studies. Shulman (1987), for example, remarked on the rarity of "richly developed portrayals of expertise in teaching" that address teachers' management of *ideas* within classroom discourse, not simply their management of student behavior. An emphasis on various forms of teacher knowledge and their relationship to teaching effectiveness, he argues, is needed "if our portrayals of good practice are to serve as sufficient guides to the design of better education."

Stanley (1991), in his chapter on teacher competence *in The Handbook of Research on Social Studies Teaching and Learning*, also comments on the lack of research on wise teaching practice. Although social studies researchers have gradually shifted their focus to "extraordinary or expert social studies teachers in an attempt to describe what levels of teacher competence are possible and how these are achieved," the teaching profession still has a unique problem because most records of excellent practice are "lost to others" as teaching takes place without peer observation. "Identification of the wisdom of practice revealed in the behavior of expert teachers," Stanley argues, should be a central goal of those who study teacher competence and effectiveness.

Shulman (1987) argues, then, that "wisdom of practice" can and must be codified through an extensive "case literature." Experienced teachers simply possess a great deal of knowledge and understandings that they have not formally articulated. One of the most important tasks of the research community, he states, is to work with these practitioners to "develop representations of the practical pedagogical wisdom of able teachers." Consistent with Davis's and Grant's statements above, Shulman argues in favor of keeping these accounts "highly contextualized, especially with respect to the content-specificity of the pedagogical strategies employed." In doing so, he reasons, it is possible to contribute to the documentation of good practice "as a significant source for teaching standards" and to "lay a foundation for a scholarly literature that records the details and rationales for specific pedagogical practice."

Stanley (1991) also calls for "knowledge of how different content and classroom contexts influence effective teaching." Echoing Shulman, he states that teachers are not trying to "teach generically"; rather, they teach toward some specific outcome related to the content. In his view, criteria for judging teacher effectiveness could be based on Shulman's categories of teacher knowledge, especially content and pedagogical content knowledge, knowledge of curriculum, and knowledge of learners and educational contexts, as well as on their ability to teach critical thinking, judgment, and problem solving. Teacher effectiveness, he states, is ultimately a blend of "technical, practical, and critical expertise" in many areas.

Clearly, teacher effectiveness in social studies must not be conceptualized too narrowly; these conceptions will continue to be both subjective and slippery. One helpful conception of "powerful teaching" in social studies was articulated by the National Council for the Social Studies (NCSS) in 1993. Informed by the goals of social studies education as well as the research literature, an NCSS task force identified five key characteristics of ideal social studies teaching and learning. These features are summarized in the task force's statement that social studies teaching is powerful when it is meaningful, integrative, value-based, challenging, and active. *Meaningful* social studies teaching encourages students to use connected, thematic networks of knowledge that will be useful to them as lifelong learners and that connects with their interests, focuses on in-depth treatment of fewer topics rather than shallow coverage of many, and incorporates authentic activities and assessments that encourage students to apply content in appropriate ways. For social studies to be *integrative*, teachers must address a broad range of forms of knowledge that crosses disciplinary boundaries with a variety of resources and activities. *Value-based* teaching means that teachers have awareness of their own values and how these influence their teaching; it also means that teachers address controversial and ethical issues appropriate to social studies and promote critical thinking and decision making. Teachers must also make the content *challenging* while ensuring that it meets students' developmental needs; such teachers encourage serious and thoughtful inquiry through the instructional activities they choose. Finally, teachers must ensure that social studies is an *active* learning experience through their development of curricula that encourage students to discover knowledge, to use a variety of instructional materials and authentic activities, to relate the content to their own lives, to engage in reflection discussion, to assume responsibility for their own learning, and to develop new understandings through a process of active construction of meaning. Finally, teachers themselves must model subject knowledge, intellectual curiosity, and the joy of learning.

Some studies of wise practice in history have informed the field of social studies more generally. The relationship between effective history instruction and the development of students' historical understanding has been explored by all of the contributors to this book. In addition, Wineburg and Wilson's (1988) case study of two history teachers constitutes a rich description of teaching approaches that engaged students through research, debate, critical thinking, interpretation, and analysis of sources beyond the textbook. These teachers were effective in stimulating class discussion and dialogue, personalizing the material, raising controversial issues, and conveying excitement about the content.

One of the most important contributions of research on effective social studies instruction is the finding that teachers' knowledge of their subject is a major factor in, perhaps the foundation of, their effectiveness. Nonetheless, we do not suggest in this book that this content knowledge alone makes better teachers. As Shulman explains, teachers' pedagogical content knowledge is also central to good practice. In other words, teachers must possess "that special amalgam of content and pedagogy that is uniquely the province of teachers, their own special form of pedagogical understanding," as well as knowledge of learners and learning that help them translate their content knowledge into forms that their students can understand. According to Shulman, teachers are familiar not only with scholarship in their discipline, but also with educational materials and structures, formal educational scholarship, and the "wisdom of practice" that guide the practices of able teachers. They also understand processes of pedagogical reasoning and action, from comprehension of ideas and translation of them for their particular students, to instructional approaches, evaluation methods, opportunities for reflection, and the generation of new comprehension from their experiences.

Some key characteristics of wise practice that emerge from the 10 chapters in this book incorporate the ideas discussed above and suggest others:

- Teachers show a good grasp of content knowledge and pedagogical content knowledge and can "translate" this in effective and interesting ways for students.
- Teachers show enthusiasm for their content, model intellectual curiosity, and interact frequently with their students, whatever the form of instruction may be.
- Teachers promote critical thinking and/or problem solving appropriate to the discipline they are teaching.
- Teachers may use different instructional approaches at different times, but whatever approach they take involves students in inquiry, meaningful issues, and classroom activities in which stimulating questions are explored and students have substantial intellectual responsibility.
- Teachers bring in meaningful material beyond the textbook and engage students in using sources appropriate to the discipline.
- Teachers attend to their students' academic skills while engaging them in social studies content; for example, they provide opportunities for reading, writing, and learning basic research methodologies.

Keith C. Barton's chapter, "'I'm Not Saying These are Going to be Easy': Wise Practice in an Urban Elementary School," identifies three elements of Leslie King's wisdom of practice. Although state standards and high-stakes testing are prominent in this setting, and although much of the school's population has traditionally been underserved by formal schooling, this teacher provides students with experiences that are consistent with principles of powerful social studies instruction. First, she treats them with intellectual respect by taking their interests and backgrounds seriously, striving to build on their prior knowledge, and giving them opportunities to engage in self-directed learning. In addition, she involves students in challenging assignments, particularly inquiry projects in which they have to locate and use a variety of resources; during these projects she is especially skilled at scaffolding their engagement in unfamiliar tasks. Finally, she organizes instruction into integrated units so that she meets required standards without breaking the curriculum into isolated topics or skills. Her commitment to these principles stems from both her ongoing reflection on practice and her commitment to learning goals that extend beyond content coverage and classroom management.

Andrea S. Libresco's chapter, "How She Learned to Stop Worrying and Love the Test...Sort Of," examines an exemplary veteran fourth-grade teacher in a suburban school in New York who must prepare her students for the state test administered in the fall of fifth grade. Before the implementation of the testing requirements, Paula Marron already exhibited many attributes of wise practice (e.g., modeling intellectual curiosity, promoting critical thinking and student intellectual responsibility, and attending to her students' academic skills while engaging them in social studies content). The imposition of a state social studies test does not stifle any of these practices. Rather, Paula is able to adapt and extend her wise practices. She translates her improved grasp of content knowledge into effective and interesting activities for students and uses meaningful primary source materials in addition to the textbook. This case study illustrates how an exceptional teacher is able to move in significantly new directions, with thoughtful, ongoing professional development, and, notwithstanding legitimate apprehensions and pressures, turn the test mandates into stimuli for new and expanded wise practices in social studies.

As increased pressures from high-stakes testing overload an already crowded curriculum, Florida teachers acknowledge the marginalization of the social studies program. The chapter by Diane Yendol-Hoppey, Jennifer Jacobs, and Keith Tilford, "Voices of Florida Elementary School Teachers: Their Conceptions of Wise Social Studies Practice," reports how 12 elementary social studies teachers, challenged by high-stakes testing and committed to teaching *all* children, conceptualize and engage in wise social studies practice. The authors delineate and explore normative conceptions of the five domains of wise elementary social studies held by the 12 teachers.

Texas has achieved notoriety as an early forerunner of high-stakes testing and as the birthplace of "No Child Left Behind." State-level policymakers, school districts, and educators have invested considerable economic, political, and educational capital in the creation and implementation of the Texas Essential Knowledge and Skills (TEKS) and the Texas Assessment of Knowledge and Skills (TAKS), the high-stakes test now used in Texas schools. Recognizing that teachers work from many "texts" of expectations and challenges that incorporate their experience, knowledge, and identity, Chapter 5, by Mary Lee Webeck, Cinthia S. Salinas, and Sherry L. Field, frames the work of an eighth-grade U.S. history teacher. In "A Good Teacher in Texas: Conversations about Wisdom in Middle School Social Studies Practice," they consider how she responds to the standardized TEKS and TAKS and present her work as a way to suggest that when teachers can respond "multilingually" and situate standards and tests *within* the culture of the classroom, rather than having the tests *define* that culture, the possibility for wise practice grows.

Stephanie D. van Hover and Walter F. Heinecke present the results of a research study that examined the influence of high-stakes testing on the planning, instruction, and assessment practices of 10 central Virginia high school history teachers identified as highly effective. This chapter, "The Impact of Accountability Reform on the 'Wise Practice' of Secondary History Teachers: The Virginia Experience," discusses the context of accountability surrounding history teaching in Virginia and elucidates the framework of "wise practice" that guided their research. Their data reveal that teachers made sense of their practice in terms of the concepts used in the professional literature on "wise practice; that the most salient aspect of testing and accountability reform for teachers was the influence on the time available for planning, instruction, and assessment; that the accountability measures associated with the standards have created a context that encourages planning, instruction, and assessment practices that conflict with history 'wise practice,' particularly teaching historical thinking; that many teachers resolved this conflict by reducing the amount of time devoted to historical thinking rather than abandoning the practice completely; and, finally, that teachers had mixed feelings about the overall success of the reform."

S. G. Grant, in "More Journey Than End," develops the construct of *ambitious* teaching through the case of Paula, a 10th-grade Global History teacher in western New York State. From interview data collected before and after the first administration of a new, high-stakes state test, he argues that Paula constructs an ambitious classroom practice, albeit one that requires constant negotiation. The key conditions are her sense of history as a discipline and as a school subject, her sense of what her students know and need to know, and the school and policy environment in which she teaches. As these conditions interact, Paula negotiates a series of compromises with which she is variously satisfied. Thus the ambitiousness of Paula's practice represents a chain of complex, mutable, and pragmatic actions, always more journey than end.

In "Wise Practice in an Innovative Public School," Diana Hess describes Joe Park's teaching in order to assess what influence new state standards and tests are having on an especially skillful social studies teacher and to learn about how his teaching has changed in response to mandated testing. She describes how he teaches students to engage in Socratic seminars about landmark United States Supreme Court cases using the standards embedded in *Powerful and Authentic Social Studies* (Harris & Yocum, 2000). She then discusses how the quality of his teaching has been enhanced, not harmed, by his state's new accountability policies, but she also raises concerns about how the tests mandated by the No Child Left Behind Act may have the opposite effect.

In "Wise Practice in High School Social Studies: The Case of Joe Gotchy," Bruce Larson examines the wise practice of a teacher who engages students in the intellectual skills of inquiry, cooperative group processes, discussion, and policymaking. By having his students engage in these skills, he intends to make social studies compelling for them by having them learn course content deeply and make use of what they learn in school beyond the classroom. Gotchy's work with students not only provides insight into the "look and feel" of how a teacher might have a positive impact on student learning, but it also provides an example of what Fred Newmann has called "authentic intellectual work." This chapter describes how such authentic work takes place during Gotchy's teaching of a unit about China.

"Engaging Pedagogy in an AP European History Classroom," by John K. Lee, examines the practice of Mike, a veteran history teacher in a Georgia high school. Lee focuses on how Mike teaches the course in the context of the dual constraints of the AP examination and state standards. He outlines Mike's two most common and descriptive forms of instruction, lecture and thesis presentation/defense, which he characterizes as a mix of Seixas's (2000) "enhanced collective memory" and "disciplinary" approaches to history. Although Mike's teaching practice primarily helps his students to construct narrative understandings of the past, they also indirectly help students to "breach" the gap that Wineburg (2001) described between the school and the academy. That is, Mike requires students to engage primary source documents and scholarly writings, and he facilitates students' development of their historical reasoning skills.

Tim Kelly and Bruce VanSledright's chapter, "A Journey Toward Wiser Practice in the Teaching of American History," is the story of Kelly's evolving teaching practice, interspersed with analytic commentary by VanSledright. Operating from the premise that good history teaching beckons students to understand both the world and themselves by engaging deeply with the past, the authors ask if common practice in the teaching of U.S. history, mainly the attempt to imbue students with knowledge of their common heritage, accomplishes this goal, and whether there are wiser alternatives than the resilient pedagogy associated with the collective memory approach. The chapter examines the conceptual shifts and pedagogical changes experienced by Kelly as he sought to develop wiser practices in teaching history. In particular, it discusses his pursuit of the disciplinary approach as a means of providing more depth and texture to his students' understanding of the American past and themselves. The path Kelly traveled, aimed at overcoming constraints on his practice, is linked to deeper knowledge of subject matter, immersion in a rich research literature, and a conviction and disposition to improving practice.

As both O. L. Davis, Jr., and Lee Shulman have argued, a knowledge base for teaching is not "fixed and final." Conceptions of teaching inevitably will be reinvented and refined. Nonetheless, the contributors to this volume agree with Shulman's assertion that "scholars and expert teachers are able to define, describe, and reproduce good teaching" and thus have chosen these tasks as the focus of the book in order to contribute to a record of "wisdom of practice" in the teaching and learning of social studies, specifically in the unavoidable, challenging context of standards and high-stakes testing.

CHAPTER 2

"I'M NOT SAYING THESE ARE GOING TO BE EASY"

Wise Practice in an Urban Elementary School

Keith C. Barton

One day about 5 years ago, Leslie King, a third-grade teacher at an urban elementary school in Cincinnati, Ohio, sat down to discuss the day's lesson with a teaching associate from a nearby university. The associate participated in Leslie's class for about 3 hours each week, and as part of her field experience she periodically taught lessons on required curricular content. A conscientious student, she had planned an extensive lesson on the food pyramid in order to address one of the district's "promotion standards" and to prepare students for the state's high-stakes "proficiency testing." She explained her goals, procedures, and use of materials. Leslie listened attentively and said, "That's a great lesson, very organized and well planned. How will you find out what students already know about the topic?" The associate responded by explaining her lesson again—her goals, procedures, and use of materials—just as she had before. Leslie nodded approvingly and said, "Yes, very good lesson, I really like it. How are you going to find out what students already know?" Once again, the associate explained key elements of her lesson, and Leslie again listened patiently and asked, "How are you going to find out what they already know?" Finally catching on that there was something worth considering in this question, the associate suggested, "Maybe I should start by asking them what they already know?" "Good idea!" Leslie confirmed.

The associate did indeed begin by asking students what they knew about the food pyramid, and as it turned out, they knew a great deal. They had studied the topic the year before, and they remembered most of the content she intended to address. Fortunately, she had planned to cover so much material and engage students in so many activities—she really had about 3 days' worth of lessons—that she could begin at a more advanced level; as a result, there was little wasted time for the students or herself. Without Leslie's question about background knowledge, though, the lesson would have been a waste, because the level at which she started would have been too rudimentary for these students. This preservice teacher had done exactly what she thought was called for: She planned a lesson that addressed required standards and prepared students for testing. But if she had proceeded with that plan, she would have accomplished neither, because students already knew the content. Leslie, on the other hand, understood how to avoid this problem. Although she had no idea what students knew about the food pyramid, she recognized that a teacher cannot begin any topic without finding out what the students already know. The associate took this principle to heart, and just 3 years into her career she received Teacher of the Year honors in another local district.

As a teacher educator, I am continually intrigued—and frustrated—by the disparity between preservice candidates' understanding of teaching and that of experienced practitioners like Leslie. What is the essence of this difference, and what accounts for it? How can we ensure that more beginners develop into effective professionals, as this one did? We have to do more than develop their knowledge of teaching methods, because even though preservice teachers repeatedly learn to activate and build on background knowledge in their preparation programs, they routinely fail to act on this principle in the classroom. And although we can point to the importance of experience in developing effective teachers, this too fails to explain why some are so much better than others. After all, many teachers, with just as much experience as Leslie, still fail to teach in ways consistent with contemporary perspectives on learning. Leslie's instruction suggests we might benefit from considering key elements of her "wisdom of practice" that can be accounted for by neither knowledge nor experience.

PROFESSIONAL BACKGROUND AND SCHOOL SETTING

Leslie grew up in a white, suburban, middle-class family. As a child, she always took the role of teacher when she and her friends played school.

Since third grade, she said, she had always wanted to be a teacher, and when she attended her first education course, she knew it was where she wanted to be. Although a native of the Cincinnati area, where she now teaches, Leslie's undergraduate preparation came at Eastern Michigan University, and her field experiences were in schools near there. Upon completing her degree she returned to Cincinnati, and after a few months as a long-term substitute, she took a permanent position in an inner-city elementary school. She taught at that school for 10 years—in third, fourth, and fifth grades—and during that time completed a master's degree in education from Northern Kentucky University. She also became certified as a Middle Childhood Generalist by the National Board for Professional Teaching Standards (NBPTS), and soon afterward, she began training teachers to evaluate NBPTS candidates' portfolios for the Educational Testing Service. After 10 years of teaching, Leslie left the classroom for a 3-year appointment in the district's Teacher Evaluation System, and during that time she also served as a mentor to teachers seeking national certification. At the time of this writing, she was preparing to return to active teaching—in kindergarten this time—at another elementary school in inner-city Cincinnati.[1]

Leslie's 10 years of classroom teaching occurred at a school in the urban core of Cincinnati. The Cincinnati Public Schools constitute the third largest district in Ohio, with 42,000 students in more than 70 schools. The student population is approximately 70% African American and 25% white, and more than 60% of students are eligible for the free and reduced-price lunch program. The Ohio Department of Education classifies the district as being in "academic emergency"—the state's lowest ranking—based on standards related to test scores, student attendance, and graduation rate (Cincinnati Public Schools 2003a, 2003b). The school at which Leslie taught, with just over 700 students in kindergarten through eighth grade, was one of the district's 22 elementary magnet schools. Parents applied for their children to be admitted to the school, which focused on the Paideia approach, but because students were enrolled on a first-come basis, the school's demographic characteristics were similar to those in the rest of the district. Sixty percent of students at the school were African American, and most white students there were Appalachian migrants, a population that traditionally has been underserved by urban districts (Borman, 1991; deMarrais, 1998; Klein, 1995); a large majority qualified for free and reduced-price lunch. Leslie also suggested that learning problems were more common than in most of the city's schools, and she estimated that the majority of students there would be tested for special programs. She also noted that many of the school's students had particularly difficult home lives, and that a large portion of them did not live with their biological parents.

LESLIE'S "WISDOM OF PRACTICE"

As Yeager (2000) and Davis (1997) point out, the teaching profession would benefit from thorough and systematic descriptions of teachers' "wisdom of practice"—the knowledge and understanding that they develop in their careers but that remains largely unarticulated and inaccessible to others (Shulman, 1987). As they further suggest, such descriptions must be highly contextualized and reflect the challenging settings in which many of today's teachers work. Leslie was from a white, middle-class background and had enjoyed a lifetime of academic success. Her students, meanwhile, were members of ethnic minorities or other underserved groups, and their backgrounds and experiences were very different than her own. Often, these students had achieved limited success in school. Moreover, like most teachers, Leslie worked in a context in which curriculum standards and high-stakes testing were an inescapable part of the educational and political reality of schooling.

What wisdom can guide a teacher in such settings? In Leslie's case, three principles stood out—intellectual respect, challenging assignments, and curriculum integration. The following sections illustrate how these principles influenced teaching and learning in her classroom. These descriptions are based on numerous formal and informal conversations with Leslie over the years, as well as several months of classroom observation as she taught social studies to third-graders.

Intellectual Respect

The National Council for the Social Studies (1994) has characterized powerful social studies education as *meaningful* and *active*. These labels refer to a number of distinct qualities, but a central feature of such instruction is that it enables students to construct their understanding of important content. This effort requires, first of all, that the content students encounter in social studies actually be important; students should study topics that help them make sense of the social world, both past and present. Moreover, instruction should enable students to develop an understanding of why these topics are important and how their activities in school help them accomplish significant educational goals. This requires that students be engaged in authentic activities that enable them to "develop new understanding through a process of active construction" (p. 169), rather than passively receiving or copying curriculum content. Such activities involve making decisions and solving problems, and they provide students the chance to pursue their own interests, as well as to relate new learning to previous knowledge and experience. Ultimately, participation in social studies should be guided by a sense of purpose, and students should be motivated "by appreciation and interest, not just by accountability and grading systems" (p. 163).

These characteristics of powerful instruction depend on teachers' respect for students' intellectual abilities. In order to engage students in such activities, teachers must believe that students will benefit from authentic activities, that their prior knowledge and experiences are important, that they are capable of constructing new knowledge, and that they can be motivated by appreciation and interest. Intellectual respect, however, is rarely a prominent feature of discussions of teaching methods, particularly for inner-city students like those at Leslie's school. Such discussions may emphasize respect for students as individuals, or respect for their cultural backgrounds, or respect for their ability to manage their own behavior, but they rarely involve any mention of students' intellectual curiosity and motivation, even when students are assumed to possess these characteristics. Moreover, many beginning teachers—and perhaps some experienced ones—assume that students are not curious and motivated learners and that they have few intellectual resources to draw upon. Such teachers may lament their inability to build on prior knowledge because they believe students are from such deprived backgrounds that they have none (Barton, McCully, & Marks, 2004). Combined with the frequent perception that inner-city students and their families "just don't care about education," this disrespectful attitude toward students' intellectual abilities can result in a highly controlled, transmission-oriented approach to teaching in which students have little involvement in the direction of their learning.

Leslie was not unaware of the obstacles that her students faced or of the ways in which their backgrounds differed from her own, but this recognition did not prevent her from taking seriously their interests and experiences. First, she constantly strove to build on their background knowledge. Her third-graders began their study of history, for example, by constructing personal timelines, on which they recorded information from their own lives by bringing in pictures of themselves to arrange in chronological order. Students found this activity very interesting, and they were excited about showing off their products to each other and to classroom visitors. Although they were more interested in discussing the substance of events from their lives than their chronology, they were successful in constructing timelines and sequencing pictures and events; the use of familiar experiences permitted them to make sense of the historical content. Later in the year, during a unit on transportation, Leslie began by having students brainstorm what they already knew about several forms of transportation, compare their information with each other, and then compile it into a single classroom chart. As students took part in this task, their conversations often focused on personal experiences—stories about their relatives' cars and trucks, for example—but by sharing this information, they remembered details they could include in their brainstorming lists. Leslie's recognition that students had relevant background knowledge enabled her to draw them into the topic.

An even more impressive example came during a unit on the Westward Movement of the 1800s. Leslie began by having students interview their parents about their own movement—how many times they had relocated, where they had come from and gone to, and their reasons for moving. Then they shared their information with each other and compiled the results as a class. In addition to engaging students in collecting and analyzing data, this exercise provided a basis for discussing how and why people move, and during the remainder of the unit Leslie asked students to compare and contrast their own families' experiences with those of people in the 1800s. By focusing on movement—a subject familiar to many of these students and their families—Leslie helped them connect what they already knew with what they needed to learn. This is the challenge teachers face as they try to build on background knowledge: They must find aspects of students' experiences that enable them to better understand new content. As Leslie explained, doing so "enables students to successfully learn and apply the new information, because they're adding to a solid foundation rather than trying to start from ground zero."

But students were not merely passive recipients of Leslie's instructional strategies. She constantly called their attention to the purpose of their activities and allowed them to direct their own efforts. For example, she had not decided ahead of time which forms of transportation students would study; they made that decision themselves after the brainstorming activity. As Leslie explained to them, "We want to pick the ones that will help us learn the most." Similarly, during the Westward Movement unit, students developed their own questions, which they would try to answer during the course of their studies. Leslie pointed out to students that these should be questions they "sure would like to find out," and as the class developed a group "KWL" chart, she modeled this intellectual curiosity by emphasizing the topics that she, too, would like to learn more about. As the list below shows, students did in fact have questions about the topic. Most of these concerned everyday experiences ("What did people drink?"), but some related to more complicated ideas, such as the involvement of African Americans and Native Americans in the Westward Movement. Students knew from books displayed in the room that both groups were involved in some way, but they were not sure how, and they wanted to know. This activity illustrated the heart of true inquiry: Students had questions that genuinely interested them, and they pursued information that would provide answers (Barton & Levstik, 2004; Levstik & Barton, 2001). Leslie provided them the freedom and encouragement to take part in such inquiry. Students' questions about the Westward Movement included the following:

> Did they celebrate holidays when they moved west?
> Why did they kill animals?
> How did they get across rivers?
> What did the Indians do with the buffaloes?
> How did they make butter?
> How long did it take to move west?
> What people were slaves?
> What did people drink?
> Did they find treasure?
> How did Indians get drinks?
> Did animals get hungry?
> Did any wagons crash?
> What kind of shoes did they have?
> What did they do when it snowed?
> What did they cover the wagon with?
> Where and when do they sleep?

Moreover, Leslie made the nature of these activities transparent to students. By explaining the purpose of activities, and by calling attention to how they could better direct their own learning, she helped students understand not only the content of education but also its process. Leslie explained the purpose of brainstorming, for example, by pointing out, "I want to find out what you already know about these forms of transportation." When they began more detailed research, she explained that the assignment was a "research paper that we're going to try," and asked, "Why do you think I said, 'We're going to *try* this?'" One student suggested, "Because we don't know how to do it," and Leslie agreed: "Yeah, I don't know if it will work, but if it does, we'll have learned something. If not, then we'll know how to fix it so it works better next time." Later, as students prepared to study Ohio history and geography, Leslie led a discussion of how these subjects might help them in the future and which aspects of each were most important; students then planned projects based on their own conclusions about their purpose. Not only did Leslie give students choices and honor their initiative, she helped them understand how their efforts were related to broader educational goals.

Meanwhile, as students read, observed, and took notes, Leslie constantly drew their attention to how they could more effectively learn what they wanted to know. She talked with them about the information that could be obtained from pictures and from text; she modeled scanning for information in expository prose; and she asked them to evaluate the usefulness of information they had written down. Moreover, when students asked questions, Leslie rarely gave them a straightforward answer. Instead, she helped them understand where they could find answers on their own. As she explained,

> It just seems to make more sense, like in that old saying, "Do you give somebody a fish, or do you teach them how to fish?" If I tell them the answer, if I tell them right where to find it, then the next time they're in that situation, they're going to come and ask me again. My point is that if they want to know—if they come across something unknown or they want to find out something else about their topic—then I'd rather guide them in figuring that out, and hopefully the next time they can do it on their own.... Rarely do I simply tell them the answer and move on; that would be a missed opportunity.

Leslie's ultimate goal was to make students independent and resourceful. She noted that by helping students take ownership of their work, "they become independent learners, instead of always saying, 'Ms. King! Ms. King! I need this! I need that! What do I do next?' When teachers complain that students can't do anything by themselves, and that 'they always need me,' well, that's the teacher's fault, because the teacher has to be the one instilling that in them." She further explained, "If students leave my room and they're resourceful, I've been successful. I don't care if they're not the top reader, if they're not the top mathematician; they *will* be one day, because they'll have it in them—they'll know where to go and what to do." Obviously, Leslie was not interested in having students "passively receive or copy curriculum content." She had a clear sense of meaningful educational goals, and because she had faith in students' ability, curiosity, and motivation, she designed instruction accordingly.

Challenging Assignments

The National Council for the Social Studies (1994) has also identified *challenge* as a key component of powerful social studies education. Challenging activities do not simply involve "retrieval of information from memory" but "deepen understanding of the meanings and implications of content"; this requires "thoughtful participation in lessons and activities and careful work on assignments" (p. 167). During challenging instruction, students work with a variety of sources, encounter varying perspectives and conflicting opinions, develop conclusions and arguments based on evidence, and collaborate with others as part of a learning community. Looking into such classrooms, a visitor would expect to see students using trade books, reference works, and technological resources; taking notes, drawing pictures, developing presentations, and engaging in simulations; and perhaps most noticeably, talking with teachers and each other as they plan investigations or share information. This is hard work, and students will not always succeed, especially on the first try. After all, if such tasks were easy, they would not be called *challenging*.

Unfortunately, many elementary students have no opportunity to take part in this kind of careful, thoughtful, challenging instruction. Instead, they spend their days looking up questions from the back of textbook chapters, filling in worksheets, defining vocabulary words, or copying reports on assigned topics. The only challenge in such tasks lies in overcoming boredom. (Yet even active and engaging tasks may present no real intellectual challenge; building a sugar-cube pyramid may be more fun than defining vocabulary words, but it is unlikely to result in deeper understanding of important content.) These practices have been common for many years, but the increased importance of state standards and accountability systems provides them a new rationale. Many teachers claim that standards determine both the content and the method of instruction and that they preclude open-ended investigations or the construction of knowledge by students. If standards require students to "identify the impact of important individuals" in state or national history, they believe, then instruction must transmit such information through prepackaged curricular materials. The students' job, meanwhile, is to absorb that information and reproduce it on tests.

Leslie, on the other hand, consistently engaged students in inquiry projects and other challenging tasks. Some of these were of her own design, whereas others resulted from students' initiative, but all involved asking and answering authentic questions, locating information from a variety of sources, and constructing new understandings. During the transportation unit, for example, students conducted research on how various forms of transportation had changed over time, how they moved people or products, and how they were related to the history of Cincinnati. In the Westward Movement unit, students took notes from videos, pictures, and trade books; completed Venn diagrams comparing life then and now; drew pictures of life along the Oregon Trail; calculated prices of provisions; and wrote letters from the perspective of children moving westward. Still later, in studying Ohio history and geography, they developed criteria for research reports on important individuals from the state's history and made decisions about the kinds of maps they wanted to construct.

Students often encountered difficulties as they began these tasks. They had trouble identifying appropriate resources, they could not find information when they did have these resources, and they were not sure what notes to take. Some even had trouble, at first, coming up with questions on the Westward Movement, presumably because they had so little previous experience developing questions of their own. Yet despite these difficulties, students generally remained on task. That is, they persevered in the face of their troubles, they took notes as best they could, and their discussions focused on the topic at hand. Moreover, they remained enthusiastic about their work, even when it did not come easily. And they got better at what they were doing: The second day that they spent locating information on changes in transportation was much more productive than the first, and the research projects they did later on the Westward Movement were more productive still. By the end of the year, when they wrote reports on important figures in state history, they were developing their own criteria for research projects. These third-graders took part in challenging tasks and learned from them.

Leslie's patience during these tasks was particularly remarkable. Because she asked students to take part in activities with which they had little previous experience, she was not surprised when they had trouble. As she told students at the beginning of one set of projects, "I'm not saying these are going to be easy." Many teachers, when faced with students who are not succeeding, either scale back the difficulty of the task or intervene immediately to provide direct assistance; they seem to believe the only assignments students should encounter are those that are easy to complete. Leslie, on the other hand, allowed students to face difficulty and uncertainty; she was not disturbed when they flitted from one book to another, when their notes were not the most relevant, or when their discussions occasionally veered off topic. In fact, she dismissed "easy" assignments:

> If they can fill out a worksheet on how to use an encyclopedia, then they didn't need to do the worksheet in the first place. It's skill and drill, and they don't care about it, it's not meaningful. What's more meaningful to me is to walk around the room while they're doing research projects and hear them excited about what they found—"Here's some information!" or "How can I write this out?" or "Can we make a copy of this picture?" Then they care about their projects.

An important element of Leslie's wisdom of practice, then, was her commitment to challenging projects and her willingness to stay with them in spite of difficulties.

This is not to say, however, that Leslie simply assigned such tasks and then let students work through them on their own. Far from it: Her teaching closely matched the forms of scaffolding identified by Rogoff (1990) and Good and Brophy (2000). She pointed out that "you have to believe that your students can learn, and you have to give them the structure to be successful." The first way in which she provided this structure was by breaking complex projects down into more manageable parts. As Leslie explained, if students were simply assigned to do research and given a due date, many of them would have no idea where to start or what to do; some would refuse even to participate, and others would produce sketchy or plagiarized reports. In order for students to succeed in this kind of research, they had to learn how to complete each component of the process. When students were to write reports on important people in state history, for example, Leslie began by engaging them in a discussion of the topics that should be covered in each report and compiling their suggestions; from this discussion, students produced an outline to guide their note taking. Leslie also taught them how to take notes (a focus of lessons throughout the year, in fact) and conducted mini-lessons on organizing notes into paragraphs. Another component of the project focused on helping students support their research with drawings, photographs, and other visual images. (During earlier projects, Leslie had devoted attention to finding information in trade books and reference sources, but by this point students were more accomplished at this element of research.) The overall project, then, was broken down into making plans, developing outlines, taking notes, organizing writing, and producing a final project. These were taught as separate skills, but not isolated ones: Leslie addressed each within the context of the assignments in which students were engaged.

Leslie also helped students structure their research through graphic organizers. Sometimes she prepared these in advance: She distributed timelines to use in developing personal histories, gave students Venn diagrams to compare present-day life to that of a family moving to Ohio in the 1800s, and produced a large KWL on chart paper so the entire class could record information about the Westward Movement. Other times, she had students make their own graphic organizers. To aid in their brainstorming on transportation, for example, Leslie had students fold sheets of paper into eight sections, list a different form of transportation in each, and record information in the appropriate spaces. Similarly, before reading a book about the Westward Movement aloud, she had students fold their papers into four sections so they could divide their notes into categories related to dangers, food, weather, and supplies. During other activities, students drew upon a variety of diagrams, outlines, and charts to organize the information they collected. Such graphic organizers were an indispensable part of these complicated research projects; without them, students might have become overwhelmed by new information, and they would have been unlikely to record what they learned in a useful format. By providing students with simple but systematic ways for structuring their notes and other written products, Leslie helped them manage and organize their encounters with a variety of resources.

Another way in which Leslie assisted students was through probing questions. When students had difficulty with a task, or when their attention began to lag, she helped them to sustain their productivity, but not with warnings and commands, or even rewards and incentives. Instead, she asked questions that stimulated their interest, reminded them of previous knowledge, or called attention to relevant components of the task. When one group had trouble brainstorming information about covered wagons, for example, she asked, "When did they use covered wagons?" and "How did they move, what gave a wagon power?" After one student mentioned horses, she asked, "And does anyone know another animal that could pull them?" When another group had similar trouble writing about steamboats, she asked, "What did steamboats look like?", "Why do you think it's called a steamboat?", and "Where is the steam coming from?" With still another group that was working on airplanes, she asked, "How does an airplane move?" and "How old are airplanes?" With each of these questions, Leslie helped students bring their prior knowledge to the surface, yet she allowed them to retain control over their own learning. She simply reminded them of what they already knew.

These were fairly simple questions, of course, but other times more complicated responses were necessary. In an activity during the Westward Movement unit, for example, one group had trouble deciding which route a group of settlers might choose; Leslie's questions focused their attention on factors these migrants would have considered. She asked what they might have encountered in each direction, what potential problems they would have faced with each choice, and what could have been frightening about each route (and whether their fears were likely to be similar to ours today). These questions were exactly what students needed: After hearing them and trying to answer, a silent and unproductive group became a thoughtful and vocal collaboration. The same approach was evident in another activity, when a student placed an event that occurred in 1811 after one from 1886—the "6" in the final position of the year apparently confusing him as to their order. Leslie asked, "Would 1886 come before 1811?" When the student remained unsure, she asked, "Would 86 come before 11?", and then, with more emphasis, "Would 86 come before 11?" The student probably knew after the first question that his arrangement was wrong (and so he simply could have reversed them), but Leslie's questions drew his attention to the aspect of the problem required for a solution—comparing the order of the last two numbers. In both these examples, Leslie used questions not just to help students arrive at correct answers, but to better understand how they could approach these problems in the first place. This is when real teaching and learning takes place: when teachers help students accomplish challenging tasks.

Curriculum Integration

A further characteristic of powerful social studies is *integration*. Again, the National Council for the Social Studies has identified a number of distinct components of this element of teaching and learning, but two are particularly important. The first is the crossing of disciplinary boundaries in order to promote students' social understanding. If students are to understand how the social world operates, they cannot study history or geography or economics or any of the other components of social studies in isolation. People do not experience these things in isolation (e.g., our decisions about resources always take place within a time, a place, and a cultural and institutional context), and students cannot understand them in isolation. If they do not understand economic concepts like taxation and political ones like representation, for example, they will be unable to make sense of the American Revolution (Barton, 1997). This means that the most effective topics of study will be those that enable students to learn content from a variety of disciplines; in the primary grades, these include cultural universals such as food, shelter, or clothing (Alleman & Brophy, 2001, 2002, 2003), and in the intermediate grades these usually revolve around time periods (the Colonial Era, Ancient Egypt, etc.) or geographic regions (the southwestern U.S., South Africa, etc.). Grades three and four sometimes include a mixture of the two approaches.

Leslie accomplished such integration by organizing her instruction into units. Usually, these were topical ones (Immigration, the Westward Movement, Transportation, Ohio), but other times they revolved around themes such as "change" or "roots" (Barton & Smith, 2000). In both types of units she combined objectives from most, if not all, strands in the state's curriculum framework for social studies. The unit on the Westward Movement, for example, addressed economics when students studied general stores and engaged in simulations of resource allocation; geography when they considered how landforms affected movement and how trails could be traced on maps; and culture and society when they discussed the contrasting experiences of men and women, as well as those of differing ethnic groups (and the interactions among them). History objectives were included when students examined the causes and consequences of the Westward Movement, the attitudes and beliefs of people at the time, and the way accounts had been constructed from diaries, letters, and other sources. Each of Leslie's units included similar integration across the social studies disciplines.

Unfortunately, beginning teachers sometimes have trouble understanding the value of this kind of unit integration. Often, they appear to believe that because the curriculum guide is divided into separate strands—10 objectives on history, eight on economics, 12 on geography, and so on—their instruction must also be divided into separate strands. They insist on teaching "units" on economics or map skills, despite the fact that these lessons include no integration of content and cannot properly be called units at all. A connected series of lessons on such topics is simply that—a connected series of lessons, not a unit. As Leslie pointed out, some schools set no higher standard than this, and students may be lucky to find that their lessons are connected in any way. But teaching the strands of social studies in isolation is, according to Leslie, a "missed opportunity," and she justified unit integration on a number of grounds.

First was the necessity of combining disciplines in order more fully to understand a single time period, place, or issue. With regard to the Westward Movement unit, for example, Leslie noted, "You need the map skills to understand where they traveled; you need to understand economics because they had resources that they had to deal with, and they had to make decisions about wants and needs; you also had different people and different cultures they encountered along the way, so you had to cover that." Without integrating this content, Leslie insisted, the unit literally would be meaningless. Efficiency was a second reason for organizing instruction into units. Without units to provide focus and coherence to the curriculum, long-range planning becomes impossible; teachers "aimlessly cover" objectives, in Leslie's words, and when they approach the end of the year they are surprised to find that they have failed to include many required standards.

Finally, units more effectively developed students' understanding because they allowed them to return to required content throughout the year. Leslie noted that many teachers, when they realize students are expected to construct timelines, simply start doing lessons on timelines; they fail to recognize that timelines can be incorporated into each social studies topic. Spreading an objective like this over the course of a year spares those students who do not initially understand it from a week or more of sustained agony. Doing one timeline in each unit is more likely to meet their needs than doing five in a single week. Even for students who appear to have mastered the objective, this one-time-only approach is ineffective: Spending a week on timelines and then saying, "We're done with timelines, you passed timelines!" results in short-term retention, at best, and when students encounter them again on high-stakes tests, they are unlikely to remember what they learned. Leslie argued that "teachers who complain that their students know something one day and forget it the next are typically the ones who do day-to-day lessons rather than units."

Revisiting such objectives in each unit reinforces some students' understanding, and it gives others who were not ready the first time around a second (and third, and fourth) chance to make sense of the subject.

Another form of integration extended beyond the objectives found in the social studies curriculum; this involved reading and analyzing literature and other written texts, communicating orally and in writing, exploring and creating artwork in a variety of forms, and collecting and synthesizing data. The National Council for the Social Studies (1994) has observed that social studies is a "natural bridging subject across the curriculum" (p. 165), and this kind of integration usually is easier for beginning teachers to understand and embrace. In fact, it is difficult to imagine how social studies could be taught without such integration: How would students learn the content if not through text, visual images, and the collection of data? How would they construct their understanding if not through speaking, writing, drawing, and other such displays? But not only should students be making use of skills and understandings from other subjects, their participation in social studies should enhance those abilities; that is, teachers should not only expect them to use reading and writing in social studies, but also help them become better readers and writers through their work in the subject. The challenge lies in achieving the right balance among content areas: With too little attention to other subjects, students' skills in those areas may show little improvement, and they may not even be able to complete their social studies assignments successfully. With too much attention to other subjects, however, social studies content may lack coherence and become little more than a vehicle for teaching language arts or mathematics (Crocco & Thornton, 2002; National Council for the Social Studies, 1994).

This integration with other subject areas also was evident in Leslie's units. In constructing timelines, for example, students used mathematics to sequence and place events. In considering how a family moving west should supply itself, they calculated the cost of varied quantities of multiple items. When they used trade books and reference works to find out about unit topics, Leslie showed them how to use tables of contents, indexes, and glossaries, as well as how to scan text for information. As they read works aloud, Leslie called students' attention to the genre conventions of the books they read and the literary devices they employed. And instruction in written composition was an ever-present feature of students' activities, as they wrote sentences to describe events on timelines, composed letters and diaries from the perspective of people moving west, and completed research reports on important figures in state history. In each of these activities, Leslie had clear objectives related to mathematics or language, and she provided systematic assistance to help students meet those goals. The specific objectives she chose, though, derived from the demands of the social studies content: In writing a letter from the perspective of a child moving westward, students naturally had to learn how to write letters; in looking up information in reference sources, they had to learn to use indexes. The integration of social studies with other content areas, then, was pervasive, but it was also seamless.

For elementary teachers, integration across subject areas is a practical necessity. As Leslie pointed out, "Self-contained elementary teachers already have a great demand on their time, and if you try to look at everything you have to teach, it can be overwhelming." If teachers fail to capitalize on opportunities for teaching more than one subject at a time, they will be hard-pressed to address any component of the curriculum effectively. Leslie noted that her initial motivation for subject integration was "simply because I couldn't see how I could get everything accomplished, in any depth, by doing it in isolation." Although many elementary teachers attempt such integration through topics like "bears" or "apples," Leslie rejected these as superficial and as lacking in any substantive social studies content (Barton & Smith, 2000). She admitted that more authentic forms of integration could be challenging, but she suggested that teachers begin with language arts because it so clearly overlaps with all areas of the curriculum:

> Finding books of various genres that match curricular topics is a great start, and understanding that writing a research report is about more than just finding information—it includes using various resources, note-taking skills, skimming/scanning skills, organization of ideas into cohesive thoughts, editing/revising, incorporating other media, and so on. When you step back and look at the bigger picture, it becomes clear how to connect the content areas.

Rather than thinking of content standards and integrated units as contradictory or incompatible approaches to curriculum, Leslie saw them as inseparable.

SOURCES OF WISDOM

The previous section described how three basic principles of Leslie's wisdom of practice influenced her classroom instruction, but an important question remains: What accounted for Leslie's embrace of these principles? Why did she respect students' intellects, for example, when other teachers may dismiss them? Why did she assign challenging tasks instead of worksheets? And why did she integrate the curriculum instead of following a list of objectives in lock-step fashion? Two factors accounted for much of Leslie's outlook on teaching and learning. First, she constantly reflected on students' learning. As a long line of scholarship on reflective practice makes clear, effective teachers must continually interrogate their own instruction (e.g., Adler, 1993; Bullough, 1989; Goodman, 1991; Merryfield, 1993). As Leslie noted, "You have to step back and see if students are learning as much as they could; maybe they're getting the minimal amount, and getting some skills, but if you find that when they revisit a topic, they've forgotten it—even when they knew it a month ago—those are signs that your teaching is not really effective." This kind of reflection requires not only introspection but also action: Teachers have to make changes based on their ongoing assessment of student learning. This means more than summative evaluation at the end of a unit; a teacher cannot just "teach her unit—a week or two weeks, whatever—and then the next week start something new." Rather, teachers must be willing to change the way they do things. As Leslie explained, "If something's not working, if my kids don't get it, if they aren't engaged in the learning, if they aren't making progress—then I stop doing it, I don't do it that way anymore, I change!"

Reflection is difficult. As Leslie pointed out, "It's much easier to blame students for not learning than to look back at your teaching and try to figure out ways to be a better teacher, to help them learn." This willingness to change one's practice rests on a simple but elusive foundation: a commitment to student learning. That idea may not seem like a radical proposition, but many teachers appear to be motivated not by student learning, but by two goals distinctly at odds with learning—control of behavior and coverage of content (Barton & Levstik, 2004). Leslie recognized that many teachers avoid such challenging, inquiry-oriented tasks precisely because they make classroom control more difficult. She noted, "It's easier to manage the classroom if students aren't really learning." If teachers expect students to behave in an "orderly manner," they are likely to rely on simple assignments, because giving students worksheets they already know how to do results in "excellent" behavior:

> They'll sit there and be so quiet, because it's so easy; there's no challenge, no one's going to get frustrated, they're not going to have any questions for you. Your management issue's going to be when they're all done and they're looking for the next thing they have to do, because they're going to be bored. But while they're filling out that worksheet, your classroom is going to look like you have perfect control over them.

Leslie had little interest in maintaining a silent classroom. Sometimes students were quiet and still (such as when they were taking notes on a book being read aloud), whereas at other times they talked and moved about (such as when they were conducting research).

Nor was Leslie driven exclusively by coverage of content. This highlights the second dimension of her view of teaching and learning: She had a vision of education that extended beyond the objectives of the required curriculum. She covered everything in the state standards, and she took those standards very seriously; she did not consider the standards themselves—or the tests based on them—to be impediments to her teaching. The problem for some teachers, she argued, arises when they believe that state or local standards are the curriculum, and that they must be covered in the same format as in official documents—as a checklist. She noted, "That's not necessarily the way students learn, that's just the way the information's organized so that teachers can better understand what they have to teach. But too many people take that as curriculum; I feel like that's the *springboard* to your curriculum." (She also had a more accurate knowledge of the required curriculum than many teachers. She complained, "If one more person tells me the kindergarten social studies standards are holidays and map skills, I'm going to scream! No they're not! They're not!"). Leslie was particularly disdainful of those who believe that examples in curriculum documents constitute required topics of study or—still worse—that textbooks determine topics. She wondered, "Are they saying that the textbook companies are the master teachers of the nation?"

For Leslie, the curriculum was what she had to construct, together with her students, based on their needs and interests. It had to include required content, and it had to prepare students for high-stakes tests, but these constituted only a portion of Leslie's goals. She justified her use of integrated units and inquiry projects, in part, by their ability to combine content standards with skills and knowledge that had broader meaning and that would prepare students for the future. As she said,

> You have to see past that test, you have to believe that you're preparing them for the next grade level, for the next level of schooling, and for their lifetimes. You have to think of it that way, in the bigger picture. That's what drives my instruction to be more challenging and to be more integrated, because the real world is challenging, the real world is integrated.

Research indicates that the purposes that guide social studies teachers' activities have more impact on practice than their knowledge of either disciplinary content or instructional techniques (Barton & Levstik, 2004), and Leslie's purposes clearly extended beyond the coverage and control that dominate so many classrooms. She aimed to prepare students for a lifetime, and this goal drove her teaching.

CONCLUSIONS

Many educators have argued that the recent emphasis on standards and accountability has had serious, negative consequences on teaching and learning, and the evidence is mounting that this is so (e.g., Amrein & Berliner, 2002; McNeill, 2000; Ohanian, 1999; Wright, 2002). Yet as Leslie King's example makes clear, there is no necessary connection between content standards and high-stakes tests on the one hand, and low-level, rote instruction on the other. Teachers play a crucial role in mediating educational policy, and their intentions and interpretations have at least as much influence on classroom practice as does the content of standards and high-stakes tests (Cimbricz, 2002; Grant, 2001; Thornton, 1991; White, 1987). This makes it all the more crucial to identify the wisdom of practice that enables teachers like Leslie to engage students in "powerful" educational experiences. Specific characteristics of this wisdom are likely to differ from one context to another. The intellectual respect, challenging assignments, and curricular integration found in Leslie's classroom may look very different in other settings, or they may be overshadowed by other wise practices. Nevertheless, the sources of this wisdom—reflection on students' learning and broader educational goals—may have more universal relevance, and beginning teachers would benefit from taking them seriously.

NOTE

1. With Leslie's permission, I have used her real name. In two other descriptions of her teaching, she is referred to by her former surname, Kreimer (Barton & Kreimer, 2001; Barton & Smith, 2000).

REFERENCES

Adler, S. A. (1993). Teacher education: Research as reflective practice. *Teaching and Teacher Education, 9,* 159–167.

Alleman, J., & Brophy, J. (2001). *Social studies excursions, K–3, Book 1: Powerful units on food, shelter, and clothing.* Portsmouth, NH: Heinemann.

Alleman, J., & Brophy, J. (2002). *Social studies excursions, K–3, Book 2: Powerful units on communication, transportation, and family living.* Portsmouth, NH: Heinemann.

Alleman, J., & Brophy, J. (2003). *Social studies excursions, K–3, Book 3: Powerful units on childhood, money, and government.* Portsmouth, NH: Heinemann.

Amrein, A. L., & Berliner, D. C. (2002, March 28). High-stakes testing, uncertainty, and student learning. *Education Policy Analysis Archives, 10*(18). Retrieved August 6, 2002, from http://epaa.asu.edu/epaa/v10n18/

Barton, K. C. (1997). "Bossed around by the Queen": Elementary students' understanding of individuals and institutions in history. *Journal of Curriculum and Supervision, 12,* 290–314.

Barton, K. C., & Kreimer, L. A. (2001). Teaching social studies in an urban elementary school: Collaboration for integration and inquiry learning. In M. Christenson, M. Johnston, & J. Norris (Eds.), *Teaching together: School/university* collaboration to improve social studies education (pp. 21–30). Washington, DC: National Council for the Social Studies.

Barton, K. C., & Levstik, L. S. (2004). *Teaching history for the common good.* Mahwah, NJ: Erlbaum.

Barton, K. C., McCully, A. W., & Marks, M. J. (2004). Reflecting on elementary children's understanding of history and social studies: An inquiry project with beginning teachers in Northern Ireland and the United States. *Journal of Teacher Education, 55*(1), 70–90.

Barton, K. C., & Smith, L. A. (2000). Themes or motifs? Aiming for coherence through interdisciplinary outlines. *The Reading Teacher, 54*(1), 54–63.

Borman, K. M. (1991). *Overwhelmed in Cincinnati: Urban Appalachian children and youth.* Washington, DC: Office of Educational Research and Improvement. (Eric Document Reproduction Service No. ED 360437)

Bullough, R. (1989). Teacher education and teacher reflectivity. *Journal of Teacher Education, 40*(2), 15–21.

Cimbricz, S. C. (2002, January 9). State-mandated testing and teachers' beliefs and practices. *Education Policy Analysis Archives, 10*(2). Retrieved January 24, 2002, from http://epaa.asu.edu/epaa/v10n2.html

Cincinnati Public Schools. (2003a). *Overview of Cincinnati public schools.* Retrieved June 10, 2003, from http://www.cps-k12.org/general/Overview/overview.html.

Cincinnati Public Schools. (2003b). *State report card.* Retrieved June 10, 2003, from http://www.cpsboe.k12.oh.us/general/StRptCard/StRptTitle.html.

Crocco, M. S., & Thornton, S. J. (2002). Social studies in the New York City public schools: A descriptive study. *Journal of Curriculum and Supervision, 17*, 206–231.

Davis, O.L., Jr. (1997). Beyond "best practices" toward "wise practices." *Journal of Curriculum and Supervision, 13*, 1–5.

deMarrais, K. B. (1998). Urban Appalachian children: An "invisible minority" in city schools. In S. Books (Ed.), *Invisible children in society and its schools* (pp. 89–110). Mahwah, NJ: Erlbaum.

Good, T. L., & Brophy, J. E. (2000). *Looking in classrooms* (8th ed.). New York: Longman.

Goodman, J. (1991). Using a methods course to promote reflection and inquiry among preservice teachers. In B. Tabachnick & K. Zeichner (Eds.), *Issues and practices in inquiry-oriented teacher education* (pp. 56–76). New York: Falmer Press.

Grant, S. G. (2001). An uncertain lever: Exploring the influence of state-level testing in New York state on teaching social studies. *Teachers College Record, 103*(3), 398–426.

Klein, H. A. (1995). Urban Appalachian children in Northern schools: A study in diversity. *Young Children, 50*, 10–16.

Levstik, L. S., & Barton, K. C. (2001). *Doing history: Investigating with children in elementary and middle schools.* Second edition. Mahwah, NJ: Erlbaum.

McNeill, L. M. (2000). *Contradictions of school reform: Educational costs of standardized testing.* New York: Routledge.

Merryfield, M. M. (1993). Reflective practice in global education: Strategies for teacher educators. *Theory into Practice, 32*(1), 27–32.

National Council for the Social Studies. (1994). *Expectations of excellence: Curriculum standards for social studies.* Washington, DC: Author.

Ohanian, S. (1999). *One size fits few: The folly of educational standards.* Portsmouth, NH: Heinemann.

Rogoff, B. (1990). *Apprenticeship in thinking: Cognitive development in social context.* New York: Oxford University Press.

Shulman, L. S. (1987). Knowledge and teaching: Foundations for the new reform. *Harvard Educational Review, 57,* 1–22.

Thornton, S. J. (1991). Teacher as curriculum-instructional gatekeeper in social studies." In J. P. Shaver (Ed.), *Handbook of research on social studies teaching and learning* (pp. 237–248). New York: Macmillan.

White, J. J. (1987). The teacher as broker of scholarly knowledge. *Journal of Teacher Education, 38*(1), 19–24.

Wright, W. E. (2002). The effects of high stakes testing in an inner-city elementary school: The curriculum, the teachers, and the English language learners. *Current Issues in Education, 5*(5). Retrieved July 8, 2002, from http://cie.ed.asu.edu/volume5/number5/

Yeager, E. A. (2000). Thoughts on wise practice in the teaching of social studies. *Social Education, 64*(6), 352–353.

CHAPTER 3

HOW SHE STOPPED WORRYING AND LEARNED TO LOVE THE TEST... SORT OF

Andrea S. Libresco

This story is about Paula Marron, an excellent veteran fourth-grade teacher by any standard of evaluation. Because of new state-mandated social studies tests in New York, Paula has had to examine both her curriculum content and her teaching methods. My primary goal in studying Paula was to ascertain the extent to which this exemplary teacher has been able to stay true to her lofty goals and wise practices, as well as her love for learning, in the face of pressure from the fourth-grade assessments in English/language arts, mathematics, science, and social studies.

For veteran teachers and those with less experience, external mandates present a special set of challenges. To what extent do teachers simply teach to the test? Can teachers regard the test as a stimulus to new ways of thinking about social studies and engaging students in the subject? How do teachers find the time, support, and skill to move in new directions? As a result of my study of Paula Marron, I accomplished another goal: I found evidence to illustrate how an exceptional teacher has been able to move in significantly new directions, and, notwithstanding legitimate apprehensions and pressures, turn the test mandates into stimuli for new and expanded wise practices in social studies.

Paula already exhibited many of the attributes of wise practice (Davis, 1997; Yeager, 2000), such as modeling intellectual curiosity, promoting critical thinking and student intellectual responsibility, and attending to her students' academic skills while engaging them in social studies content. The imposition of a state social studies test did not stifle any of these practices. Rather, Paula has extended her wise practices. She translates her improved grasp of content knowledge into effective and interesting activities for students and uses meaningful primary source materials in addition to the textbook.

According to her principal, the K–12 social studies director, and her colleagues, Paula is an excellent teacher. Additionally, she is the new lead teacher for elementary social studies and science districtwide. This research focuses on 2 years of her fourth-grade teaching in Oceanside, a suburban system on the south shore of Nassau County, Long Island. New York State designated the fourth grade as a marker year in elementary school in which students are tested in English/language arts, mathematics, and science. Although the social studies test is administered in the fall of fifth grade, the state education authority considers it to be a fourth-grade test. Therefore, all fourth-grade teachers in New York State recognize that they must prepare their students for tests in the four core subjects.

Paula acknowledges the pressure the entire accountability apparatus places on her and her students, but she also appreciates the fact that the social studies test has introduced her to document-based instruction that she and her students find to be thoughtful and interesting (instruction with which she had no experience in her preservice teacher education). Paula recognizes that the test has prompted increased staff development and collaboration among teachers. Moreover, she is aware of her power as a curricular instructional gatekeeper (Thornton, 1991), and this position helps her to use test knowledge as a guide, not a control, for her instruction in order to stimulate student inquiry activities (as opposed to simply handing out test-preparation packets). Thus, her exemplary practice is not sabotaged by the test. Rather, as she gains new information about the content and pedagogy of social studies through additional staff development activities, she believes that she actually improves her social studies instruction. For Paula, then, the general testing crisis has produced some useful opportunities.

WISE PRACTICES AND STATE ASSESSMENT

Before turning to how Paula Marron responds to state mandates, a brief perspective on the emergence of the state testing requirements is helpful. The recent imposition of high-stakes testing in all major school subjects at the secondary level in New York State was accompanied by the imposition of achievement testing at the middle and elementary school levels. Elementary social studies testing began annually in November 2001, and it parallels the eighth-, 10th-, and 11th-grade social studies tests, the latter two being high-stakes tests required for high school graduation. Testing at the elementary and secondary levels shares some similarities; however, significant differences also exist. Because fourth-grade instruction is not departmentalized, and because in New York State the fourth grade houses the English/language arts, science, and mathematics statewide tests, teachers must allot time for all of the major subjects during the school day. In addition, unlike their secondary school colleagues, elementary teachers must teach all subjects. Consequently, they are unlikely to be well versed in all of them, including, and perhaps especially, social studies.

Although Paula is keenly aware of the time pressures that come with all of the fourth-grade tests and expresses ambivalence about state testing (wanting to avoid "standardization of children" and wanting to address "the multiple intelligences of students"), she believes that the "test has changed instruction in a positive way." She points to the test's emphasis on upper-level document-based instruction and on "doing the stuff of historians that teaches students how to think and analyze." Paula finds the state standards and assessments helpful in teaching her students to read, write, and speak better, and she reports that the social studies assessments will "give students the social studies skills they need to walk away with...skills that can enhance their roles as citizens." She adds, "If there were no state test, teachers might not know about these skills; the test has focused us." Although Paula acknowledges that bad document-based instruction is certainly possible with too much "worksheeting," she does not see it. In fact, she sees teachers "discover DBQs [document-based questions] and essential questions and change their teaching for the better." Paula explains:

> Because the test is a thinking test, it produces a thinking curriculum. The test requires students to read critically and write to make a point. Testing has changed teaching, instruction, and learning, and it helps with differentiation of instruction. The upper and lower students used to learn nothing; this new test in the hands of good teachers (even in the hands of not-so-good teachers) allows all students to think and make connections in other subject areas. We owe it to all students to teach them how to interpret information.

And Paula notes another benefit: The time pressures of the tests result in teachers' greater integration of subjects and information because they cannot possibly teach all four basic subjects and simultaneously prepare the students for the tests in the time allotted.

On the other hand, the negative impact of the time pressures often overwhelms teachers. Paula reveals that, had I not been observing her teaching, she would "probably not teach social studies [except for her ongoing MST (math/science/technology) colonial panels project] until after the science and math tests in May" because of all of the test-preparation packets she is required to use. Her reasoning?

> There's just no time for social studies. The tests get in the way; I didn't feel I could do the MST project [in which students created panels to represent different groups of people in colonial New York], or a mock trial of John Peter Zenger, or the American Revolution tea [in which students role-play and quote from actual characters as they participate in a tea on the eve of the Revolutionary War] until the ELA [English/language arts test] was over.

In addition, Paula believes that the state requirements lean too far on the side of breadth over depth: "If there were no state standards and assessments, I might teach all of social studies through the American Revolution. Although the students wouldn't get all the other content the state wants, their own investigations would guide instruction." Her statement can be interpreted as an argument for the desirability of state control of the curriculum to ensure balance, particularly at the elementary level where teachers did not, for the most part, major in the subjects that they teach. However, in this situation, Paula's case argues that the state has not made enough hard decisions about what curriculum is most important: "They put more content in the curriculum than we can possibly teach." Her sophisticated analysis of the political nature of how topics are included in the state curriculum leads her to question the wisdom of state choices.

Nonetheless, Paula clearly is cognizant and proud of her power as decision maker, and she finds ways to make the time pressures work for her. A key factor in Paula's ability to do this—and to develop new social studies approaches—is her sustained involvement in a staff development program. She was one of a committee of four teachers that worked throughout a year to revise the entire district's fourth-grade social studies curriculum through the use of an essential questions approach—that is, using overarching, higher-level questions that guide units of study (Wiggins & McTighe, 1998). She also participated in all-day sessions that introduced fourth-grade teachers to methods of searching out and teaching with source documents. Out of her staff development work, she created an essential question for ELA that supports social studies: "How do particular books change the way people think about tolerance and social justice?" She also has learned how to integrate and manage her social studies and ELA instruction time to teach students the skills of reading a nonfiction text (e.g., break down the vocabulary, look for context clues, chunk pieces of text together, bullet information, draw a picture or diagram, reread the text), and the "habits of mind" that students need in order to think, analyze, read, and write in any subject. Given her classroom posters (e.g., "Developing a Writing Project," "Inquiry Skills," "Ways to Solve Problems," "Photo Analysis"), one can see that the boundaries between social studies and ELA are indistinct in Paula's classroom.

Another point about Paula's approach to teaching that her staff development activities have enhanced: before she enters the classroom, Paula thinks long and hard about why she teaches what she teaches in both social studies and literature, even as she perceives them to be inextricably linked. She highlights parallel skills used in each subject (e.g., using text evidence in literature to substantiate one's view of a character, and using primary source data to support one's conclusions in social studies). Paula also stresses perspective taking in both subjects (e.g., understanding the motivations of a fictional character, as well as a historical actor). She values the concepts of social justice, tolerance, and students' "understanding of who you are as an American." Paula wants to teach students to be "citizens of the school and of the nation." As an example of her beliefs, she mentions with pride the evolution of her students' thinking about candidates in the last presidential election:

> When I first asked my students how many of them were voting for Gore and how many for Bush, all hands went up. When I asked them why, not a hand went up. After the unit, which culminated in a class debate and an essay, a father confided to me that his daughter had convinced him to change his vote.

ESSENTIAL QUESTIONS AND DOCUMENT-BASED INSTRUCTION

Paula's typical class sessions involve students working to gather data to answer an essential question. The New York State curriculum for grade four focuses on New York state history; Paula uses a districtwide curriculum document that poses an overarching question for the whole year: "Has the history of New York State been a history of progress for all?" She also creates what she calls subessential questions for each unit (e.g., "Did colonization of New York state result in progress for all?" "Did the modernization of New York State result in progress for all?"). Paula's use of essential questions reveals her emphasis on reflection about knowledge rather than on knowledge acquisition alone. Her assumption that big ideas, themes, and concepts must be the starting point for instruction is consistent with research on the elements of effective teaching (e.g., Good & Brophy, 1991), thoughtfulness (e.g., Newmann, 1990), and depth over breadth (e.g., Whitehead, 1929; Wiggins & McTighe, 1998).

At the beginning of each unit, Paula shares with her students the final assessment question she has created (e.g., "Did the American Revolution and Constitution result in progress for all?"). She explains, "We start with the end first, then go back to the beginning." She guides her students through an analysis of the question itself. Students pull apart the question, define words like *progress*, and discuss the various groups that constitute the "all" in "progress for all." After parsing the question, students spend several days completing a glossary of approximately 20 crucial vocabulary words for the unit. They use dictionaries, texts, and conversations with adults to define and give examples of terms. For example, the Revolution unit includes words and phrases such as "democracy," "representation," and "consent of the governed." The glossary is the only part of the unit that is completed as homework. Data gathering, which comprises the bulk of the unit, occurs during class sessions through a variety of activities, including computer research and "history mysteries." In the latter activity, students analyze a variety of documents in order to find the answer to a historical question such as "What became of the Matinecock Indians?" or to analyze data that support or refute a statement such as "The lives of slaves in New York were not as bad as the lives of southern slaves." Students can collect research evidence to create a character collage in which they draw and decorate people of the time period (e.g., Charity Clarke, a Long Island patriot) and surround them with accurate historical information, including excerpts of their own quotations about issues of the day. Students find their sources in packets derived from the district curriculum binder; they also rely heavily on a comprehensive website on Long Island history created by *Newsday*, the newspaper of Long Island (www.lihistory.com).

Each unit concludes with students writing an essay that responds to the essential question. At the beginning of the year, Paula spends time with her class to prepare a planning page on chart paper, but in the second half of the year, students construct their own planning pages. After the English/language arts (ELA) assessment at midyear, Paula explains that she can afford to include nonwriting activities as end-of-unit assessments in social studies. For example, the end of the colonial unit includes a project that combines social studies with mathematics, science, and technology (MST). MST projects do not have to be connected to other disciplines, but Paula chooses to use the MST experience to further her social studies objectives. Most teachers in the district, however, are not able to find the time to work on MST projects with their students.

To answer the question, "Did colonization lead to progress for all?", groups of students construct a three-panel display. Students use one panel to display an aspect of culture for Native Americans, another for European Americans, and a third for African Americans. At the end of the American Revolution unit, students participate in a simulation of a tea on the eve of July 4, 1776, in which they role-play patriots and loyalists and use actual primary source quotations as part of their presentations. Paula is convinced that students remember little content. Instead, "they remember what they did and then associate the concepts that went with the activity." This conviction is supported by Alleman and Brophy's (1993) research with college students, indicating that what they remembered of their elementary social studies class were the activities and the concepts connected with those activities, rather than a compendium of specific dates and events.

Not surprisingly, Paula's preparations outside of class are considerable and extensive. She spent about 4 hours, for example, to create a list that contained websites on different colonial groups for the MST project. That preparation is merely one of several during her colonial unit. In fact, Paula reveals that, after 9 years of teaching, she actually spends more time planning now than when she began, although she believes her time now is better spent and her activities are more productive. A key influence on her practice has been Grant Wiggins's notion of backwards assessment; she explains: "I give my students my unit up front. Students have to be in on the hunt if they're going to be invested in it. Then they need specific information to answer the question, so activities are always content-based. However, they are not 'give me the answer' exercises."

In addition to having the essential question for the year posted on the classroom wall, Paula posts Wiggins's six facets of understanding as well: "Wiggins is in my head and in their heads and up on the wall." Indeed, when discussing the impact she hopes to have on her students, she mentions "empathy" and "self-knowledge," which are two of his primary forms of understanding.

I observed Paula formally and informally for more than 2 years. For the purposes of the discussion here, I selected five observations to analyze, for several reasons: They stem from the most upper-level unit of the year, Colonial New York and the American Revolution; they represent conscious attempts at interdisciplinary instruction, an important goal of Paula's instruction; they employ several methods of instruction; and they illustrate the use of a variety of primary sources in several different contexts.

The first observation centers on a Math–Science–Technology (MST) project in which students are in the design phase of creating panels to represent different groups of people in colonial New York. Students discuss physical design for half the class period, and then spend the remaining time in the computer lab acquiring information from websites on colonial

New York selected by their teacher. In the next class period, different groups of students read about different events that led to the American Revolution as preparation for their sharing this information with their classmates, and later to create a timeline about how the American Revolution occurred. In a subsequent class session, some students discuss connections between a historical fiction book (*The True Confessions of Charlotte Doyle*) and the Declaration of Independence, while other students monitor this discussion. During the fourth observation, each of five different groups of students read two documents about one event that led to the American Revolution. Each group then reports about its particular event to the rest of the class. Then, group members stand in the order in which their event occurred, thereby creating a human timeline. During the final observation, students analyze articles on weather and slave life and the connection between climate and way of life from a yearlong *Newsday* series on Long Island history in order to gather information to place on the panels of their MST projects.

PAULA'S WISE PRACTICES

Paula's wise practices may be grouped into seven categories. She involves her students in "doing the work of historians/citizens"; she brings in issues of perspective taking and historical empathy through students' historical investigations; she teaches skills to help students to be successful with upper-level materials; she checks for understanding; she is aware of the large gaps in her students' knowledge; she connects to other subject areas; and she acts as a facilitator of student learning.

Doing the Work of Historians/Citizens

Paula's emphasis on students doing the work of historians/citizens is a classroom commonplace. She uses the term "historian/citizens" to indicate that the work of historians in analysis and evaluation of data, in actuality, is the work of citizens. When she asks elementary students to read, interpret, and think critically about primary and secondary sources, she does so in the hope that they will be able to make informed judgments on personal, community, national, and global issues as citizens in a deliberative and participatory democracy.

Before students are to discuss a social studies topic, Paula asks them to bring their "research" folders to the circle. With respect to the design and creation of their MST projects, she reminds them that, "We are after a representation of your research, not just out of your head." Her questioning of students focuses on what she believes they know and the sources that they have examined: "How did you understand they were growing tobacco? Were there any photographs or text documents? What other documents might help? How will you find out if your source is authentic?" Following this discussion, the class lists on chart paper the possible documents they might find on the websites (e.g., photos, sketches, handwritten documents, journals, text documents, graphs, videos). In another lesson, when students use packets of information that include primary and secondary sources in order to construct a timeline on the American Revolution, Paula reminds them that this is "just like historians use data to figure out the order of events." Indeed, the district curriculum binder (created in a staff development project) contains more than 400 pages of a combination of primary and secondary sources for use in elementary social studies. When Paula uses articles from the yearlong *Newsday* series on Long Island history, she reminds the students that the articles were "written by historians who used primary sources in their work." The emphasis in the lessons is always on the use of evidence to substantiate points of view. When students discuss historical fiction, she reminds them that to "be accountable in the discussion, you must lift text evidence."

On another occasion, Paula asks students to take 15 minutes to "get 10 facts and three quotes on what it was like to be a slave at Lloyd Manor" in order to find out "whether or not Jupiter was treated poorly like the stereotype we'd expect." This lesson is followed later in the year by a field trip to Lloyd Manor so that students gain a sense of context about how this particular enslaved man lived. In addition, she asks students to interact with and question their readings. When examining an account about a particularly severe winter in the 1770s, Paula queries, "Why do historians care about weather? Why are we reading this piece?" Several students connect this study to their MST projects; knowing the weather helps them represent the location and climate on their panels. Another student connects the weather to the historical fiction the class is reading by noting that the British soldiers' uniforms showed they were better dressed than the minutemen in their rag-tag outfits, that must not have protected them from the frigid air.

Focusing on Perspective Taking and Historical Empathy

Hand in hand with students doing the work of historians is Paula's focus on perspective taking and historical empathy (e.g., Davis, Yeager, & Foster, 2001). Her instruction is consistent with research showing that even first-graders can "do" history and explore multiple voices (Barton, 1997; Brophy & VanSledright, 1997; Levstik, 1994; VanSledright & Brophy, 1995).

With the three-panel MST project, Paula acquaints students with three perspectives within the same time period: African Americans, European Americans, and Native Americans. Indeed, the essential question the students answer with their projects is based on the issue of perspective: Did colonization result in progress *for all?* The organization of the assignment into three different panels encourages students to distinguish among the three groups' experiences. Nearly all students decide that Native Americans and African Americans did not experience progress as a function of their treatment by European Americans. Students reveal divided conclusions with respect to European Americans. Those who emphasize progress focus on democratic institutions; others recognize several categories within "European Americans," including poor women, poor men, affluent women, and affluent men. Paula's use of historical fiction (e.g., *The True Confessions of Charlotte Doyle*; *Will You Sign Here, John Hancock?*, *What's the Big Idea, Ben Franklin?*, *Why Don't You Get a Horse, Sam Adams?*, *And Then What Happened, Paul Revere?*, *Where Was Patrick Henry on the 29th of May?*, *Can You Make Them Behave, King George?*) in conjunction with an examination of the Declaration of Independence makes the document come alive and reminds students that historical documents reveal the impact of the times on real people's lives.

Incorporating Skills Instruction

As her 9-year-old students analyze the U.S. Declaration of Independence, Paula is abundantly aware that they need strategies for studying this and other complicated documents; consequently, she offers advice about reading skills. In any upper-level reading assignment, Paula helps students to decode unknown words. She also teaches them how to skim: "If you're looking for information for your timeline, how do you find it without reading the whole packet?" Students seem to internalize many of these strategies. For example, when Paula answers a telephone call as a student defines a word, the student continues her definition only to be corrected by another student for "using the same word in the definition." When students in a group have to analyze and then present information to the class based on a challenging text, different groups use strategies with which they clearly are familiar. One group moves to another part of the room in order to get the quiet that its members need to think; then the group decides that one of its members will read the selection aloud while the others take notes. This procedure devolves into a mini-discussion over who will get to read; the group decides that whoever takes the most notes will get to read next.

Paula attends to note-taking skills as well. When she reads aloud excerpts from a historical fiction book (Jean Fritz's *Will You Sign Here, John Hancock?*), she asks her students to list in their notebooks the grievances that they hear in the story. When a discussion is about to begin, Paula points out that she has her notebook to record good information in the discussion and that students need their notebooks as well. Students then keep their notebooks open throughout the discussion; sometimes they jot down information, while at other times they verbally refer to previous information.

In addition to their having internalized reading and note-taking skills, these students clearly have internalized discussion skills. Students who are not chosen to be discussants are assigned other roles. Recorders, for example, listen for specific process skills, such as words they can use to help them add to another comment, the number of people who invite others into the discussion, how they invite other students in, and the number of times students revise their original ideas and weave other ideas into their thinking. At the end of the historical fiction discussion, the students have notes that they give orally to the discussants; these include specific phrases that show how people have added to others' comments (e.g., "So you're saying that…" and "So now I think that…" and "Can you support that with another part of the Declaration of Independence?").

Even as Paula focuses on a variety of skills to help students process what they read, see, and hear, she is mindful to teach students how to search for and talk about the main idea. Essential questions posted in the room keep her students focused on overarching issues, but Paula also uses questions to keep students on track. For example, the creation of a timeline of events leading to the American Revolution begins with the question, "What will be a *major* date?" When different events are given to different groups, Paula asks students to find out the "who, what, when, where, and why" of the event, reminding them that the "why is most important."

Checking for Understanding

Because the readings are challenging, Paula often checks for students' understanding. Several times during a discussion, she stops and has each student talk with the person next to him or her about a point just made; then some of the students report to the entire group about their understanding of the point. In the middle of an Internet research activity, Paula asks students to pause in their work to share what they have found so far. At the end of a discussion, Paula assigns students to record how they are now thinking about the topic: "Everyone write four quick sentences on how your original thinking was revised and who in the room changed your thinking." Sometimes she employs a quick check to assess the gaps in students' knowledge: "Okay, thumbs up or thumbs down; was it America yet?"

Identifying Gaps in Students' Knowledge

Students inevitably and routinely display gaps in their knowledge. Paula is attentive to this concern, and she is flexible enough to slow down and ask a series of questions to ascertain what students do not know. During one class session in which a group of students presents its assigned event (the Stamp Act) leading to the Revolution, she whispers in my ear, "Isn't it amazing what they don't know?" These particular children think the stamps being discussed were postage stamps and that the colonists were protesting the price of such stamps rather than the "taxation without representation" issue. Sometimes what students do not know totally changes the meaning of the discourse. During the Declaration of Independence/ *True Confessions of Charlotte Doyle* discussion, for example, one student states, "I looked it up; consent means authority." Authority certainly is one possible definition; however, Paula's probing reveals that this student has a different and unwarranted definition of authority in mind. Aware of the misconceptions around the idea of "consent of the governed," Paula subsequently teaches a lesson to clarify the grievances outlined in the Declaration by having students bullet them as she reads from a Jean Fritz book (*Will You Sign Here, John Hancock?*). Meanwhile, the students continue to read and take notes from their own Jean Fritz books (*What's the Big Idea, Ben Franklin?*, *Why Don't You Get a Horse, Sam Adams?*, *And Then What Happened, Paul Revere?*, *Where Was Patrick Henry on the 29th of May?*, *Can You Make Them Behave, King George?*). Paula uses historical fiction in conjunction with appropriate primary source documents to humanize history and to provide students who have reading difficulties with another way to master the content, yet she also acknowledges the importance of distinguishing between the different uses of historical fiction and historical texts.

Making Connections across Subject Areas

A ubiquitous aspect of Paula's teaching is her ability to make content and skill connections across school subjects. Her assigned projects are often interdisciplinary. For example, the MST panels connect math and science skills with social studies content, and an English/language arts (ELA) project asks students to address issues of social justice found in literature. As a follow-up to the social justice emphasis in the literature project, Paula's students use their American Revolution research to write their own declaration of grievances in an imperfect world. The communication skills in ELA readily carry over to historical fiction book discussions; students are quite comfortable as they monitor the process of their discussion in any subject. Also, Paula does not hesitate to insist on correct spelling in all subject areas; she reminds students to use their glossaries to check the correct spelling of unfamiliar words.

Facilitating Learning

Throughout all of the varied activities, Paula is careful to act as a learning facilitator rather than simply as a lecturer/authority figure, even if this role means that students do not have their misinformation corrected until future lessons. Her frequent strategy of having students sit together on the rug to share information and to monitor their own discussions pays off in the students' self-starting capabilities and in their many opportunities to learn from each other. Paula's comments during such discussions are brief and strategic. "Stop and think; you're onto something big," she tells her students when they link the concept of "consent of the governed" in the historical fiction book to the Declaration of Independence. "Substantiate it," she challenges students when they make a statement that is not fully supported. Even her physical presence in the classroom illustrates her role as facilitator. She circulates in the computer room, pausing at different groups of students to listen to their hypotheses and evidence, asking a question or two, and then moving to the next group. She is another member of the discussion circle with notebook in hand, recording, as her students do, meaningful comments about content and process. She gives periodic time bulletins (rather than mandating what portion of the assignment students should be working on by a set time) so that students can manage their time effectively. She shies away from praising a correct answer immediately; rather, she asks other students to agree or disagree, or to add to the previous remark. She also tries not to reexplain directions. Her first response to students who are unclear on an assignment is to direct them to ask a group member or another classmate for clarification.

THE POSSIBILITY OF STAFF DEVELOPMENT
FOR TEACHER AGENCY

Clearly, Paula is able to maintain her wise practice during the imposition of state-mandated testing. In fact, she believes that she has become a better teacher of social studies because of the test's emphasis on the use of primary sources to answer meaningful questions. She attributes her use of rich sources to the staff development activities in her district, but she admits that this staff development is not the type available to most teachers. She characterizes her experience as "being in a classroom and seeing good teaching, then planning together with someone who is knowledgeable, then trying it out yourself"; in other words, she is describing the "lead teacher" model that her district uses. Through this approach, teachers contact lead teachers (one for each major school subject) to meet with them and mentor them. All of the lead teachers confirm that Paula invites them into her classroom more than any other teacher in the district. Consequently, she has become a "turnkey teacher" (an expert who helps other teachers understand and deliver the curriculum) in her own building. That is, she does her own staff development (on her free periods and lunch hours) with teachers at her grade level and with others at different grade levels. Paula also values being tapped to give presentations at conferences and views these experiences as affirmation of her ability to learn and transmit important information and techniques.

Paula recognizes that her district provides her with opportunities to expand her professional knowledge, which in turn expands the opportunities for her students. This process reinforces Eisner's (1994) idea that "the school must be a growth environment for the teacher if it is to be an optimal growth environment for the student" (p. 376). Paula echoes Eisner's warning against "teacher-proof" materials, acknowledging that the imposition of statewide tests has the potential to "deskill" teachers (Apple, 1990), unless there is worthwhile and thoughtful staff development. Given the tendency of teachers to underestimate their potential to shape curriculum and the context of their work (e.g., Thornton & Wenger, 1990), this limited conception of the teacher as deliverer of prepackaged review materials, unfortunately, may be a more likely model in the world of standardized testing than the one offered by Paula Marron. Certainly, in the enacted curriculum, the key factor is the teacher and her or his sense of purpose (Ross, 1994; Thornton, 1991). However, the teacher needs to know her or his power in order to use it. Thus, professional "consciousness-raising" is a crucial issue for teachers. Staff development leaders can play an important role in helping teachers understand what they want to do and why they want to do it (Thornton, 1992).

Paula's observations about teachers' expertise and on staff development in one's own classroom and school (as opposed to a districtwide, one-size-fits-all initiative) are consistent with research that advocates bringing teachers back into the professional development process in a localized setting (Fullan & Hargreaves, 1996; Hargreaves, 1989, 1995; Lieberman, 1997; McLaughlin, 1997; Paris, 1993). Paula's district's new approach to staff development is also consistent with this research. Districts that are scrambling to accommodate new testing mandates would do well to develop similar models in which teachers are actively involved at the center of the process.

Clearly, good professional development is exceedingly difficult (Lieberman, 1997). Researchers have asserted that it requires the creation of a community of learners, collegiality, and the integration of work and learning (Joyce & Showers, 1996; Smylie, 1995). Successful staff development also requires time and meaningful support (Adelman, Walking Eagle, & Hargreaves, 1997; Eraut, 1995); it must be ongoing with feedback and follow-up (Guskey, 1995). Moreover, the development of a professional learning culture in school must be part of a teacher's job, not an afterthought or extracurricular activity (Fullan, 1995). Thus, the literature on school reform outlines some specific conditions of collaborative culture and interactive professionalism (Fullan & Hargreaves, 1996), and researchers argue that teachers cannot create and sustain contexts for productive learning unless those conditions exist for them. Little evidence exists, however, that this has ever been a priority of schools (Sarason, 1996). Indeed, Paula remarks that teacher agency requires these conditions, and she notes the need for "someone with vision (e.g., a lead teacher, a turnkey person in the school, a principal who is willing to free people up, a visionary social studies director) because teachers are too overworked already, especially fourth-grade teachers."

Despite this comment, Paula's awareness of her power as a curricular and instructional gatekeeper helps her to use the state social studies test as a guide, not a directive, for instruction that values inquiry over "drill materials." Of course, if the tests are guiding instruction, then the type of test matters, and in the case of the teacher-created New York State elementary social studies test, document-based analysis trumps memorization. A "good" test, as Paula illustrates, can be an impetus for powerful teaching and learning, but, as she suggests, only if there is commitment to meaningful staff development, including providing teachers with a solid grasp of content.

Paula's experiences also demonstrate that the New York State requirement for professional development can be an opportunity for teacher educators to connect with school districts in order to provide elementary teachers the content and skills they need to offer rich social studies instruction. Even the best social studies methods course taken by preservice elementary teachers, while an important starting point, is woefully inadequate to guide these teachers through the testing maze they face when they enter the profession. This story of one exemplary teacher suggests that a combination of mandatory elementary social studies assessments and ongoing professional development requirements could produce more social studies teachers like Paula Marron.

REFERENCES

Adelman, N., Walking Eagle, K., & Hargreaves, A. (1997). Racing with the clock: Making time for teaching and learning in school reform. New York: Teachers College Press.
Alleman, J., & Brophy, J. (1993). Teaching that lasts: college students' reports of learning activities experienced in elementary school social studies. *Social Science Record 30*(2), 36–48.
Apple, M. (1990). Is there a curriculum voice to reclaim? *Phi Delta Kappan 71*, 526–530.
Barton, K. (1997). History—it can be elementary: An overview of elementary students' understanding of history. *Social Education 61*, 13–16.
Brophy, J., & VanSledright, B. (1997). *Teaching and learning history in elementary schools.* New York: Teachers College Press.
Davis, O.L., Jr. (1997). Beyond "best practices" toward wise practices [Editorial]. *Journal of Curriculum and Supervision 13*(1), 1–5.
Davis, O.L., Jr., Yeager, E., & Foster, S. (Eds.). (2001). *Historical empathy and perspective taking in the social studies.* Lanham, MD: Rowman & Littlefield.
Eisner, E. (1994). *The educational imagination: On the design and evaluation of school programs.* New York: Macmillan.
Eraut, M. (1995). Developing professional knowledge within a client-centered orientation. In T. Guskey & M. Huberman (Eds.), *Professional development in education: New paradigms and practices.* New York: Teachers College Press.
Fullan, M. (1995). The limits and potential of professional development. In T. Guskey & M. Huberman (Eds.), *Professional development in education: New paradigms and practices.* New York: Teachers College Press.
Fullan, M., & Hargreaves, A. (1996). *What's worth fighting for in your school?* New York: Teachers College Press.
Good, T., & Brophy, J. (1991). *Looking in classrooms* (5th ed.). New York: HarperCollins.
Guskey, T. (1995). Professional development in education: In search of the optimal mix. In T. Guskey & M. Huberman (Eds.), *Professional development in education: new paradigms and practices.* New York: Teachers College Press.
Hargreaves, A. (1989). *Curriculum and assessment reform.* Philadelphia: Open University Press.
Hargreaves, A. (1995). Development and desire: a post-modern perspective. In T. Guskey & M. Huberman (Eds.), *Professional development in education: new paradigms and practices.* New York: Teachers College Press.
Joyce, B., & Showers, B. (1996). *Student achievement through staff development: Fundamentals of school renewal.* White Plains, NY: Longman.
Levstik, L. (1994). Building a sense of history in a first-grade class. In J. Brophy (Ed.), *Advances in research on teaching: Case studies of teaching and learning in social studies* (Vol 4). Greenwich, CT: JAI Press.
Lieberman, A. (Ed.). (1997). *Rethinking School Improvement: Research, Craft, and Concept.* New York: Teachers College Press.
McLaughlin, M. (1997). Rebuilding teacher professionalism in the United States. In A. Hargreaves & R. Evans. (Eds.), *Beyond educational reform: bringing teachers back in.* Philadelphia: Open University Press.

Newmann, F. (1990). Qualities of thoughtful social studies classes: An empirical profile. *Journal of Curriculum Studies, 22*, 443–461.

Paris, C. (1993). *Teacher agency and curriculum making in classrooms.* New York: Teachers College Press.

Ross, E. (1994). Teachers as curriculum theorizers. In *Reflective practice in social studies* (pp. 35–42). Washington, DC: National Council for the Social Studies.

Sarason, S. (1996). *Revisiting "The culture of the school and the problem of change."* New York: Teachers College Press.

Smylie, M. (1995). Teacher learning in the workplace: Implications for school reform. In T. R.Guskey & M. Huberman (Eds.), *Professional development in education: new paradigms and practices.* New York: Teachers College Press.

Thornton, S. (1991). Teacher as curricular-instructional gatekeeper in social studies. In J. P. Shaver (Ed.), *Handbook of research on social studies teaching and learning.* New York: Macmillan.

Thornton, S. (1992). How do elementary teachers decide what to teach in social studies? In E. Ross, J. Cornett, & G. McCutcheon (Eds.), *Teacher personal theorizing: Connecting curriculum practice, theory, and research.* Albany, NY: State University of New York Press.

Thornton, S., & Wenger, R. (1990). Geography curriculum and instruction in three fourth-grade classrooms. *Elementary School Journal, 90*, 515–531.

VanSledright, B., & Brophy, J. (1995). "Storytellers," "scientists," and "reformers" in the teaching of U.S. history to fifth graders. In J. Brophy (Ed.), *Advances in research on teaching* (Vol. 5). Greenwich, CT: JAI Press.

Whitehead, A. (1929). *The aims of education.* New York: The Free Press.

Wiggins, G., & McTighe, J. (1998). *Understanding by design.* Alexandria, VA: Association for Supervision and Curriculum Development.

Yeager, E. (2000). Thoughts on wise practice in the teaching of social studies. *Social Education 64*(2), 352–353.

CHAPTER 4

VOICES OF FLORIDA ELEMENTARY SCHOOL TEACHERS

Their Conceptions of Wise Social Studies Practice

Diane Yendol-Hoppey
Jennifer Jacobs
Keith Tilford

The National Council for the Social Studies (1993) has defined social studies as "the integrated study of the social sciences and humanities to promote civic competence." In addition to this statement, an NCSS Task Force (NCSS, 1994) described powerful social studies as meaningful, integrative, value-based, challenging, and active. Consistent with these statements, several researchers have identified skills that a teacher should possess in order to provide quality social studies instruction. Stanley (1991), for example, argued that teacher effectiveness is a blend of technical, practical, and critical expertise, whereas Shulman (1987) outlined a need for teacher knowledge that includes substantive pedagogical content knowledge. However, the often discrepant cultures of public schools and higher education

(Leming, 1989) prompts wonder about how elementary teachers who work in a high-stakes testing context conceptualize wise social studies practice.

More recently, Yeager (2000), drawing on Shulman and Stanley, extended the discussion of "wise social studies practice" by assembling a set of portrayals of such teaching, agreeing with Shulman that wise social studies teaching could be codified through extensive case literature. Nevertheless, in light of many efforts to define the purpose, components, and characteristics of sound social studies practice, more studies are needed that report and interpret how elementary social studies teachers, challenged by high-stakes testing and committed to teaching *all* children, conceptualize and engage in wise social studies practice.

This issue has become a particularly pressing dilemma for teachers in Florida. They face state-mandated curriculum frameworks and standardized testing in the areas of reading, writing, and mathematics, which are emphasized in classrooms increasingly at the expense of the nontested social studies curriculum. Elementary school teachers in Florida who face pressures of "raising their school grade" appear to have shifted their curricular attention away from social studies. As increased pressures from high-stakes testing overload an already crowded curriculum, Florida teachers acknowledge the marginalization of the social studies program. Thus, this chapter illustrates how several elementary school teachers, described by colleagues and school leaders as highly effective, conceptualize and engage in elementary social studies practice.

METHOD

Given that the purpose of this chapter was to portray how teachers make sense of their social studies teaching as they interact with the social and organizational forces of the context in which they teach, we used an interpretive and naturalistic research paradigm (Denzin & Lincoln, 1994) to capture teacher stories that responded to our research questions. This chapter does not try to impose a definition of wise practice or measure the extent of wise practice in each context. Instead, we explore teachers' thoughts about teaching elementary social studies within a high-stakes testing context. Accordingly, phenomenology became the theoretical lens for this study. The goal of phenomenology is to describe the essence of a phenomenon through intense and careful study (Moustakas, 1994; Seidman, 1991) that seeks to "determine what an experience means for a person who has had the experience and is able to provide a comprehensive description of it" (Moustakas, 1994, p.13). Thus, this study combined ethnographic methods of prolonged observation[1] with a phenomenological positioning

(Maso, 2001), in order to provide description and analysis of how teachers conceptualized and enacted their work.

The 12 teachers interviewed and observed for this study taught grades two through five in two different schools, Keene Elementary (KE) and Belle Elementary (BE), each of which possessed their own contextual and student challenges. Both of these schools would be considered somewhere in the middle on a continuum of socioeconomic and cultural diversity in this north central Florida area. Although these schools were culturally diverse and relatively similar to each other (see Table 4.1), they were not plagued by the seemingly insurmountable contextual challenges faced by "failing" Florida schools.[2] Opportunistic or emergent sampling (Patton, 2002, p. 240) provided the basis for the selection of these 12 "reputationally" noted teachers. Although only four of these 12 teachers had a reputation for strong social studies teaching practice, both school leaders and the research team identified all of the teachers as strong in their general elementary practice.

Table 4.1. Select Demographics of the Teachers' Schools

	School	
School Characteristic	KE	BE
Grades	K–5	3–5
Total School Population	360	463
Students Absent 21+ days	4.4%	6.6%
Average Class Size K–5	25.7%	22.5%
Pupils with Disabilities	15.6%	17.8%
Pupils Who Receive Free and Reduced-Price Lunches	29.4%	55.9%
Pupils Identified as Gifted	13.33%	12%
Stability Rate of School Population	98.3%	94.4%
Grade Assigned to School by State DOE	A	B
Teachers with Advanced Degrees	83.9%	57.1%
Average Years of Teachers' Experience	14	15.5
Title One	N/A	Title I School
Pupil Ethnicity: White Non-Hispanic[*]	53.6%	65.4%
Pupil Ethnicity: Black Non-Hispanic	24.7%	28.8%
Pupil Ethnicity: Hispanic	13.6%	3%
Pupil Ethnicity: Asian/Pacific Islander	1%	.9%
Pupil Ethnicity: Multiracial	7%	1.9%

[*] Racial Ethnic Category information reported to Florida DOE for Fall 2002

Table 4.2 presents a snapshot of each school's performance as measured by the Florida Comprehensive Achievement Test (FCAT). Schools KE and BE demonstrated similar levels of student achievement in the tested areas of reading, mathematics, and writing.

Table 4.2. Comparison of FCAT (2003) Scores by School and Grade Level

	Percent of Pupils Scoring Three and Above on the FCAT					
	3		4		5	
School	KE	BE	KE	BE	KE	BE
Reading	62	65	76	65	76	53
Mathematics	52	51	53	61	60	43
Writing	NA	NA	96	88	NA	NA

NA, Not applicable; KE, Keene Elementary; BE, Belle Elementary

Six of the 12 teachers participating in this study taught at KE[3] Developmental Research School. The elementary portion of the school served about 360 students in kindergarten through grade five. As noted in Table 4.2, KE enrolled a range of students from differing socioeconomic, racial, and ethnic populations. All KE teachers held a master's degree and had at least 3 years' teaching experience. In addition to a master's degree, many teachers on this faculty held doctoral and specialist degrees. Led by the school's research director who is committed to teacher leadership, the school's mission is to develop, evaluate, and disseminate exemplary programs of education as well as to serve as a vehicle for research about, demonstration of, and evaluation of teaching and learning.

The other six participants taught at BE, a rural school located about 20 miles from the university in a small, stable rural community. BE is one of the oldest continuously operating schools in the county, with its first building erected in 1895. At the time of this study, the intermediate school served 463 pupils in grades three through five. BE comprised a socioeconomically and culturally diverse student population. The principal had been at the school for 12 years and engaged in leadership through shared decision making. BE's mission statement is "Excellence through initiative, innovation, and involvement." Both KE and BE have been involved in a school/university partnership for the past 3 years; university professors place a cohort of preinterns at each school each semester to work alongside a mentor teacher.

Researchers had the opportunity informally and regularly to observe teaching, schedules, and planning for a period of 18 to 36 months in these contexts. These observations typically occurred once each week. The duration of the researchers' involvement in each context enabled them to develop probing interview questions and added to the credibility of their conclusions (Patton, 2002). In an effort to discern the teachers' perceived experiences in the area of elementary social studies, the researchers also asked the 12 teachers to participate in a lengthy semistructured interview during May and August 2003. Table 4.3 identifies the grade-level representation, the years of experience possessed, ethnicity, and educational attainment of each teacher who participated in this study.

Table 4.3. Teacher-Participants' Teaching Assignment, Total Years of Experience, Highest Degree Held, and Ethnicity

	Teacher	*Grade*	*# of Years*	*Degree*	*Ethnicity*
KE	Megan	3	9	M.A.	White
	Kim	1/2	15	Ph.D.	White
	Jon	5	25	M.A.	White
	Carolyn	4	21	M.A.	White
	Jessica	4	3	M.A.	White
	Jennifer	1/2	5	M.A.	White
BE	Joyce	5	31	M.A.	White
	Robert	5	35	M.A.	White
	Colin	4	5	M.A.	White
	Karen	4	19	M.A.	White
	Ali	5	18	M.A.	White
	Nancy	3	4	M.A.	White

Given the focus on understanding elementary teachers' conceptions of wise practice, researchers utilized an organizational framework for pedagogical content knowledge in the analysis. Building on Shulman (1986. 1987), Yeager (2000) asserted the importance of pedagogical content knowledge (PCK) in the construction of wise practice. As a result, the teacher interview protocols (see Appendix A) consisted of 24 questions that probed the five domains developed by Silva and Mason (2003), who considered these key to teacher pedagogical content knowledge: content, students, teacher, teaching, and context. This framework for PCK draws on the work of several researchers (e.g., Grossman, 1990; Magnusson, Krajcik, & Borko, 1999; Shulman, 1986, 1987) who defined PCK as a teacher's personal transformation of content knowledge into subject-specific pedagogical knowledge. In this regard, PCK seems to be central to teachers' work as they organize and represent appropriate knowledge and processes of a subject area in light of particular contexts and students.

Because of the potentially contentious or ambiguous nature of the term "wise practice," participants were not asked specifically to define their "wise practice" in social studies. Rather, they were asked to describe and explain the knowledge base they used when planning for teaching social studies to their students in their particular context. Because these teachers were nominated as strong elementary generalists, the researchers believed that they would represent the strongest social studies teachers within the two contexts and that their insights would make possible the development of a normative-based practitioner conception of wise practice.

After the interviews were transcribed, the researchers used HyperResearch 2.0 (1999) to analyze the collective set of interviews. This analysis resulted in 41 codes. In a review of the 41 codes, the researchers sorted the codes by assigning them to one of the five overarching PCK domains. These codes easily connected to the domain examples and led the researchers to construct a normative description of wise practice as understood by these elementary educators.

In addition to the interview data, field notes collected over the course of the past 2 years served to triangulate the themes that emerged from the interviews around instructional strategies. Finally, a questionnaire also served to triangulate and shed light onto the contextual challenges experienced by these teachers. The Adjusted School Improvement Questionnaire (ASIQ) is a version of the original School Improvement Questionnaire (SIQ) developed by Webb and Pajares and described in Sindelar, Webb, and Miller (2002). This questionnaire included demographic items and Likert-scale items. The anchors on the Likert-scale items include "disagree totally" to "agree totally," "no confidence" to "complete confidence" or "near perfect confidence," and "no say or influence" to "total say or influence." These items are divided conceptually into nine scales that provide a gauge of (a) collegiality (5 items), (b) faculty inventiveness (5 items), (c) district support for learning (6 items), (d) professional commitment (8 items), (e) willingness to adapt instruction to fit the needs of individual students (2 items), (f) personal sense of efficacy (5 items plus the 3-item scales for language arts teachers, eighth-grade language arts teachers, and mathematics teachers), (g) ability to influence decision making at work (11 items), (h) mutual influence on teaching (4 items), and (i) collective efficacy (15 items). The ASIQ served as a final data source that helped us triangulate the stories emerging around the role of context.

HOW DID THESE TEACHERS CONCEIVE OF THE PHENOMENON OF WISE PRACTICE?

The data culled from the interviews and observations indicated a variety of characteristics that teachers viewed as central to their own conception of the phenomenon of wise elementary social studies practice. Table 4.4 presents the threads and characteristics within the five domains of PCK held by the 12 teachers in this study.

In the first domain of PCK, knowledge of content, these teachers also noted a number of key characteristics that reasonably could be conceptualized as related to wise practice. For example, teachers noted the importance of depth over breadth, even in light of the current high-stakes testing climate's pressure to stress only the latter. They also described a preference for teaching and assessing "big ideas" rather than isolated facts. In addition, the majority of the teachers indicated the need to possess a personal interest in social studies content. They believed that this personal interest was essential to successful teaching because most of their content knowledge in social studies had resulted from independent effort and interest. Also consistent across the teachers' responses was their belief in the importance of teachers possessing content knowledge across the social sciences and not just history. Yet while they consistently noted the importance of content knowledge, none of the teachers could name any aspect of their social studies content preparation, beyond general high school and undergraduate course requirements.

The second domain of PCK, knowledge of/role of students in learning, demonstrated the teachers' belief that children needed to have choices, to be active participants, and to understand the relevance of social studies. Teachers also acknowledged that they must possess a deep knowledge of the individual differences—academic, cultural, and emotional—of children in their classroom. This knowledge seemed key to these teachers' ability and efforts to provide examples of differentiated instruction and alternative assessment. Although most of the teachers discussed student differences in generic terms (e.g., independent/dependent learners, behavioral characteristics), they also emphasized their belief that teachers must possess an understanding of child development in order to teach, for example, time and space as social science concepts.

The third domain of PCK, role of the teacher, also exemplified a number of practical characteristics that appeared to shed light on wise practice. Most teachers identified the importance of the teacher's fundamental commitment to teaching social studies, as well as a belief in and understanding of how to engage in "integrated instruction" (e.g., using social studies as the content focus for teaching reading, writing, critical thinking, and oral language). A clear distinction emerged between the way teachers in this

Table 4.4. Normative Conceptions of Five Domains of Wise Elementary Social Studies Practice Held By 12 Teachers

PCK Thread	Characteristics of Wise Practice
Knowledge of Content	Comfort with depth over breadth in content
	Teacher possesses a personal interest in the content area
	An understanding of social studies as an integrated approach to the social sciences
	Focus on "big ideas" (concepts/generalizations) and not just facts
Knowledge of and Role of Students	Providing children with choices
	Relevancy of topic to children's lives, Understanding of individual differences within the classroom
	Differentiated instruction and assessment
	Knowledge of children's conception of time and space
Role of Teacher	Commitment to teaching social studies
	Understanding of integration
	Willingness to challenge status quo and to take a risk
Knowledge of Instructional Strategies	Integration of technology
	Integration of literature
	Simulations
	Role play
	Use of primary resources
	Inquiry
	Field trips
	Discussions
	Current events
	Models
	Maps
	Projects
	Storytelling
	Assignments that reinforce FCAT skills
	Reading skill for content acquisition
Knowledge of Context	Adequate materials and resources
	Flexible scheduling
	Opportunities to integrate
	Blocks of time
	Teams of teachers working together

study described themselves as committed and how they described many of their colleagues who were less committed to teaching social studies. In fact, they stated their belief in the idea of teachers as leaders who are willing to challenge the status quo on behalf of children (Silva, Gimbert, & Nolan, 2000), as well as to take risks (e.g., not rely on FCAT preparation materials) in their own instructional practice. This conception meant that teachers at BE taught against the grain (Cochran-Smith & Lytle, 1990) by "usurping" mathematics, reading, and writing time to engage in social studies instruction. The most skilled of these teachers described how they connected social studies instruction to their responsibility to teach reading and writing.

The fourth domain of PCK, knowledge of instructional strategies, revealed a variety of strategies common across the teachers' social studies teaching practice. Many of the teachers emphasized generic use of simulations, role-play, drama, primary sources, field trips, wax museums, models/maps, discussion, and storytelling; they clearly indicated that they understood a menu of instructional choices that extended beyond the adopted textbook. However, in probing for how teachers determined which of these strategies to use for teaching specific concepts, we found that teachers rarely offered content-specific reasons for making such a choice. In fact, their choices most often were connected to what the children in their classroom enjoyed doing, what they themselves believed to be an engaging instructional strategy, or what had worked for them in the past.

In the final domain of PCK, knowledge of context, teachers' responses focused on the importance of adequate materials and resources, opportunities for flexibility in scheduling, opportunities to integrate subject areas by moving away from departmentalized structures, providing blocks of time dedicated to social studies, and creating an organizational structure for effective teaming. These teachers noted that the context has had a dramatic effect on their social studies teaching. They believed that high-stakes testing of mathematics, reading, and writing had stolen time previously specified for social studies instruction. For example, at BE, the untested social studies curriculum area had become a second-tier subject that often received little attention until after March when the testing was over.

EXAMPLES OF TEACHERS' CONCEPTIONS OF WISE PRACTICE

The following examples of instruction provide windows into the way the teachers conceptualized and enacted these wise practice characteristics. For each example, a narrative is provided in the teacher's voice, followed by our interpretation with connections to the characteristics of wise practice.

Example One: Joyce

A fifth-grade teacher, Joyce, described the way her team incorporated the teaching of current events into a spontaneously generated unit on the war in Iraq. As her teaching team acknowledged the relevancy of the topic and the students' interest in it, they adjusted the traditional U.S. history curriculum accordingly:

> I enjoyed the unit we did on the war because it was relevant to what was going on in their lives. We tied it into current events. They got points for bringing in newspaper and magazine articles and Internet things that related either to World War I and II or what was going on in the Middle East. We incorporated political cartoons of what was happening and we wrote letters to the editor. That was the culminating thing. We were constantly panning back and forth between the U.S. history text and today, looking for similarities and differences. They loved it. I was originally "iffy" on the whole thing. I had never gotten to the 1900s in fifth grade. We were always stopped at the Civil War. This really stands out. (Joyce, BE, 4102, 4929)

This anecdote indicates what happened when a team of teachers worked together to identify and capture teachable moments that occur as a result of dealing with relevant events in children's worlds. In fact, because Joyce's team developed this idea as a group, they believed in their power and flexibility to seize the moment and redirect the focus of their instruction beyond the established Civil War topics. Through this experience, Joyce integrated technology, and her instruction panned back and forth between the war in the Middle East by using current events and the exploration of the 20th-century world wars. This change offered children the opportunity to expand their conceptions of time and space. In addition, Joyce attended to children's writing and the use of the media as she conceived of social studies as an area that legitimately could be related to language arts. As Joyce described her work on this unit, she said that she focused on depth over breadth and on developing children's "big ideas" about the sources and reality of war rather than the details of each battle. Evidence from this example underscores the importance of teachers' possessing a personal interest in the content area, as well as being both committed to teaching social studies and being willing to take risks in their teaching. Furthermore, this anecdote illustrates that Joyce attended to all five domains in her construction of PCK.

Example Two: Colin

Colin described how he used simulation as a way of making social studies meaningful to the children in his fourth-grade classroom:

> This time I really went beyond my Florida history curriculum. It was a tangent that came out of a part of our Florida textbook. My children were intrigued with the notion of the Loyalist and the Patriot, but they really didn't have a sense of where those words came from or what they meant. We decided to divide the class. Some of them became Loyalists and others became Patriots. That defined their whole personality. They chose a name, they chose a career, they chose everything and they became those people. We had a third group that was a British royal family. And so they did research and found out who Queen Charlotte was.... And then after they learned about these people, they acted things out. They engaged in a formal debate around the conflicting ideas of the time. It was just the coolest thing ever. The whole year they would call each other King George or Queen Charlotte. They would call each other by their names like Paul Revere.... They just identified with it. So it became more than something they read. They became a part of it. They also began to see how people held different perspectives around the same issue. (Colin, BE, 5328, 5591)

In this example, Colin used simulation and role-play, as well as multiple types of discourse and discussion, including some of the components of Socratic seminar and debate, as they discussed the conflicting ideas of the time (Parker, 2001). The children in this classroom spent time around an inquiry question: What were the roles of the Loyalists and Patriots, and how did they influence our existing government? This was a question of relevancy to the children as it emerged from their own discussion. Indeed, Colin realized that a gap in their knowledge base existed, and he was concerned about providing both background and conceptual clarity. Finally, Colin's example once again demonstrated the importance of challenging the status quo of mandated curriculum on behalf of his students.

Example Three: Jessica

Jessica, a fourth-grade teacher, shared an example of what she conceived as her best social studies practice:

> We are learning about the geography of Florida right now and, you know, it is hard for kids to grasp the idea of space unless they are really involved with it. After we have spent some time investigating the unique geography of Florida, we are going to work in small groups to create a map or model of the state. I have them bring in play dough and they make the map of Florida using the

dough. So where there is water they put blue play dough, where there is land they put green play dough. So Lake Okeechobee is huge and it will be on their maps too. They make the Keys and then they've got a sheet of paper that we make together of the places that need to be on the map: Tallahassee, Gainesville, Orlando, The Keys, the Atlantic Ocean, the Gulf of Mexico, the Straits of Florida, bordering states, etc.... It is really hands-on and the project really helps them remember and visualize the geography of the state. They work in partners and this makes it possible for all kids to participate in social studies. They are "doing" geography. Assessment becomes a project grade based on the expectations defined by our class. (Jessica, KE, 3940, 5242)

This example highlights this teacher's belief that *maps and models* as well as "hands-on" involvement with a project helped her children construct meaning of place. Jessica's small group project approach supported the needs of her diverse classroom of learners as they all engaged in the same work. Additionally, Jessica appeared to be comfortable with alternative forms of assessment that departed from traditional textbook tests. Missing from Jessica's example, however, is an articulation of the underlying generalizations and concepts she hoped the children in her classroom would generate as a result of this map construction.

All 12 teachers offered insights into a normative conceptualization of wise social studies teaching practice. They also lamented the challenges and voiced a collective sense of deep frustration with their ability to engage routinely in such wise practices. Yet these frustrations were handled differently in each context.

THE FRUSTRATIONS OF WISE PRACTICE

Given the intensity of Florida's high-stakes testing in reading, writing, and mathematics, these 12 teachers each voiced substantial frustration in teaching the untested subject of social studies. However, although teachers in both schools admitted that social studies did not receive the same emphasis that it had prior to the FCAT era, they asserted differences in the way high-stakes testing impacted social studies instruction. For example, Robert (BE) described a type of field trip that he routinely conducted with his fifth-grade students before his district shifted personnel and support from social studies:

For example, we used to have a mock court that we went to that was connected to our study of the judicial system and the Bill of Rights. We would go to the courthouse each year and local attorneys would work with the fifth grade. The attorneys, judges, law students, and others would hold a mock court for the kids. The kids were selected to sit on the jury and there were one or two scenarios that they would use and go through the trial process. They had direct examination, cross-examination, witnesses, to see how the court system worked in our country, and the kids or jury would go and deliberate and come back with a verdict. We decided not to go to it anymore for a bunch of reasons. For example, they started turning all the responsibilities for planning and teaching it to the teachers because we lost the district social studies curriculum coordinator. They also started limiting our field trips because of FCAT. Our school day is so short and there is so much to cover for FCAT. (Robert, 5817, 6687)

Robert's account was typical of the experiences of BE teachers, who often viewed themselves as curriculum implementers, not curriculum developers, or, in Apple's term (1979), as having been "deskilled." Teachers shared that in many schools across their district, field trips were not even allowed until after the FCAT administration. The reality for teachers at BE was that FCAT pressures forced a dramatic decrease in the time and resources dedicated to social studies instruction.

On the other hand, because the teachers at KE university research school considered themselves curriculum developers as well as curriculum implementers, they did not feel the same pressure to diminish social studies in the curriculum in order to focus solely on reading, writing, and mathematics. Jessica and Carolyn, for example, described the freedom they had to make curricular choices even in light of FCAT:

We do have the freedom to go on as many field trips as we want. We can bring in guest speakers. I think our campus is a wonderful place to get a good glimpse of a variety of social studies opportunities. I really am given a lot of freedom as far as my teaching goes to develop lessons the way I want to. (Carolyn, 9497, 9910)

There is a lot of support for making life concepts a reality for the kids and not something they just read about. (Jessica, 9130, 9586)

In light of these two quite different responses, the frustration associated with teaching social studies, to some degree, seemed to be related to the school's culture and organization. This is supported by the results of a culture survey given in both schools (see Table 4.5). The degree of satisfaction with their district was quite different for the two schools' faculties. Additionally, the responses to the question "How much say do you have in deciding what you teach?" highlights a plausible difference in the teachers' perceived roles concerning curriculum. The responses for teachers at KE to this question produced a mean score of 7.26 with a standard deviation of just over 1.5, whereas the BE teachers' mean score was 5.27 with a standard deviation of more than 2. The teachers at BE also indicated that they believed they had less input into the form and content of in-service programs than did the teachers at KE. Importantly, BE's school district mandates that certain tests aligned with the adopted texts be administered to students throughout the school year. The results of the survey appear to reveal that the teachers at BE, in comparison to the teachers at KE, saw their role largely as "curriculum implementers" rather than "curriculum developers." We concluded that the school and district culture, a factor that is never measured in Florida's performance assessment system, appears to be a key difference between KE, which embraces curriculum integrity, and BE, which does not.

Table 4.5. Means Responses by Teachers at BE and KE about Specific Aspects of School Improvement

Survey Questions	BE	KE
I would accept almost any class or school assignment in order to keep working for this district.	2.48	5.11
I feel that this district inspires the very best in the job performance of its teachers.	3.34	7.63
I am proud to tell others that I work for the district.	5.31	8.21
How much say do you have in deciding what you teach?	5.27	7.26
How much say do you have about the form and content of in-service programs?	4.97	6.37

FINAL THOUGHTS ABOUT WISE PRACTICES IN ELEMENTARY SOCIAL STUDIES INSTRUCTION

This study described two dimensions of these teachers' stance toward wise elementary social studies practice. The first dimension related to the teachers' pedagogical content knowledge, which undergirded their elementary social studies pedagogy. The second dimension focused on the teachers' perceived ability to resolve the contextual challenges that limited implementation of the social studies practice that they deemed wise.

In terms of the first dimension, teachers in this study were able to identify key characteristics within each of the five domains. However, although these teachers showed promise in their knowledge of each domain, few could offer insight into how they made curricular decisions. Additionally, given the breadth of content explored in the elementary social studies curriculum, few of these teachers could demonstrate depth of content knowledge in the form of specifying key generalizations or big ideas inherent in a specific area of inquiry.

Connected to the second dimension of wise practice, this study's findings also revealed that these elementary teachers experienced great frustration regarding their efforts to teach elementary social studies, and they identified contextual barriers to teaching social studies with the curriculum integrity that they believed social studies deserved. These kinds of barriers certainly complicate and constrain wise practice when social studies is situated within a larger curricular and high-stakes testing framework for which the elementary teacher is responsible.

The stories of practice offered by these teachers reveal that, although few preservice and in-service opportunities have been offered to these elementary teachers in social studies, these teachers are nonetheless considered wise in their general practice and collectively possess pedagogical content knowledge that could serve as a foundation for building wise social studies practice. Schools and school districts could capitalize on this collective knowledge by bringing groups of teachers together in professional learning communities (Lieberman, 1995; Sergiovanni & Starratt, 2002) to share their wise practices and ideas about teaching social studies through integrating the five domains and related characteristics of teacher PCK. This collaboration would enhance their individual collective practice, strengthen their curriculum, and empower them to make curricular changes. These professional learning communities might work with shared inquiry questions: "What is wise practice in elementary social studies?" and "How do we resolve our dilemmas of practice?" The learning community would engage in and wrestle with school-based action to define wise practice, resolve dilemmas, and restructure their current social studies practice. This focus on teachers as curriculum developers and implementers within a learning community would encourage teachers themselves, rather than stakeholders outside the classroom, to bring about second-order changes (Cuban, 2001)—that is, altering the ways the school develops curriculum through new goals, structures, and roles that transform the familiar ways of enacting curriculum.

Although portraying the dynamics and intricacies of how teachers construct their pedagogical content knowledge is often difficult for researchers, we found that the 12 teachers who participated in this study felt comfortable describing what they believed social studies should look like and were able to provide examples of their engagements in wise social studies instruction. However, none of these teachers considered themselves to be regularly engaging in a wise practice of social studies. Additionally, none of these teachers were able to articulate how they combined the elements of the PCK framework to make instructional decisions. Future research must probe more deeply into this thinking, as well as identify structures that support the development of PCK, and thus, a wise practice of elementary social studies within a high-stakes testing context.

APPENDIX A: WISE PRACTICE IN ELEMENTARY SOCIAL STUDIES INTERVIEW PROTOCOL

(This protocol was constructed in an effort to capture the different elements of pedagogical content knowledge that a teacher integrates in conceptualizing subject matter instruction.)

PART A: SELF

Tell me about your professional life as a teacher.

Tell me about your beliefs about teaching elementary social studies. How did you come to hold these beliefs?

How do you think students learn social studies best?

What makes a good and not-so-good elementary social studies teacher?

PART B: CONTENT

What kind of content preparation have you had for social studies (courses, workshops, organizations)?

Where do you learn the content for what you teach in social studies?

PART C: PLANNING, TEACHING, ASSESSING

What methods do you find least effective in teaching elementary social studies?

Describe two of your favorite elementary social studies lessons.

What units/topics do you teach in elementary social studies?

How do you plan for social studies (SSS, county curriculum, and team planning)? Talk me through your planning process.

What are your favorite strategies for teaching social studies?

What kinds of assessment do you use? Why?

What would I see in your classroom as evidence of social studies?

PART D: CONTEXT

What features of your context support the teaching of elementary social studies?

What features of your context inhibit the teaching of elementary social studies?

How does your team and school organize the school day?

Does everyone on your team teach social studies?

What role do you think your principal believes social studies should play in a student's school day?

How has FCAT influenced social studies?

Do you think social studies should be tested? Why? Why not?

How does the county support social studies?

PART E: STUDENTS

Do all kids in your school get social studies (ESE, GIFTED, ESOL, etc.)? How do you feel about that?

How would the children in your classroom describe their elementary social studies experience this year?

How do you accommodate the needs of diverse learners as you teach elementary social studies?

NOTES

1. In this case, prolonged observation came about through 18 to 24 months of researcher presence in each of these classrooms as a result of a school–university partnership in which a cohort of interns was placed with a group of university instructors at the school. Both coursework and supervision were integrated into the field experience, a combination that permitted a high degree of familiarity with the teaching practice of each participant.
2. In this case, failing refers to schools that received a D or F as measured by the Florida Comprehensive Assessment.
3. All schools and teachers are referred to by pseudonyms.

REFERENCES

Apple, M. (1979). *Ideology and curriculum.* London: Routledge.
Cochran-Smith, M., & Lytle, S. (1993). *Inside outside: Teacher research and knowledge.* New York: Teachers College Press.
Cuban, L. (2001). *How can I fix it?: Finding solutions and managing dilemmas.* New York: Teachers College Press.
Denzin, N. K., & Lincoln, Y. S. (1994). Introduction: Entering the field of qualitative research. In N. K. Denzin, & Y. S. Lincoln (Eds.), *Handbook of qualitative research* (pp. 1–18). Thousand Oaks, CA: Sage.
Grossman, P. L. (1990). *The making of a teacher: Teacher knowledge and teacher education.* New York: Teachers College Press.
Leming, J. S. (1989). The two cultures of social studies education. *Social Education, 53*(6), 404–08.
Lieberman, A. (1995). *The work of restructuring schools.* New York: Teachers College Press.
Magnusson, S., Krajcik, J., & Borko, H. (1999). Nature, sources, and development of pedagogical content knowledge for science teaching. In J.Gess-Newsome & N. G. Lederman (Eds.), *PCK and science education* (pp. 94–132). Hillsdale, NJ: Erlbaum.
Maso, I. (2001). Phenomenology and ethonography. In Atkinson, Coffey, Delamont, Lofland & Lofland (Eds.), *Handbook of ethnography* (pp. 136–144). London: Sage.
Moustakas, C. (1994). *Phenomenological research methods.* Thousand Oaks, CA: Sage.
Parker, W. (2001). Classroom discussion: Models for leading seminars and deliberations. *Social Education, 65*(2), 111–115.
Patton, M. Q. (2002). *Qualitative research and karenluation methods.* London: Sage.
Sergiovanni, T. J., & Starratt, R. J. (2002). *Supervision: A redefinition.* Boston: McGraw-Hill.
Shulman, L. S. (1986). Those who understand: Knowledge growth in teaching. *Educational Researcher. 15*(1), 4–14.
Shulman, L. S. (1987). Knowledge and teaching: Foundations of the new reform. *Harvard Educational Review, 57,* 1–22.
Siedman, I. E. (1991). *Interviewing as qualitative research: A guide for reasearchers in education and the social sciences.* New York: Teachers College Press.
Silva, D. Y., Gimbert, B., & Nolan, J. (2000). Sliding the doors: Locking and unlocking the doors to teacher leadership. *Teachers College Record, 102*(4), 779–804.
Silva. D. Y., & Mason, T. C. (2003). Developing pedagogical content knowledge for civics in elementary teacher education. *Theory and Research in Social Education, 31*(3), 366–387.
Sindelar, P. T., Webb, R. B., & Miller, M. B. (2002, April). *School culture: Can it predict student achievement?* Paper presented at the annual meeting of the American Educational Research Association, New Orleans, LA.
Stanley, W. B. (1991). Teacher competence for social studies. In J. P. Shaver (Ed.), *The handbook of research on social studies teaching and learning* (pp. 249–262). New York: MacMillan.
Yeager, E. A. (2000). Thoughts on wise practice in the teaching of social studies. *Social Education. 64* (6), 352–353.

CHAPTER 5

A GOOD TEACHER IN TEXAS

Conversations about Wisdom in Middle School Social Studies Practice

Mary Lee Webeck
Cinthia S. Salinas
Sherry L. Field

O.L. Davis, Jr., has suggested:

> For American schools, increasingly robust visions of *wise practices* may exist alongside the dream of best practices. Three assumptions drive this possibility. Many teachers and administrators understand what guides their professional endeavor. *They possess wisdom of practice.* Some individuals are able to articulate their reflections, legitimations, and rationalizations. Certainly, for others, their wisdom is inchoate, but their practices exhibit their tacitly held understandings. Best practices are never contextualized, and individuals portrayed as best-practitioners are always exemplary individuals. *Wise practices are always situated thoroughly in their context.* Recognizable and ordinary individuals use them in real, specific circumstances. And consequently, when other professionals learn about these wise practices, they acknowledge the reports' enhanced authenticity and credibility. The reports ring true.... Another assumption is *the central importance of the practical to educational decision making.* Circumstances and life seldom unfold as individual teachers and administrators wish they would. Consequently, reality *will* be—not just *must* be—a central consideration of their teaching and administration. (1997, p. 1)

What, then, does wise practice look like and sound like in action and reflection? What dimensions of context should be considered in conversations about wise practice? How is wise practice described in the middle school social studies teaching?

With Davis's assumptions and these questions in our minds, we were intrigued by a recent conversation between two ninth-grade students. Their conversation took place in the back seat of a car during the spring semester of their freshman year in high school, as they reflected on their learning experiences in an eighth-grade U.S. history class. We took their dialogue as a starting point for our further conversation and inquiry.

> Lee: Mrs. E[1] was one of my favorite teachers in eighth grade because I felt really involved in how we learned in her class.
>
> Kathy: Oooh, I didn't like her very much.
>
> Lee: Why? I thought you liked her? I learned so much in her class, especially from the projects and the way we did history.
>
> Kathy: I liked her. I didn't like the way she taught social studies. We just did things all the time, we had to find answers, and we always had to work.
>
> Lee: But Kathy, that's what I liked.
>
> Kathy: Well, I think a good teacher in Texas doesn't teach that way. If they are going to put so much emphasis on testing, then a good teacher in Texas should just spend time teaching what exactly is on the TAKS test instead of making us do projects and write and think. A good teacher in Texas should just *tell* us what we need to know. It would be easier for everybody.

As social studies teacher educators who work within the environment and contexts that high-stakes testing promotes, this conversation compelled our questions and our critical examination of educational policy, high-stakes testing, and the influence of such policy on the work of teachers. At the same time, the conversation opened doors of inquiry into the notion of wise practice from the perspectives of teacher educators, a practicing teacher, and that teacher's former students.

How is it, we ask, that teachers make choices about their practice in light of the standards and high-stakes testing climate in contemporary schools? How do teachers, practicing wisely, create spaces in which to balance curriculum enactment with the stresses many teachers feel in response to mandated testing? Our inquiry, conducted deep in the heart of Texas, is offered as an aid to current understandings that are emerging about wisdom in middle school social studies practice, especially in an era in which focus may be perceived to have drifted away from the notion of quality and contextualized learning and toward test-based teaching and learning.

THE CONTEXT OF WISE PRACTICE: A CASE STUDY

In this chapter, we develop a construct for understanding wise middle school social studies practice through the use of a single case study that examines the understandings and responses of a respected and outstanding social studies teacher, Terry, during the first years of the Social Studies Exit Level Texas Assessment of Knowledge and Skills (TAKS). Terry, in our judgment, is a teacher who exemplifies the notion of wise social studies practice in the middle school setting; she was also the focus of the students' conversation. We assert that this case study of Terry, an eighth-grade U.S. history teacher and social studies department head in central Texas, provides notable moments to explore social studies curricula and pedagogy in a high-stakes testing setting (e.g., Merseth, 1996; Stake, 1994).

Using data from an interview, assignment artifacts, and online communications from Terry's classroom and practice, we attempt to explicate what Terry does in her classroom, how she understands and thinks about her pedagogy, her curricular and teaching choices, and her approach to middle school social studies students. We also return to the idea raised by the ninth-graders in their casual discussion of Terry and her teaching: What does a *good* teacher in Texas do in the environment of high-stakes testing? We assert that Terry is a "good" teacher for a number of reasons, but that in her "goodness," she is also a "wise" teacher.

SOCIAL STUDIES AND THE HIGH-STAKES TESTING LANDSCAPE

The use of high-stakes tests translates to a measure of "competence" for all those associated with schooling (e.g., Koretz, 1988, 2002). In particular, publicized ratings of "accountability" are now being used to link student performance to teacher and administrator capability and adequacy (e.g., Black & Valenzuela, 2004; McNeil, 2000). Since the early 1990s, Texas has rewarded/punished each district and campus with an accountability rating based on standardized test results (Koretz, 2002).[2] Likewise, students' promotion and eventual high school graduation depend on their performance on the statewide test. Texas public schools are a case in point of the broader national landscape of high-stakes testing. And now, two American history high-stakes examinations at the 8th- and 11th-grade levels have been added to the menu. Thus, our attention now focuses on how the implementation of these examinations is manifested in the teaching of social studies. In particular, we focus on the eighth-grade American history course and a single case study analysis.

Research evidence about high-stakes testing in Texas reveals that it exerts intense pressure on schools (e.g., Black & Valenzuela, 2004; McNeil, 2000). The question at hand is: How does this pressure manifest itself in school settings? In particular, how do social studies teachers change, resist, ignore, defy, acquiesce, and/or succumb to the tumultuous presence of a high-stakes standardized exam?

The assumption is that the power of high-stakes tests certainly influences curriculum and instruction. Studies, some of them conducted in Texas, have concluded that these tests *profoundly and negatively* impact curriculum and instruction as well as minority student learning opportunities (Black & Valenzuela, 2004; Bustos-Flores & Riojas-Clark, 2003; Hoffman, Assaf, & Paris, 2001; McNeil, 2000; Shepard, 2000; Valenzuela, 2002; Wiggins, 1989).

Admittedly, knowledge about high-stakes testing and social studies is limited. The late entry of the social studies to high-stakes testing systems has precluded long-term studies. A few studies on the effects of high-stakes testing on social studies have been conducted (e.g., Brooks, 2001; Grant, 2000, 2001; Grant et al., 2001; Kurfman, 1991). For example, Grant and colleagues concluded that, with the group of New York teachers they studied, "...testing has failed to show that teachers' practices improve with more testing" (2001, p. 247). Even so, additional studies of how high-stakes tests influence classroom teaching and student learning in specific content areas are needed (Cimbricz, 2002). Texas social educators, now in the throes of the ever-expanding testing schema, would certainly benefit from this research.

SETTING A CONTEXT

In our recent work, in an effort to focus our ideas about the realities of social studies teaching, we have begun to examine the lives and work of teachers. We have conceptualized that "boundaries, expectations, challenges, and possibilities" play important roles in the professional experiences of social studies teachers (Webeck, Field, & Salinas, 2004). These four categorical distinctions help us to contextualize the experiences of teachers and better understand the decisions they make in response to their context. Once teachers have reflected critically upon their experiences, these experiences serve as a "basis for professional growth" (Chant, 2002, p. 517).

Working Within/Outside the Boundaries

For 10 years,[2] Texas teachers have been bound by an elaborate accountability design, the Academic Excellence Indicator System (AEIS), which includes content standards and high-stakes testing. The Texas Essential Knowledge and Skills (TEKS) constitute the state-mandated curriculum, and the Texas Assessment of Knowledge and Skills (TAKS) is the corresponding high-stakes test. The heavy-handed public ratings of schools utilize single performance indicators in determining children's and/or schools' academic failure or success.[3]

The testing of social studies was implemented in Spring 2003. Two extremes frame the teaching of social studies within these standards/testing boundaries. In lower grades (K–7), in which social studies are not tested, the "squeezing out" of the social studies occurs. With heavy emphasis on the content areas that "count" for high-stakes purposes, few if any material or human resources are allotted to social studies. On the other hand, in the upper grades at which social studies are tested, any extra resources that are available are most likely to go toward test preparation and test-related professional development.

Bound by rigid policies and an externally designed role for social studies in the school curriculum, teachers may or may not recognize the multiple forces that now influence their curriculum, instruction, and assessment choices. As a result, we are not sure of the overall implications for curriculum, teaching, and assessment in social studies. For example, elaborate curricula matrices and rigid scope and sequence requirements have been distributed; however, we are unsure of the degree of allegiance teachers have to these guides. Likewise, we assume that social studies teachers are now aligning classroom instruction with the testing format of the TAKS, which includes the use of primary sources, document-based questions, critical thinking/problem solving, and map and graph/chart skills. Initial indications are that schools have developed benchmark examinations and/or purchased software that provides item analysis data (Salinas & Reidel, 2003). Nevertheless, we are unsure as to whether or not teachers have changed their everyday assessment practices.

In sum, federal and state testing policies and the testing rhetoric are public boundaries that determinedly portray schools as spaces for education reform. The enactment of No Child Left Behind (NCLB) legislation is the latest and most far-reaching demonstration of the reasoning that equates successful schooling with institutionalized high-stakes testing systems. Nonetheless, the boundaries surrounding curriculum, instruction, and assessment call for a closer examination.

WITHIN TERRY'S REALM

A bejeweled crown rested on the overhead stand at the front of the room on the day that Mary Lee met with Terry in her middle school classroom. Terry wore that crown during class, affecting the role of a monarch in the simulation in which her class participated. Her students were studying the early colonization of America, reenacting the experiences and decisions made by early colonists as they boarded ships and crossed the ocean to North America. Her room was arranged with tables in groups, and with artifacts, books, maps, resource materials, and computers that invited students to inquire. Clearly, this was a room that welcomed activity and interaction, arranged with eighth-graders in mind.

This was not Mary Lee's first visit to the classroom. Two years earlier, her daughter had been a student in Terry's class, and Mary Lee came to view Terry as an exemplar of possibility for middle school social studies. Thus, we began our conversation with an established trust and quickly turned to discussing Terry's work.

When asked how she became the teacher she is, Terry described two college instructors who had influenced her through their active teaching styles and high expectations. They showed her that hands-on learning could be challenging and rigorous, taught history from a wide variety of perspectives, and encouraged their students to learn history "from the inside" and from various primary sources. Terry decided that the types of learning experiences she wanted to occur in her classroom would be purposeful and engaging. Also, when Terry and Mary Lee discussed the notion of "powerful" teaching promoted by the National Council for the Social Studies—meaningful, integrated, value-based, challenging, and active—Terry laughed and said, "That's what social studies is all about. That is what we—the students and I—try to do here."

Terry believed that one of the most important goals of her teaching was to help students to find, process, and analyze information as they proceeded toward new levels of understanding and new levels of responsibility for their work. She routinely embedded social studies content, process, and skills within her instructional strategies. Moreover, students typically understood that their experiences in Terry's class would be challenging; Terry believed that students should be "a little bit frustrated" and "a little bit on the edge" for their learning experiences to be productive. Although learning in her classroom was a "brain-jarring experience," Terry said she still recognized that such experiences must be scaffolded and constructed by other forms of structure and support.

Terry reported that she regularly reminded her students that she was "not simply preparing them for a one-time TAKS test or an end-of-unit assessment"; she was "preparing them for life," which would assess them in different ways. She jokingly told them that she wanted to see them on the *Tonight Show with Jay Leno* for something positive, "not on Jay Walking" to display their poor social studies knowledge.[4] Terry believed that she could help prepare her students for life by engaging them with substantive content knowledge, helping them to make meaningful connections between early American history and contemporary times, and encouraging them to develop a spirit of continuing inquiry and exploration.

Terry also treated her students with respect, urged students to respect themselves and to act responsibly, to take a stand on historical and current issues, and to support their positions with reason and evidence. She told her students that they would someday be the "producers" of society, that each of them would be responsible for what society becomes.

Terry and Mary Lee also discussed the idea that most knowledge about good teaching never makes it into the public sphere, because most good teaching occurs between teacher and students in the privacy of classrooms. Yet that private sphere also helped to foster trust; Terry believed that her teaching style and methods had evolved through the trust she built with her students. She also made some of her pedagogical decisions with what she described as a "gut feeling" that was, nonetheless, informed by what she knew about her profession and appropriate pedagogy, her expertise in the content of U.S. history, and her knowledge about her students. Pedagogical awareness and wisdom, according to Terry, are thus constructed from practical experience and reflection about who she as a teacher has become.

Some of the challenges that Terry perceived also impacted her thinking about wise practice. For example, she recalled that when she was a student, her teachers were her primary source of information, but that today's students have many sources of information so she must remain current in her content, her thinking, and her understanding of students. Another challenge Terry recognized was that parents sometimes were uninformed about the purposes underlying her instructional approaches and wanted to set up the boundaries for the kind of teaching they expected. Helping parents to understand why she taught the way she did, when this style of teaching differed significantly from how many parents remembered their own school experiences, often was difficult when parents frequently checked to see if what their child was learning was connected to the TEKS. One way that Terry negotiated these concerns was through online communication with the students on her team and with their parents. For example:

> I want to thank all of you who have worked with me to maintain high standards of performance we require of our students in the... team. We all realize that the methods, assignments, and assessments may not be what you have experienced in the past.... We are working hard to ensure proper learning

opportunities for your child, and we thank you for your support.... Students are periodically being assessed both formally and informally about their present and past learning. Assessments will ask about major TEKS topics covered throughout the year.

Terry also maintained a weekly online dialogue about her classroom activities, what students were currently doing, and what they would be working on next, in order to keep parents "in the loop" while also supporting her students' ability to manage tasks:

(Monday–Thursday) We are continuing to research government topics in order to build a database of information of the history, structure, function, and operation of our government. Students are being self-paced, with opportunities to learn in many different ways. I have a special topic I discuss each day in the "Discussion Pit," and students have access to the library, the computers, films, audiotapes, and many handouts that help convey the information.

(Friday) Students will need to stop and reflect on the information gathered so far, organize the information, and complete a short written reflection today. They will begin planning for their product and unit test. Both will need to be completed in 2 weeks.

In addition to parents, Terry noted that sometimes, in what was perceived to be in the best interest of the students, her school district created boundaries for her teaching goals. For example, when the September 11th attacks occurred, administrators and teachers in her school were told by district administrators not to discuss these events with their students. Terry reflected:

How odd, in a social studies class, not to talk about things that at the time seemed such a turning point in a society's history. Later, this event will be taught about, and "we" will build monuments, but the students who lived through it did not benefit from the kinds of conversations that could have taken place in a U.S. history classroom in the immediate aftermath of the event. Oddly, we were asked not to talk about social studies in social studies.

When asked if she identified the TEKS and TAKS as boundaries, Terry responded, "Yes, they are." However, to her, these standards simply served as a basic guide for what she should expect of her students. She reported that she used the TEKS as an organizational tool with which she framed her units, and as a structure from which she could "bounce off" and extend her students' learning. Terry firmly believed that a teacher could choose to see the TEKS/TAKS as a huge wall that blocks creativity, or as a stepping-stone that facilitates learning and provides a minimal structure for teaching. She explained that, from the beginning of the year, she made her students aware of the TEKS objectives and how these objectives drove the

TAKS exam. Because she included TEKS with each unit of instruction, they became an accepted part of the language of the classroom, and each student was responsible for correlating their mastery of learning objectives with the TEKS for the unit. For example, in an end-of-unit portfolio, one student marked a TEKS objective, "to locate places and regions of importance in the United States during the 18th and 19th century," as one that he still needed to master. As the year progressed, Terry gave the students more freedom and responsibility in determining the ways in which they would meet the TEKS objectives. For example, in the spring semester, they had an opportunity to develop a unit they wanted to study based on a set of TEKS they had yet to master.

The variety of Terry's instructional choices reflected her unwillingness to be "bounded" by external pressures; they included direct instruction, problem-based learning, inquiry, interactions with primary and secondary sources, and the frequent use of technology. She created complex and integrated WebQuests for several units, including Ye Old Survivor: A Study of U.S. Colonization; Rebels with a Cause: Monumental Personalities of the American Revolution; The Constitution and Government; Zesty Qwesty Stations: A Self-Directed Study of America's Teenage Years (1800–1860); Westward HO!; and Raiders of the Lost Artifact, during which students created a virtual museum Web page about the Civil War period. The following text introduced the students to the WebQuest on "America's Teenage Years (1800–1860)":

> You know how difficult it can be to be a teenager, right? Well, our country went through its teenage years as well, and you could say the same types of issues and questions that affect teens affected our country. What were some of these growing pains and changes affecting America during the rapid growth period of 1800–1860? It's time to go explore and delve into these special topics!

During this unit, students worked together as a class to generate a list of topics that could be researched about America between 1800 and 1860. Then students worked individually, following a set of guidelines that Terry established for the project. Each student researched a selected topic, used a compilation of resources, and organized and built their WebQuest, complete with a learning station for other students to use. Each student also created two test questions about his or her topic to be included on the unit test.

Terry also frequently assigned writing throughout each of the units, including reflective essays at the conclusion of each 6-week grading period that became increasingly demanding throughout the year. Her essay prompts were intended to help students organize and express ideas about social studies knowledge, skills, and dispositions; she noted that students' writing was indicative "of the content they are internalizing and also of how they are learning." The following excerpt from Terry's instructions illustrates her reflective essay assignment for the fifth 6-week grading period, after students had studied federal government and westward expansion:

> Please look back over the fifth 6-week period, and reflect upon the projects you participated in or you developed, and address the following issues in a short reflective essay:
>
> Which project helped you to develop a system for solving a problem or completing a task, and how did it help you do this?
>
> In what ways can you connect the historical information that you learned from the projects to your present-day world?
>
> What skills or processes did you learn or enhance that you will be able to apply and use in your present and future work, whether it be in school or the work world?

Terry also incorporated writing because she believed that it offered another way to make social studies learning experiential and to encourage empathic responses to history. Throughout the unit's activities and in the reflective essays, she asked students to think about multiple aspects of the history that they studied, about the places and people, about what people had hoped for and imagined, and about what kinds of changes had taken place. Students were also asked to talk about how their thinking might have changed because of their work. In this way, Terry's pedagogy seems consistent with research on efforts to increase student voice and agency in the classroom (Mitra, 2004). From her interactions with students and her responses to their reflective essays, Terry truly got to know her students and encouraged them to think about how their ideas and voices shaped the nature of what took place in their classrooms, school, community, and society. She encouraged them to look to the past as they thought about the future.

Indeed, a teacher's classroom choices, often made when time is limited and content is rich, are essential to who students can become. Terry wanted her students to know that they were developing a "beginning framework" for learning about history and the world, and that high school and college would help them to gain more in-depth understanding. She wanted to excite her students about the possibilities of social studies. One student wrote at the end of the second 6 weeks of study, "Over the last 6 weeks, it has felt as if the history has come alive to me, which has made me want to learn more about the history of our country; so I go home and read more about it."

TEACHING AS A WAY OF BEING

One of the most compelling issues in educational research today is locating possibility amidst the boundaries, expectations, and challenges that we can easily pinpoint. Opportunities for teachers, students, and administrators increasingly are limited by external policy. Yet this problem is not unique in present times. In 1940, John Dewey advanced the following idea:

> The system which makes no great demands on originality, upon invention, upon the continuous expression of individuality, works automatically to put and keep the more incompetent teachers in the school. It puts them there because, by a natural law of spiritual gravitation, the best minds are drawn to the places where they can work most effectively. The best minds are not especially likely to be drawn where there is danger that they may submit to conditions which no self-respecting intelligence likes to put up with; and where their time and energy are likely to be so occupied with details of external conformity that they have no opportunity for free and full play of their own vigor. (p. 67)

Dewey's words ring true today. Much work supports the notion that many bright and energetic teachers leave the field. So, why speak of wise practice and "ambitious teaching" (Grant, Chapter 7, this volume) in an era that seems to ask teachers to conform to an externally constructed norm? In response to Dewey and in support of the many teachers who choose to remain in teaching and who work to surmount and sometimes circumvent boundaries, we suggest that investigating wise practice within the culture of today's schools is increasingly necessary, and that such study must be undertaken locally and contextually.

Clearly, many teachers across our country teach children well. Explication of their work at this moment helps us understand how teachers make choices in day-to-day practice. Feldman, for example, has suggested that seeking out new ways of looking at the work of teachers, recognizing teaching as "a way of being," has merit (1997, p. 757). Teacher educators have long been aware that individual characteristics and beliefs are fundamental aspects of a teacher's work. Cornett and Setenyi's (2002) study of teachers suggested a need for further study of teacher theorizing as teachers construct and use personal practical theories. These theories inform teachers' identities, their approach to teaching materials, and their approach to children; moreover, they are informed by teachers' personal experiences outside the classroom and by practical experience gained during teaching (Chant, 2002; Miller Marsh, 2002a, 2002b, 2003). Kagan has described teaching as "rooted in personality and experience," and he further noted that "learning to teach requires a journey into the deepest recesses of one's self-awareness, where failures, fears, and hopes are hidden" (1992, p. 137). In addition, "pedagogical content knowledge requires the teacher to be a skilled decision-maker who integrates and crafts the features of content, context, students, self, and pedagogy in unique ways" (Mason & Silva, 2001, p. 70).

How teachers choose to approach their work depends on their stance toward themselves, their career, their students, and their society. As teacher educators, we know that pedagogical choices made by teachers are part of the complex, contextual, and intertextual process of teaching. The complexity of the process is indeed fascinating and invites an inquiry stance (Cochran-Smith, 2003) as teacher educators further explore the construct of wise practice, situated in context. As teacher educators, we also recognize that wise practice can serve as an exemplar for beginning teachers and an impetus for reflection on the part of practicing teachers. For example, the following statement made by a secondary social studies teacher suggests understanding of her practice:

> Teaching social studies requires attention to and consideration of creative tensions. An engaged social studies teacher choreographs materials and questions to challenge students to make connections—between past and present, between stasis and movement, between textbook dryness and soap opera interesting, between objective distance and subjective closeness, between institutions and people, and between particular issues or events and more general considerations. (Delaney, 2001, p. 125)

In this text, Delaney describes the functions of her decision making as an accomplished social studies teacher. She is aware of content knowledge in her field and comfortable with a range of instructional methods. We assert that Delaney's statement provides insight into the way she situates herself as a teacher (Clark, 2001; Duckworth, 2001; Roney, 2001) and reflects her personal practical theories (Chant, 2002; Cornett, 1990; Cornett & Sentenyi, 2002; Marland, 1998; Richardson, 1996), as well as her professional pedagogical content knowledge (Mason & Silva, 2001; Shulman, 1986, 1987, 2000). Within this statement, Delaney positions herself and states her ideas about the ways in which a teacher of social studies defines some central aspects of her practice. When we read Delaney's statement from the perspective of teacher educators and in light of the ninth-grade students' reflective conversation that introduced this chapter, we found it useful for understanding Terry and her work.

POSSIBILITIES AND WISE PRACTICE IN THE MIDDLE

A number of studies conducted between 1981 and 2001 add to our understanding of middle-level teaching. Several studies have identified characteristics of effective teaching at the middle grades level. For example, The National Middle School Association (NMSA, 1981) identified such characteristics, as did Buckner and Bickel (1991) and Arth and colleagues (1995). Roney (2001) added six characteristics to the accumulating lists. Interestingly, three of the four studies shared the same "top 15" identifiers/characteristics (Roney, 2001). Common professional characteristics described across the studies included understanding the development of young adolescents, adapting curriculum to the students' developmental needs, using varied materials and activities, teaching communication skills, encouraging self-responsibility, and knowing subject matter. Synthesizing these characteristics, Roney suggested that effective middle-level educators "blend knowledge of young adolescents with knowledge of self in working with their colleagues to create developmentally responsive middle school" experiences for learners (2001, p. 96). Based on an earlier analysis of literature on effective middle-level teaching, Davies (1995) reported a number of personal and professional qualities: having a positive self-concept, and showing optimism, a sense of humor, and flexibility.

We suggest that another aspect must also be considered in middle-level teaching: that a teacher be considered as a unique person, because teaching, as Feldman (1997) has asserted, is a way of being. As Palmer suggested, "Good teachers join self, subject, and students in the fabric of life because they teach from an integral and undivided self; they manifest in their own lives, and evoke in their students, a 'capacity for connectedness' " (1997, p. 16). Drawing upon Palmer, Roney's recent work described an effective middle school teacher as being "inwardly integrated, outwardly connected" (2001, p. 100). At the conclusion of her study, Roney suggested that "middle school teachers need to know themselves inside out" (p. 100).

These ideas brought to our attention the special nature of middle school teachers and the possibilities that might arise from approaching teacher preparation and teacher study with a focus on what an inwardly integrated and outwardly connected teacher might do—or be—in practice. We "teased out" these conceptions of middle-level teaching with respect to Terry and her practice, and we connected them to Feldman's notion of conceptualizing wise practice as a *way of being* within the context of the complex set of boundaries, expectations, challenges, and possibilities that define Terry's work.

SPEAKING IN THE LANGUAGE OF "REALITY"

We have situated much of our discussion within the context of high-stakes testing in Texas. Certainly, Terry works in a district that pays strict attention to student achievement. Within the suburban community in which Terry teaches, test scores are vitally important to the public perception of student success and school quality. The district expects teachers to teach in such a way that students master the TEKS curricular objectives by passing the TAKS test, preferably scoring in the top percentile. The district's website claims that the district has achieved curricular alignment and correlations to TEKS and TAKS expectations. This assertion is one language of "external reality" in Texas that teachers must learn to speak. As suggested earlier, we remain fascinated with how this language works in the lives of teachers. Texas teachers do "speak" in ways consistent with the culture of the TEKS and TAKS, but what else are they saying though their approaches, choices, and articulations of practice? Do teachers speak with different degrees of sincerity and compliance—in the classroom, in the community, and at the university?

Using the analogy of language usage, we might ask how teachers speaking the language of TEKS and TAKS compose texts through their teaching. In some schools and classrooms, the language of reality is spoken in such a "monolinguistic" manner that alternative "languages" are denied. In others, teachers have become "multilingual" as they talk about the expectations of TEKS and TAKS. Some teachers use the TEKS/TAKS "language" while simultaneously creating classroom environments that support effective teaching and wise practice. Others, believing they are doing what is necessary to help students succeed, use the TEKS/TAKS language to structure learning entirely around test success. We suggest that in social studies teaching, "multilingual" skills can be used in ways that address the pressing reality of high-stakes testing while also promoting learning experiences that are meaningful, integrated, value-based, challenging, and active (National Council for the Social Studies, 1994). Burroughs explained, "Social studies teachers can play a part by helping optimize the positive and minimize the negative impacts of testing to make sure schools stay focused on the goal of enhancing learning" (2002, p. 315).

In our linguistic metaphor, Terry is a skilled "multilinguist." Because we propose that Terry is an educator who practices wisely, we further suggest that Terry's "multilingual" skills are an important aspect of her wisdom of practice. We posed questions to her about her pedagogical choices and her notions of wise practice, and we asked her about the boundaries, expectations, challenges, and possibilities that she located in her work and how they shaped her experiences of teaching middle school social studies.

INTERPRETING WISE PRACTICE

We suggest that three aspects of Terry's work are the common threads that weave through her teaching and interactions with students. First, Terry had a clear sense of her identity as a teacher; after 19 years of teaching, this self-understanding is not surprising. Second, Terry held a philosophy of teaching social studies that she articulated through her approaches to the content and the ways she communicated and interacted with students, colleagues, and parents. When conversing with Terry about her work, and in analyzing the transcript of that interview, we clearly understood that Terry developed her philosophy based on what she knew about herself, her teaching, her students, and the broader society in which her students and she lived. Third, based on her identity, philosophy, content knowledge, and understanding of her middle school students, Terry has created structures that scaffold and support the innovative learning experiences typical of her classroom.

Earlier, we mentioned Terry's introductory words to her students: "Our class is about learning social studies, but it is also preparing you for life. Life will test you in many ways." Terry's identity as a teacher and her philosophy toward her work situated her in such a way that she valued and supported students as members of society both within and outside the school community. To think about her work with students is to recall Walter Parker's observation about democratic citizens:

> Democratic living is not given in nature, like gold or water. It is a social construct, like a skyscraper, school playground, or new idea. Accordingly, there can be no democracy without its builders, caretakers, and change agents: democratic citizens. These citizens are constructs, too. Who "builds" and cares for them? (2003, p. xvii)

If, as Parker states, democratic living is not a "given," then neither is a disciplinary and nuanced understanding of ocial studies. Terry seemed to understand that both must be built, experience upon experience.

When we think about wise practice and the promise that this term suggests for student learning and involvement, John Dewey's notion again comes to mind. Rich leaning experiences in social studies classrooms open new ways of seeing and thinking. And because education and democratic life were closely interwoven in Dewey's work, in reflecting about Terry's wise practice we returned to Dewey's statement: "Democracy is belief in the ability of human experience to generate the aims and methods by which further experience will grow in ordered richness" (1998, p. 343).

One of the last comments Terry made during her interview is that she comes to school each day "with a sense of wonder at what will happen that day." She asserted that she looks forward "…to each tomorrow of my teaching…. I want my last day of teaching to be as good, as exciting, as the days I now approach with wonder." We are convinced that Terry's experiences as a teacher have grown—and will continue to grow—in ordered richness.

CONCLUSION

The rhetoric of high-stakes testing has permeated Texas classrooms, entering the discourse of teachers, administrators, parents, community members, and children. This much is abundantly clear. Regarding Kathy's comment about Terry being "a good teacher in Texas," Terry laughed and remarked, "Strictly, if all people are worried about is tests, I'm not the best Texas teacher—but really I am, because life will ask a whole lot more of my students than any test."

Undoubtedly, high-stakes testing is changing the landscape of American education, and it is making the culture of classrooms in Texas even more complex. Sometimes there are highly negative implications for teachers and students. But when teachers can respond "multilingually" and situate the tests *within* the culture of the classroom rather than having the tests define that *culture*, the possibility for wise practice grows. Classrooms are where teachers make choices at the intersection of boundaries, expectations, and challenges. Teachers work from many "texts" of expectations and challenges, speaking through their experience, knowledge, and identity. How well versed they are in interpreting and dealing with these texts is, largely, a function of who they are as individuals. Clearly, Terry has ventured beyond the status quo to become "multilinguistic" in her wise social studies teaching and learning, while still meeting and surpassing externally imposed standards and assessment expectations.

NOTES

1. Throughout our discussion, pseudonyms are used for the teacher and students to whom we refer.
2. The educational onslaught can be dated to 1983 (Ross Perot–generated), including two standardized content curricula—the Essential Elements (EE), first adopted in 1985, and the Texas Essential Knowledge and Skills (TEKS), adopted in 1998—as well as four iterations of standardized exams: Texas Assessment of Basic Skills (TABS), Texas Educational Assessment of Minimum Skills (TEAMS), Texas Assessment of Academic Skills (TAAS), and Texas Assessment of Knowledge and Skills (TAKS).
3. The Academic Report Card is a much more comprehensive description of schools' performance through the use of multiple indicators. However, the report is eclipsed by the more public discussion surrounding the ratings/standards associated with the high-stakes test.
4. "Jay Walking" is a regular feature on the popular late-night television program *The Tonight Show with Jay Leno*. In this segment, the host, Jay Leno, interviews people on the street in Los Angeles. He usually asks them questions about history, geography, or current events. Almost all of the

responses featured on the television show portray that the interviewees have little to no knowledge of American history, geography, and current events.

REFERENCES

Arth, A., Lounsbury, J., McEwin, C., Swaim, J., & Eighty-three Successful Middle Level Educators. (1995). *Middle level teachers: Portraits of excellence.* Columbus, OH: National Middle School Association and National Association of Secondary School Principals.

Black, B., & Valenzuela, A. (2004). Educational accountability for English language learners in Texas: A retreat from equity. In L. Skrla & J. Scheurich, J. (Eds.), *Educational equity and accountability: Paradigms, policies, and politics* (pp. 215–234). Albany: State University of New York Press.

Brooks, S. (2001). High-stakes in New York: From a "last chance, first chance" classroom. *Educational Foundations, 15*(4), 57–70.

Buckner, J., & Bickel, F. (1991). If you want to know about effective teaching, why not ask your middle school kids? *Middle School Journal, 22*(3), 26–29.

Burroughs, S. (2002). Testy times for social studies. *Social Education, 66*(5), 315–318.

Bustos-Flores, B., & Riojas-Clark, E. (2003). Texas voices speak out about high-stakes testing: Preservice teachers, teachers, and students. *Current Issues in Education, 6*(3). Retrieved from http://cie.ed.asu.edu/volume6/number3/

Chant, R. (2002). The impact of personal theorizing on beginning teaching: Experiences of three social studies teachers. *Theory and Research in Social Education, 30*(4), 516–540.

Chapter 113, Texas Essential Knowledge and Skills for Social Studies. Retrieved from http://www.tea.state.tx.us/rules/tac/chapter113/index.html

Cimbricz, S. (2002). State-mandated testing and teachers' beliefs and practices. *Education Policy Analysis Archives, 10*(2). Retrieved from http://epaa.asu/adu/apaa/v8n14.html

Clark, C. (Ed.). (2001). *Talking shop: Authentic conversation and teacher learning.* New York: Teachers College.

Cochran-Smith, M. (2003). Learning and unlearning: The education of teacher educators. *Teaching and Teaching Education 19*(1), 5–28.

Cornett, J. (1990). Teacher thinking about curriculum and instruction: A case study of a secondary social studies teacher. *Theory and Research in Social Education, 28*(3), 248–273.

Cornett, J. W., & Setenyi, J. (2002). Teacher theorizing in civic education: An analysis of exemplary teacher thinking in the United States and Hungary. In J. J. Patrick, G. E. Hamot, & R. S. Leming (Eds.), *Civic learning in teacher education: International perspectives on education for democracy in the preparation of teachers* (Vol. II, pp. 177–204). Bloomington, IN: ERIC Clearinghouse for Social Studies/Social Science Education.

Davies, M. (1995). The ideal middle level teacher. In M. Wavering (Ed.), *Educating young adolescents: Life in the middle* (pp. 149–169). New York: Garland.

Davis, O. L., Jr. (1997). Editorial: Beyond "best practices" toward wise practices. *Journal of Curriculum and Supervision 13*(1), 1–5.

Delaney, M. K. (2001). Understanding the presidency." In E. Duckworth (Ed.), *"Tell me more": Listening to learners explain* (pp. 125–146). New York: Teachers College Press.

Dewey, J. (1940). *Education today.* New York: Greenwood Press.

Dewey, J. (1998). Creative democracy—the task before us. In L. Hickman & T. Alexander (Eds.), *The essential Dewey: Volume 1. Pragmatism, education, democracy* (pp. 340–343). Bloomington: Indiana University Press.

Duckworth, E. (Ed.). (2001). *"Tell me more": Listening to learners explain.* New York: Teacher's College Press.

Feldman, A. (1997). Varieties of wisdom in the practice of teachers. *Teaching and Teacher Education, 13*(7), 757–773.

Grant, S. G. (2000). Teachers and tests: Exploring teachers' perceptions of changes in the New York state testing program. *Educational Policy Analysis Archives, 8*(14), 1–16.

Grant, S. G. (2001). An uncertain lever: Exploring the influence of state-level testing in New York state on teaching social studies. *Teachers College Record, 103*(3), 398–426.

Grant, S. G., Derme-Insinn, A., Gradwell, J., Lauricella, A. M., Pullano, L., & Tzetzo, K., (2001). Juggling two sets of books: A teacher responds to the New York state global history exam. *Journal of Curriculum and Supervision, 17*(3), 232–255.

Hoffman, J. V., Assaf, L. C., & Paris, S. G. (2001). High-stakes testing in reading: "Today in Texas, tomorrow?! *The Reading Teacher, 54*(5), 482–492.

Kagan, D. M. (1992). Professional growth among pre-service and beginning teachers. *Review of Educational Research 62,* 129–169.

Koretz, D. (1988). Educational practices, trends in achievement, and the potential of the reform movement. *Educational Administration Quarterly, 24*(3), 350–359.

Koretz, D. (2002). Limitations in the use of achievement tests as measures of educators' productivity. *Journal of Human Resources, 37*(4), 752–77.

Kurfman, D. (1991). Testing as context for social education. In J. P. Shaver (Ed.) *Handbook of research on social studies teaching and learning* (pp. 310–320). New York: Macmillan.

Marland, P. (1998). Teachers' practical theories: Implications for preservice teacher education." *Journal of Teacher Education & Development, 1*(2), 15–23.

Mason, T., & Silva, D. (2001). Beyond the methods course: civics as the program core in elementary teacher education. In J. J. Patrick & R. S. Leming (Eds.), *Principles and practices of democracy for education of social studies teachers* (pp. 65–86). Bloomington, IN: ERIC Clearinghouse for Social Studies/Social Science Education.

McNeil, L. (2000). *Contradictions of school reform: Educational costs of standardized testing.* New York: Routledge.

Merseth, K. K. (1996). Cases and case methods in teacher education. In J. Sikula, T. J. Buttery, & E. Guyton, (Eds.), *Handbook of research on teacher education* (2nd ed., pp. 722–744). New York: Simon & Schuster Macmillan.

Miller Marsh, M. (2003). *The social fashioning of teacher identities.* New York: Peter Lang.

Miller Marsh, M. (2002a). Examining the discourses that shape our teacher identities. *Curriculum Inquiry, 32*(4), 453–469.

Miller Marsh, M. (2002b). The shaping of Ms. Nicholi: The discursive fashioning of teacher identities. *International Journal of Qualitative Studies in Education, 15*(3), 333–347.

Mitra, D. L. (2004). The significance of students: Can increasing "student voice" in schools lead to gains in youth development? *Teachers College Record, 106*(4), 651–688.

National Council for the Social Studies. (1994). *Expectations of excellence: Curriculum standards for social studies.* Washington, DC: Author.

National Middle School Association. (1981). Preparing teachers for the middle grades. *Middle School Journal, 12*(4), 17–19.

Palmer, P. (1997). The heart of a teacher: Identity and integrity in teaching. *Change, 29*(6), 15–21.

Parker, W. (2003). *Teaching democracy: Unity and diversity in public life.* New York: Teacher's College Press.

Richardson, V. (1996). The role of attitude and beliefs in learning to teach. In J. Sikula, T. J. Buttery, & E. Guyton, (Eds.), *Handbook of research on teacher education* (2nd ed., pp. 102–119). New York: Simon & Schuster Macmillan.

Roney, K. (2001). The effective middle school teacher: Inwardly integrated, outwardly connected. In V. Anfara (Ed.), *The handbook of research in middle level education.* Greenwich, CT: Information Age.

Salinas, C., & Reidel, M. (2003, November). *Has our time come? A multiple case study of five Texas high schools preparing for high-stakes testing in the social studies.* Paper presented at College and University Faculty Assembly (CUFA), National Council for Social Studies (NCSS) Chicago.

Shepard, L. (2000). The role of assessment in a learning culture. *Educational Researcher, 29*(7), 4–14.

Shulman, L. S. (1986). Those who understand: knowledge growth in teaching. *Educational Researcher 15*, 4–14.

Shulman, L. S. (1987). Knowledge and teaching: Foundations of the new reform. *Harvard Educational Review 57*, 1–22.

Shulman, L. S. (2000). Teacher development: roles of domain expertise and pedagogic knowledge. *Journal of Applied Developmental Psychology, 25*(1), 129–135.

Stake, R. (1994). Case studies. In N. K. Denzin & Y.S. Lincoln (Eds.), *Handbook of qualitative research* (pp. 236–247). Thousand Oaks, CA: Sage.

Texas Education Agency. Texas Administrative Code (TAC), Title 19, Part II.

Valenzuela, A. (1999). *Subtractive schooling: U.S.–Mexican youth and the politics of caring.* Albany: State University of New York Press.

Valenzuela, A. (2002). High-stakes testing and US–Mexican youth in Texas: The case for multiple compensatory criteria in assessment. *Harvard Journal of Hispanic Policy, 14*, 97–116.

Webeck, M. L., Field, S. L., & Salinas, C. (2004). Tell me more: Boundaries, expectations, challenges, and possibilities for civic education in pre-service elementary methods. In G. E. Hamot & J. J. Patrick (Eds.), *Civic learning in teacher education* (Vol. 3, pp. 147–167). Bloomington: The Social Studies Development

Center of Indiana University in Association with Cititas: An International Civic Education Exchange Program.

Wiggins, G. (1989). A true test: Toward a more authentic and equitable assessment. *Phi Delta Kappan, 70*(9), 703–713.

Zancanella, D. (1992). The influence of state-mandated testing on teachers of literature. *Education Evaluation and Policy Analysis, 14*(3), 283–295.

CHAPTER 6

THE IMPACT OF ACCOUNTABILITY REFORM ON THE "WISE PRACTICE" OF SECONDARY HISTORY TEACHERS

The Virginia Experience

Stephanie D. van Hover
Walter F. Heinecke

> The History and Social Science Standards of Learning and the Standards of Learning assessment program form the core of the Virginia Board of Education's efforts to strengthen public education across the Commonwealth and to raise the level of academic achievement for all Virginia students. (Virginia Board of Education, 2001)

In the late 1990s, the Commonwealth of Virginia implemented a massive accountability reform effort that included the development of content standards, high-stakes testing, and revised standards of school accreditation. Subsequently, the Virginia Board of Education released the History and Social Science Standards of Learning (revised and rereleased in 2001), which were designed to provide a framework for history instruction across the state. These Standards of Learning (SOLs) were followed in 1998 by multiple-choice, high-stakes assessments intended to address the knowledge and skills specified in the standards (Duke & Reck, 2003). These new policies and actions unleashed extensive debate and discussion over the content of the standards, the nature of the tests, and the effects of this reform on teaching and learning (Duke & Reck, 2003; Fore, 1995). Virginia's reform efforts have spurred research studies on the history of assessment (Heinecke, Curry-Cocoran, & Moon, 2003); the role of Virginia superintendents and principals in the implementation of these reforms (Grogan & Sherman, 2003; Tucker, 2003), classroom instruction of math, language arts, and biology teachers with high SOL scores (Grogan & Roland, 2003); and attitudes of new and veteran teachers toward the SOLs (Winkler, 2002). However, scholars have paid little attention to the influence of Virginia's standards and high-stakes assessment on the classroom practices of secondary history teachers.

In the literature on teaching, several definitions of effective or wise practice exist (Shulman, 1987). In addition, researchers and professionals in several school subjects have developed discipline-specific notions of "wise practice"(e.g., Shulman, 1987; VanSledright, 1996; Wineburg, 2001; Yeager, 2000). This previous research, however, does not illuminate how Virginia's politically driven, standards-based reform efforts interact with notions of wise practice in the teaching of history as defined by the profession and as implemented by practitioners. This report offers some insights into this mainly unstudied problem: effects of standards-based reform on the "wise practice" of secondary history teachers. Specifically, we studied the influence of high-stakes testing on the planning, instruction, and assessment practices of 10 central Virginia high school history teachers identified as effective teachers. This chapter discusses the context of accountability surrounding history teaching in Virginia and elucidates the framework of "wise practice" that guided this educational research. Also, the chapter explains the research design and methods utilized, and it asserts findings that emerged from analysis of data. The chapter concludes with a discussion of the findings and analysis of implications for the teaching and learning of history in Virginia.

STANDARDS AND ACCOUNTABILITY IN THE COMMONWEALTH OF VIRGINIA

For the last decade or so, the notion of "accountability" has dominated the discourse of American educational policymakers and affected all levels of education in the United States (Heinecke et al., 2003). The reauthorization of the Elementary and Secondary Act (ESEA) in January 2001, known as the No Child Left Behind Act of 2001, calls for "accountability and results" in the form of standards and high-stakes testing (U.S. Department of Education, 2003). States across the nation are enacting their own accountability reforms. Common components of these systems include: (1) aligning standards and assessments, (2) rating schools and reporting school or district performance, and (3) creating consequences for schools that fail to perform adequately (Heinecke et al., 2003, p. 7). Virginia's reform efforts include all three of these components in the form of the Standards of Learning (SOLs), Standards of Quality (SOQ), and Standards of Accreditation (SOA) (Virginia Department of Education, 2003b).

The SOQs provide general guidelines and standards for virtually every aspect of the educational and school organizational system in Virginia (Duke & Reck, 2003). The SOAs provide benchmarks and requirements for school accreditation and introduce the notion of school performance report cards. Issued by the Virginia Department of Education, these publicly available report cards for individual schools include the following information: the school's accreditation rating, a comparison of schoolwide and statewide SOL scores, graduation rates, enrollments in advanced academic programs, and, for the schools, information on the number of students, attendance, dropout rate, teacher training, and school safety (Duke & Reck, 2003; Virginia Department of Education, 2003b).

Virginia's content-based standards, the SOLs, set expectations for teaching and learning and provide statements of knowledge and skills that every child is expected to learn. Social studies SOLs at the secondary level are established for U.S. and Virginia History, World History I and II, World Geography, and Virginia and U.S. Government (for an example, see Table 6.1). The secondary history SOLs are chronological and can be characterized as "traditional" history (Fore, 1995). The politically conservative Fordham Foundation, for example, assessed the history standards of 37 states and described Virginia's history standards as "exemplary." Its 2003 report noted:

> The Old Dominion's standards are clearly written, measurable, and descriptive of what is to be taught and learned. They are also coherent, demanding, and very specific about history content. They are based on chronology, reflect solid and warranted history, keep history in context, avoid presentism, and encourage students to develop and practice historical skills, including the use of primary and secondary sources. The Virginia standards avoid the promotion of dogma and refrain from manipulating student attitudes. Finally, Virginia's standards are centered on specific historical content from United States and world history. Virginia wasn't the model from which other standards were assessed, but this research found Virginia's standards to be the nation's "exemplary" benchmark for history standards at the present time.

Table 6.1. Example of Virginia and U.S. History Standard

History and Social Science Standards of Learning: Virginia and United States History

Civil War and Reconstruction: 1860–1877

VUS.7—The student will demonstrate knowledge of the Civil War and Reconstruction Era and its importance as a major turning point in American history by:

- Identifying the major events and the roles of key leaders of the Civil War era, with emphasis on Abraham Lincoln, Ulysses S. Grant, Robert E. Lee, and Frederick Douglass;
- Analyzing the significance of the Emancipation Proclamation and the principles outlined in Lincoln's Gettysburg Address;
- Examining the political, economic, and social impact of the war and Reconstruction, including the adoption of the 13th, 14th, and 15th Amendments to the Constitution of the United States.

Students take SOL assessments in grades three, five, and eight, and at the end of each high school content course. The eighth-grade social studies test addresses questions related to U.S. History and Virginia and U.S. government. Social studies end-of-course assessments at the high school level include U.S. History, World History I (ancient until 1500), World History II (1500 to the present), and World Geography (Virginia Department of Education, 2003a). U.S. and Virginia government are taught in the twelfth grade but, to date, do not have an end-of-course test. These assessments are four-choice multiple-choice tests. In history and the social sciences, these tests almost exclusively emphasize recall of factual content. They offer no opportunities for students to demonstrate the "historical skills" addressed in the standards (see Table 6.2). The tests are scored on a scale from 0–600. A student must receive a score of 400 or higher in order to pass the test. Scores of 500 or higher are considered "advanced-level" performances (Virginia Department of Education, 2003b). Seventy percent of students who take the SOL tests must pass them in order for a school to be considered for accreditation.

Table 6.2. Sample Questions from End-of-Course SOL Tests (1998)

End-of-Course United States History	End-of-Course World History I
Which of the following was written specifically to encourage ratification of the Constitution?	Which of the following philosophers was the teacher of Alexander the Great?
Federalist Papers	Socrates
Declaration of Independence	Plato
Articles of Confederation	Agamemnon
Common Sense	Aristotle

To assist teachers with standards-based teaching and test preparation, the Virginia Department of Education created a series of resource guides. *The History and Social Science Standards of Learning Curriculum Framework* provides a breakdown of the essential understandings, questions, knowledge, and skills related to each content standard. *The History and Social Science Standards of Learning Sample Scope and Sequence Guides* go one step further and provide an organizing topic; the essential knowledge, skills, and understandings; the related SOL; sample assessment methods; and sample resources (see Table 6.3). Additionally, the Department of Education provides a "test blueprint" that lists for each course the number of test questions by chronological time period. For example, the 2003–2004 blueprint notes that the statewide test for U.S. history will include six items related to "Early America through the Founding of the New Nation" and 15 items from "The United States since World War II" (Virginia Department of Education, 2003b).

Table 6.3. Example of The History and Social Science Standards of Learning Sample Scope and Sequence Guides

Organizing topic	Essential understandings, knowledge, and skills	Related SOL	Classroom assessment methods	Resources
U.S. Constitution	Explain that during the Constitutional Era, the Americans made two attempts to establish a workable government based on republican principles	VUS5a	Projects Quizzes Student reports Unit tests Writing assignments Class discussion	A commonwealth of knowledge Audiovisual materials Center for Civic Education Library of Congress Smithsonian Institution Textbook

What effects have these reforms had on classroom instruction in Virginia? Very little empirical research has examined this absolutely practical question. One study, however, offers important clues. Grogan and Roland (2003) conducted a study of "successful" secondary teachers of biology, English, and Algebra I. They defined "successful" in terms of students' pass rate on the SOL test and examined what nine teachers with above-average pass rates were doing to prepare their students for the tests. The profile of a "successful" teacher that emerged from the data included the following personal and professional characteristics: deep love of substantive content knowledge and love of teaching; maintenance of good relationships with students; assurance that they were available to students for extra help;

effective management and organization of the classroom; carefully made plans for instruction; demonstration of a wide range of instructional skills and strategies; maintenance of a professional stance and high expectations for all students; and maintenance of professional pride in their own development as teachers (Grogan & Roland, 2003). These descriptors certainly reflect many of the components discussed in "wise practice" research literature. However, defining classroom success solely in terms of student pass rates does not provide insight into the influence of the standards on classroom practice. Were these teachers successful before Virginia mandated the SOLs? What do these teachers do the same or differently as a result of the SOLs? The present study extends Grogan and Roland's research by examining the influence of the SOL tests on the "wise practice" of experienced history teachers identified as "effective" on the basis of their instructional practice. Also, Grogan and Roland studied teachers of biology, algebra I, and English—SOL subject areas with tests that include higher-order thinking questions as well as factual recall. The history SOL tests almost exclusively emphasize the ability of students to recall facts. What is the influence of this fact-based assessment on wise practice?

WISE PRACTICE AND EFFECTIVE HISTORY TEACHING

The conception of wise practice informing this study reflects research and writings by scholars of general educational practice and of social studies education, as well as components of effective teaching posited by the National Council for the Social Studies (NCSS) and the *National Standards for History*. In 1993, NCSS articulated "a vision of powerful teaching and learning in the social studies" by identifying and describing five principles of "excellent" and "powerful" teaching. Powerful social studies teaching and learning, according to NCSS, is meaningful, integrative, value-based, challenging, and active (*Expectations of Excellence: Curriculum Standards for Social Studies,* 1993). Meaningful teaching requires teachers to engage in reflective planning, instruction, and assessment; to emphasize in-depth investigation of a few significant topics rather than to superficially cover extensive amounts of content; to encourage students to draw connections between ideas; to engage students in meaningful learning and assessment activities that focus on "big ideas" or important themes; to integrate across the curriculum and encourage students to grapple with and consider the ethical dimensions of topics; and to examine the values, complexities, and dilemmas involved in a topic. Additionally, "powerful social studies teaching" involves utilization of a variety of instructional strategies that promote active student engagement in the learning process, emphasize authentic activities and authentic assessment, and shift the role of a teacher to encouraging students to become independent and self-regulated learners (*Expectations of Excellence: Curriculum Standards for Social Studies,* 1993, pp. 11–12).

Although the *National Standards for History* (1996) do not address effective history instructional practice as explicitly as the NCSS standards, they emphasize the importance of teaching students both historical understandings and historical thinking skills. Historical understandings define what students should "know" about history—the historical content that students should learn. Historical thinking skills, however, encompass the "doing of history," skills that:

> enable children to differentiate past, present, and future time; raise questions; seek and evaluate evidence; compare and analyze historical stories, illustrations, and records from the past; interpret the historical record; and construct historical narratives of their own.

Historical thinking includes chronological thinking, historical comprehension, historical analysis and interpretation, historical research, historical issues analysis, and historical decision making. A growing body of research has demonstrated that students as early as elementary school can begin to think historically and, as they grow older, develop increasingly sophisticated abilities to engage in historical inquiry and perspective taking (e.g., Barton, 1997; Foster, Hoge, & Rosch, 1999; Levstik & Barton, 2001).

In order for students to think historically, their teachers must be able to teach historical thinking. Thus, researchers in the teaching and learning of history argue that effective history teachers should possess extensive and deep substantive historical knowledge, as well as an understanding of how to teach historical thinking (e.g., Shulman, 1987; VanSledright, 1996; Wineburg, 1991, 2001; Yeager & Davis, 1994, 1995). Shulman (1987) refers to this combination as pedagogical content knowledge, which he defines as "the blending of content and pedagogy into an understanding of how particular topics, problems, or issues are organized, represented and adapted to the diverse interests and abilities of learners, and presented for instruction" (p. 8).

In addition to pedagogical content knowledge, Shulman (1987) asserts that several other categories should form the teachers' knowledge base, including the following: content knowledge, general pedagogical knowledge, curriculum knowledge, knowledge of learners and their characteristics, knowledge of educational contexts, and knowledge of educational ends, purposes, and values, and their philosophical and historical grounds.

In *How People Learn: Brain, Mind, Experience, and School,* the National Research Council offers a description of "expert history teachers" that reflects Shulman's categories of knowledge. The National Research Council explains:

> For expert history teachers, their knowledge of the discipline and belief about its structure interact with their teaching strategies. Rather than simply introduce students to sets of facts to be learned, these teachers help people to understand the problematic nature of historical interpretation and analysis and to appreciate the relevance of history for their everyday lives. (2000, p. 159)

Thus, our conception of wise practice includes Shulman's (1987) emphasis on content, pedagogy, pedagogical content knowledge, and knowledge of students and educational contexts; NCSS's conception of "powerful" and "meaningful" teaching; and the National Standards contention that students must learn both historical content and historical thinking skills.

In order to examine the effects of standards-based reform on the wise practice of history teachers, we divided classroom practice into three components: planning for instruction, instruction, and assessment. Teachers engaging in wise practices make innumerable decisions prior to instruction, during instruction, and after instruction. We asked: How do teachers within the context of accountability reform in Virginia make decisions about what to teach, how to teach, and how to measure student growth and learning? Shulman (1987) describes wisdom of practice as "the maxims that guide (or provide reflective rationalization for) the practices of able teachers" and urges researchers to "work with practitioners to develop codified representations of the practical pedagogical wisdom of able teachers" (p. 11). This research sought to collect, examine, and begin to codify the emerging wisdom of practice of able history teachers working within the context of standards and accountability in Virginia.

RESEARCH METHODOLOGY

Because this research centered on the sense-making and meaning perspectives of teachers, we used a qualitative research design to study 10 history teachers' conceptions of wise practice and to investigate their perceptions of the influences of state standards and accountability measures on their planning, instruction, and assessment practices. Our research examined the following two questions: (1) How do secondary history teachers define "wise practice" within the context of standards and accountability in Virginia? (2) What are the influence of standards-based reform on wise practice reflected in the planning, instruction, and assessment of secondary history teachers in Virginia?

Participants and Setting

The participants included 10 teachers: seven high school history teachers (four white males and three white females) and three middle school history teachers (three white females) (see Table 6.4 for descriptions of the teachers in this study). These teachers worked in two districts located in central Virginia near a large public university. All but one of the schools involved in this study were accredited by the state (High School B is provisionally accredited), and all of these social studies teachers had above-average pass rates on SOL testing. The researchers chose to focus on these particular teachers on the basis of several criteria. First, these teachers served as clinical instructors (teachers who mentor student teachers) for the teacher education program of the local university. The university selects social studies clinical instructors by asking district social studies supervisors and building-level administrators in the local secondary schools to provide lists of the most effective and highly qualified teachers with 3 or

Table 6.4. Participants

	Pseudonym Demographics	School	*Years Teaching*	*Educational Background*	*Classes taught*
1.	Larry White male	HS A	19	BA History & Education MA American History	American History American Studies Sociology
2.	Chris White male	HS A	7	BA History MEd Social Studies Ed.	World History Psychology
3.	Sally Hispanic female	HS B	11	BA Political Science Working toward MEd	World History American History
4.	Elaine White female	HS B	6	BA History MEd Curriculum	World History
5.	Greg White male	HS B	6	BA Govt & Philosophy JD/MA Law & Philosophy PhD Administration	World History
6.	Kara White female	HS B	28	BA History	World History
7.	Jerry White male	HS C	20	BA Social Studies MEd Social Studies PhD Social Studies	World History
8.	Julie White female	MS A	18	BS Social Work	American History
9.	Mary White female	MS A	26	BA Studio Art MEd Special Education	Humanities
10.	Paula White female	MS B	9	BS Business Administration MAT Education	American History

more years of experience. "Effective" relates to judged/perceived quality of instructional practice, not SOL pass rates, and "highly qualified" refers to teacher certification. Additionally, the teacher education program assesses the effectiveness of these clinical instructors through a series of internal evaluations related to instructional and mentoring practices that are entered into a database and reviewed each year. The researchers believed this group of able history teachers would offer insight into the perceived influence of the SOLs on planning, instruction, and assessment. Second, these teachers had 6 or more years of experience. The researchers wanted to study teachers who had teaching experience both before and after the SOL reforms. Third, these 10 teachers agreed to participate in the study. The researchers emailed all of the secondary social studies clinical instructors with 6 or more years of teaching experience who taught American or World History at the middle school and high school level (12 of the clinical instructors met these criteria) and invited them to participate in a study examining the influence of SOL testing on classroom practice. These 10 teachers agreed to permit the researchers to interview them, observe them, and collect archival evidence about their teaching.

Data Collection

The data sources for this study included interviews, observations, and classroom documents. The researchers conducted semistructured interviews with each teacher, following a protocol that addressed the teachers' educational and personal background; their approaches to planning, instruction, and assessment; their understanding of "wise practice" and "effective teaching"; and their perceptions of the impact of SOLs and SOL testing on the school, district, and Commonwealth of Virginia. The interviews lasted approximately 1–2 hours each and were audiotaped and transcribed. The researchers also conducted observations of each teacher for the duration of one unit of study (from 1–10 days). During the observations, the researchers took extensive field notes to document the instructional strategies utilized by the teacher, content covered, student and teacher movement, classroom setup, and other pertinent information. Additionally, the researchers collected classroom documents (e.g., copies of tests, handouts, graphic organizers, worksheets, etc.).

Data Analysis

The data were analyzed using methods of analytic induction (Erickson, 1996). In this two-step process, the researchers inductively derived analytic assertions from multiple readings of the data record. Then, working assertions were warranted through a rigorous search for confirming and disconfirming evidence and alternative explanations. The researchers used the conceptual framework to sensitize, but not drive, the process of data analysis. Multiple sources of data were analyzed in an effort to enhance the validity of findings. In addition, the conceptual framework, the data collection design, and the researchers' expertise and relationships with field practitioners facilitated access to the meaning-making perspectives of participants, thereby enhancing the validity of the study. Findings, in the form of empirical assertions, are presented with general description and interpretive commentary framing exemplars from the data.

FINDINGS

What happens to teaching practice when a state government implements a program to increase accountability in public schools? How do these effects converge or diverge with professionally defined conceptions of "wise practice"? In this section, we provide a set of analytic assertions about the influences of the Virginia accountability initiative on the wise practice of 10 secondary teachers of social studies. Subsequently, for each assertion, we present evidence to substantiate these assertions.

Table 6.5. Assertions

Assertion 1: Teachers made sense of their practice in terms of the concepts used in the professional literature on "wise practice"—Shulman's emphasis on content, pedagogy, pedagogical content knowledge, and knowledge of students and educational contexts; NCSS's conception of "powerful" and "meaningful" teaching; and the National History Standards contention that students must learn both historical content and historical thinking skills.

Assertion 2: The most salient aspect of testing and accountability reform for teachers was the influence on the time available for planning, instruction, and assessment.

Assertion 3: The accountability measures associated with the standards have created a context that encourages planning, instruction, and assessment practices that conflict with history "wise practice," particularly the National History Standards emphasis on teaching historical thinking. However, many teachers resolved this conflict by reducing the amount of time devoted to historical thinking rather than abandoning the practice completely.

Assertion 4: Teachers had mixed feelings about the overall success of the reform. Teachers agreed with certain components of the standards and accountability initiative, yet they disagreed with the direction of implementation and results in terms of effects on wise practice.

Assertion 1: *Teachers made sense of their practice in terms of the concepts used in the professional literature on "wise practice"—Shulman's emphasis on content, pedagogy, pedagogical content knowledge, and knowledge of students and educational* contexts; NCSS's conception of "powerful" and "meaningful" teaching; and the National History Standards contention that students must learn both historical content and historical thinking skills.

These history teachers' conceptions of wise practice varied in terms of depth and emphasis. Still, all teachers addressed some aspects of the definition of wise practice elucidated in our framework. The following two quotations illustrate teachers' comments about wise practice:

> [Teachers who engage in wise practice] relate well with the students. They know their subject area well, so they are totally confident in what they are doing. They understand how to differentiate their instruction. They have very clear expectations and they are very organized. And they are able to step back now and then and keep a perspective on things instead of getting stressed about the particulars and worry about SOLs. They balance their own goals in the big picture of education versus the specific things like meeting SOL standards and things. (Greg, Interview)

> [A teacher engaging in wise practice] knows her objectives and essential questions. [Wise practice is] using certain tools for certain things and knowing when to use them, giving the kids choices when it comes to products to show their knowledge and show they're learning. I see myself more as a facilitator. I do a lot of indirect instruction. And that's discovery—thinking like an historian, letting the kids dig for information. Using time wisely. (Paula, Interview)

Paula and Greg's remarks highlight many of the common themes that emerged across teacher definitions, despite the variance in teacher conceptions of wise practice. These common elements included extensive content knowledge, love of subject matter, knowledge of multiple instructional approaches and strategies, knowledge of curriculum, and knowing one's students.

Many of the teachers' descriptions of wise practice referred to at least three of Shulman's knowledge categories—content, pedagogy, and knowledge of students. Larry, for example, touched on knowledge of content, pedagogy, and students by stating that teachers who engage in wise practice must "love the content and you have to like kids...[and know] methodology" (Larry, Interview). Another teacher, Chris, described the importance of content and knowledge of students in this way:

> The first thing that would come to my mind is content knowledge, but I think it's the most important and the least important, all at once. You've got to understand what you're teaching, but at the same time, I could know everything and be a bad teacher. Effective teaching would be content knowledge, empathy to students, you really have to understand students.... Teachers who allow students to engage, allow students to be creative.

Interestingly, most teachers did not refer to pedagogical content knowledge either implicitly or explicitly. Also, much like Chris's quotation above, many of the teachers emphasized the importance of "empathy" with students and described important personality traits of a teacher who engages in wise practice: sense of humor, patience, and enthusiasm. Kara included attention to empathy and personality when she described wise practice as follows:

> The important things are that teachers need to (1) know their curriculum, and (2) actually like or love their subject matter...I think they need to be organized, structured, enthusiastic, and energetic. They need to have what I call the "temperament for teaching," which is to be patient and have thick skin. That's a good combination. And finally, I think they need to have kind of an "inner child," if you want to call it that, or whatever—they need to be childlike in some way so that they can have empathy with what kids are going through.

Several teachers discussed components of wise practice that reflect NCSS's conception of "meaningful" and "powerful" teaching, including the importance of teaching "big ideas," utilizing meaningful instructional and assessment activities, and engaging students in active learning. For example, Greg's quotation above addressed the importance of big ideas and differentiated instruction, whereas Paula touched on the role of teacher as facilitator for active student learning. Jerry asserted that wise practice includes trying to "engage children in those larger concepts...that will make for a better society." Also, several teachers referred to the importance of teaching both historical content and historical thinking, similar to the ideas presented in the *National Standards for History*. Paula mentioned the importance of teaching students to "think like historians." Overall, teachers' meanings of wise practice varied in terms of depth and emphasis, but generally, each of these 10 teachers listed characteristics of wise practice included in our framework.

Assertion 2: *The most salient aspect of testing and accountability reform for teachers was the influence on the time available for planning, instruction, and assessment.*

The issue of time pervaded most of the teachers' discussions of planning, instruction, and assessment. The mandated tests, administrated several weeks before the end of the school year, served as the endpoint of the formal SOL curriculum for all teachers. When they described how they structured their curriculum, 9 of the 10 teachers explained that they used the state's curriculum framework as a guide for organizing their course's curriculum and planned to finish covering the standards a few weeks before the test in order to provide students with an intensive review of material. This severely limited the amount of time per topic of study. Sally noted, for example: "The SOLs influence my planning in such a way that I will not do something unless it is covering an SOL. It is rare that I deviate from what the SOLs want me to cover. So all the planning has to correlate with an SOL." Similarly, Jerry described the SOLs as the "arbiter" of what is taught and explained that he needed to "be sure that I've covered [the SOLs] and given students a fair opportunity to pass that test."

These two quotations reflect most of the teachers' descriptions of the influence of SOLs on their planning process. Although many teachers commented that they appreciated the structure and framework provided by the SOLs in terms of topics to be taught and pacing of the course, they characterized their "race" to cover the content prior to the SOL tests as "brutal." Units of study averaged 1–4 days, versus the 1–4 weeks teachers spent on similar topics before the implementation of SOLs. That is, they seemed to have increased the number of topics taught while reducing the amount of time they spent on teaching these topics. The SOL standards dictated what teachers taught, and the test date acted as a daily reminder for teachers to "cover" the material, which then influenced their instructional and assessment decisions.

Two of the 10 teachers admitted that time constraints related to SOL testing exerted a strong influence on their instructional decision making by forcing them to rely more heavily on direct instruction and lecture. Elaine reflected that she used "mostly direct instruction" because "given the time constraints in the course of a year there is not much time to have the kids discover history for themselves, [particularly now] when they have the SOL test in 3 weeks." Sally's comments echoed Elaine's. She described the influence of time constraints on instruction in this way:

> I used to spend a lot of time with projects, which I don't do now. I used to show one or two historical movies during the year, which I no longer do. I used to do cooperative learning activities with the kids…which I no longer do because even though it's worthwhile and the kids get a lot out of [the activities] and enjoy, they are not learning the facts as quickly as when I just do the lecture and discussion. So I tend to go back to lecture and discussion more than I would if I didn't have the test hanging over my head.

Sally and Elaine both specifically mentioned that they used direct instruction and lecture because of the pressures of time. Sally addressed the influence of the "time constraints" imposed by the SOL test on her instructional decisions, whereas Elaine referred to the challenges of getting students to learn facts "quickly." All of the classroom observations of Sally and Elaine revealed content presented in a lecture format, with recall and discussion questions interspersed throughout the presentations. For example, Sally used one lesson period to present Renaissance art to students through a PowerPoint lecture (Observation, Sally); in a single lesson,

Elaine outlined Martin Luther King's role in the U.S. Civil Rights Movement through a lecture–discussion (Observation, Elaine). The two teachers lectured in a lively manner and used excellent questioning techniques that engaged students. However, the interviews clearly indicated that time constraints influenced instructional decision making, instead of other factors such as personal preference, relevance to topic and lesson objectives, or desired level of student engagement.

Seven of the 10 teachers asserted that they still used indirect instruction but had cut back on more student-centered activities perceived as time consuming, such as mock trials, movies, projects, and in-depth cooperative learning activities. Rather, in order to cover content, these teachers explained that they had become more efficient and that they paid closer attention to the time allotted for each lesson. Chris, for example, in a series of five observations, spent one class period engaging students in a cooperative learning exercise in which they read and analyzed primary sources related to Truman's decision to drop the atomic bomb on Japan during World War II. The students did not have time to complete the entire activity, but as Chris mentioned in class, they had to move on to the next topic in the interest of time. During the subsequent four observations, Chris showed video clips of the dropping of the atomic bomb, lectured, and led short discussions of the events leading to the end of World War II; engaged the students in a map activity about countries involved in World War II; reviewed World War II and gave students a multiple-choice test on the unit; provided students with outside readings and questions focused on the postwar period with special reference to Holocaust discoveries, the Marshall Plan, and the Iron Curtain; asked students to complete a Venn diagram comparing the aftermath of World War II in Europe and Japan; and assigned chapter outlines for homework. He utilized a variety of instructional approaches, used many outside readings and resources, and engaged his students in different activities, yet he maintained a very fast pace and covered an enormous amount of content within a short time period (Observation, Chris). In interviews, Chris observed:

> [I]f there weren't any SOLs, I would not cover as much content material as I do now…I would love to do more class-long group activities similar to the atomic bomb lesson, but because of time, I don't do that a lot and I feel like I can't do that a lot, but I'll try to incorporate something like that in every couple of units.

Chris also explained that he prioritized the content he chose to cover in class and relied heavily on graphic organizers, charts, and fact sheets for students' independent study. He admitted that he often had to treat an entire SOL content strand in half a class period and commented that "you can't teach these topics in half a class period, yet to get through all the content that has to be covered, you have to. I would like to be able to take more time on certain topics and go a little deeper...but that has proven to be too time-consuming."

Almost all of the teachers referred to the influence of time on their assessment decisions. All of the teachers admitted that, as a result of the time constraints of SOL testing, they tended to avoid or underutilize time-consuming, performance-based assessments such as projects and presentations; instead, they used more multiple-choice tests to assess student knowledge, and they needed a format that allowed for efficient grading. Jerry, for example, explained that "time is the key factor" in his assessment decision making. With the high number of students enrolled in his class and the wide range of topics he taught in a school year, he stated, a fill-in-the-bubble, multiple-choice test format represented the most efficient means of assessing students' ability to recall information that would appear on the SOL tests. He added that these tests also gave him the opportunity to include questions from readings and homework that minimally relieved the "burden" of covering everything in class. Other teachers mentioned that using multiple-choice assessments enabled them to test content not necessarily addressed in class, thus conserving precious instructional time. In summary, these 10 teachers often described their concerns about the SOLs in terms of the influence of intensive time constraints that the end-of-year test imposed on their planning, instruction, and assessment.

Assertion 3: *The accountability measures associated with the standards have created a context that encourages planning, instruction, and assessment practices that conflict with history "wise practice," particularly the National History Standards emphasis on teaching historical thinking. However, many teachers resolved this conflict by reducing the time devoted to historical thinking rather than abandoning the practice completely.*

The SOL test emphasizes recall of historical facts. This fact-driven approach to history clashed with 9 of the 10 teachers' conceptions of history and historical thinking. Eight of these nine teachers admitted that the nature of the test altered their teaching of history. Chris noted:

> [Since the SOLs] I see more teachers looking at history as an exercise in trivia—the SOLs reinforce that. Especially with the lower-ability kids. I think the idea of giving them time and letting them struggle with historical thinking doesn't happen. You talk to a teacher in a standard-level class, and pretty much across the board they're going to be concerned with where they are, how far they have to go, and whether or not the students know content. It is important, but in the struggle to make students memorize, you're completely bypassing the opportunity to give them a chance to think or to struggle with materials or to learn to make evaluations, do analysis, and things like that.

Greg echoed Chris's statement, observing that "the SOL tests have exacerbated the idea that teaching history is basically a lot of facts and a sequence of events rather than the idea of historical thinking and understanding a particular culture deeply."

The nine teachers who provided a rich definition of history and historical thinking commented on the interpretive nature of history, the importance of critical thinking and historical analysis, and the need to teach students how to "do history." As reflected in Chris and Greg's quotations, 9 of the 10 teachers viewed the format of the SOL test as conflicting with their understandings of history and historical thinking. Jerry, for example, observed that "the survey nature of social studies becomes detrimental to deeper understanding." He elaborated that if the SOL tests did not exist, he would

> cut the frantic pace and take more time to go deep and rich, based on a themed topic.... [For example], we develop wonderful units around the Civil War with hundreds of primary sources for students to examine. That's fine, but the SOL tests don't really allow us to do that because of the nature of the knowledge recall on the test. [The emphasis on depth over breadth] would mean that students might not be as good at trivia, but they would be much deeper thinkers.

In a similar manner, Julie commented, "I feel like we're just scratching the surface and we don't get in depth." The fact-based recall questions promoted a "trivia" approach to teaching history and led to teacher emphasis on breadth of coverage over depth of coverage.

Additionally, several observations of classroom instruction revealed that concern with student mastery of SOL factual content often caused teachers to emphasize "right" answers that agreed with the essential understandings asserted in the SOL guides, and to discourage students from developing their own interpretations and questions about history. In some classes, this change was subtle. For example, Paula would ask a question, entertain a few answers, and then write the "correct" answer (the one closest to the SOL guide) on the overhead projector. If no answer reflected the "correct" answer, she answered the question herself (Observation, Paula). This emphasis on "correct answers" was especially evident in classes whose teachers were conducting pre-SOL review sessions. Several of the observations for this study occurred 1–3 weeks prior to the SOL end-of-course tests in the classrooms of two teachers who conducted drill-like review sessions for the upcoming assessments. In one of these classes, the teacher gave students a summary of "need-to-know" facts, and the students worked in pairs to review the information (Observation, Mary). In another class, a teacher distributed review sheets and practice tests for students to take during class time (Observation, Elaine). All of the review sessions emphasized the need to know the "correct answer" on SOL tests.

The nature of the history SOL tests exerted the most significant influence on teacher assessment. Each of these 10 teachers admitted to increasing their use of multiple-choice tests that addressed content that might appear on the SOL test in order to familiarize students with the multiple-choice format. The researchers collected three examples of multiple-choice tests during observations. Each included 25–100 items emphasizing fact recall, and test questions were written in a style that clearly mirrored the sample questions from the SOL tests. Also, several teachers employed daily quizzes designed to emphasize fact recall from assigned readings and previous class lecture notes (Chris, Observation; Greg, Observation; Elaine, Observation). These tests and quizzes did not include higher-order questions that required historical interpretation or analysis. Jerry explained the influence of the SOL test on his assessment choice in this way:

> Honestly, the SOL test has not emerged to where there are big ideas or themes. You don't need a high conceptualization of the material. It encourages you to be sure that you've got the small pieces and not the big ideas on your tests.... Nobody wants to reduce to factual recall, but if we all kind of look at SOL results and eliminate teachers from the conversation, that's what we'll get as tests.

On the other hand, Larry stated that the SOL tests exerted no influence on his planning or instruction. He noted that the very nature of the test prevented him from paying attention to the standards. Rather, he used the Advanced Placement (AP) American History curriculum for all of his U.S. history courses and structured his instruction according to themes and big ideas that made sense to him. He explained:

> To me, the [American History] AP test is still the fairest assessment of real quality in historical learning. So I teach to the AP test. I don't worry about the SOLs. So if I've prepared the students for the AP test to the best of my ability and theirs, then they have a better chance of passing that SOL test than if I try to teach them to prepare for this test, which isn't really a test. I don't know what it is. That's the other thing I say about the SOL test. Even if I wanted to teach to it, I couldn't because I don't know what it is. It's smoke. It's this random trivia. I have no idea how you prepare people for random trivia. No idea...I just need to teach them how to learn about American history and to take challenging tests, and the SOLs will take care of themselves.

Nevertheless, Larry did admit that he included more multiple-choice items on his tests because of the SOLs, noting that the multiple-choice items were his "most feeble attempt to address the SOLs directly." He pointed out that the AP test also used multiple-choice items, but that these questions required thought and analysis rather than memorization of trivia.

Nonetheless, the majority of teachers noted that the nature of the SOL test influenced their teaching of history by promoting a "breadth versus depth" or survey approach to history, and encouraged them to reinforce students' recall of facts rather than to engage students in historical thinking, interpretation, and analysis. The nature of the test was antithetical to most of these teachers' understandings of history and historical thinking and, in many cases, clashed with teachers' notions of wise practice.

Assertion 4: *Teachers had mixed feelings about the overall success of the reform. Teachers agreed with certain components of the standards and accountability initiative, but they disagreed with the direction of implementation and results in terms of effects of the reform on wise practice.*

Most of the teachers expressed appreciation for the content standards because they provided a framework for the curriculum and helped teachers decide what historical content to teach. For example, Paula explained, "I came here 10 years ago. I said, OK, what do I teach? U.S. history? Where do I start? Anywhere...I never saw a curriculum during my first 2 years.... [The SOLs] do set a purpose." Jerry explained that "the SOLs are a welcome, crucial entity—they lay out 'here's what we have to cover,' they limit debate [about what history should be taught] because somebody has to." He added:

> We are constantly aware of [the SOLs] because they help direct us—it's actually comforting to know what your job asks you to do. I can plan a lesson and know that in these 20 minutes I've met my legal requirements. It's a pragmatic nuts-and-bolts question. They created a curriculum but didn't tell me how to teach it.

Many teachers also noted that the standards streamlined the curriculum. They also observed that history teachers who used to spend a disproportionate amount of time on their favorite topic soon realized that they must cover the entire stated curriculum by the end of the year. Kara reflected:

> I know I used to spend a lot more time on the Russian Revolution, as I majored in [Russian history]. Now, I cut it to its proportion on the SOL because I realize that it is not as important to the rest of the world as it is to me. Which is not a bad thing, but it changes things to a certain extent.

Several teachers stated that they recognized the need for accountability in education. Jerry, for example, said:

Positively, the SOLs reinvigorated the conversation about what we're doing. Positively, the SOLs brought a reminder back to teachers that we're accountable for what we do. Education has a tendency to be arrogant.... One more thing positive—we deceive ourselves that just when someone takes on the mantle of professional that all people do a good job.... The SOLs at least created a vehicle by which, if you can't at least do the basics of teaching, it is going to show up.

Chris, in a similar vein, noted:

The SOLs improved education in Virginia in the sense that schools realize finally, and it's unfortunate that they couldn't realize this before politicians forced them to realize it, that the public demands accountability and that the activities of the school, because they're funded by the public, are open and things don't go on behind closed doors, and teachers don't have the right to stand in front of a classroom and do whatever they want without expecting to be called on it.

At the same time, many teachers questioned the direction of implementation: namely, the fact-based, multiple-choice test that provided only one, very public measure of student learning and teacher performance. Additionally, some of the teachers questioned whether the SOL history test measured student learning or teachers' demonstration of wise practice. Larry expressed concern that "a lot of the kids are more fact-driven and have greater test anxiety than ever."

Greg reflected:

I think the process of coming up with standards and identifying what students ought to learn is a good process for the state to go through. I'm not sure about the accountability aspect of the SOLs. I think it drains resources and detracts from some of the more important programs in education. And they penalize students when they really shouldn't be penalized—they get an education but don't get a diploma. I think it has been mixed results.

He added:

I think the SOL [tests] have impacted some teachers. I think some teachers think they need to teach more toward the test and they feel burdened by it. Whether they actually are or whether they have improved their practice is a matter of subjectivity.

Chris observed that the SOLs could foster teacher complacency unless a teacher really wanted to improve his or her practice. School administrators, he believed, only looked at test scores. He explained his own struggle to improve his practice in this way:

Every year, you get the results of your SOLs—you usually get the teachers' name and the percent rate of how many of your students pass, right beside your name, and you have that for every teacher. So you know you're being judged based on how many of your students pass the SOL test. You get to the point where, well I have a pretty good pass rate now. If I don't change things very much it's probably going to continue. And I probably won't have to answer any questions about what I'm teaching, why I'm teaching it, or what's happening to my pass rate.... At the same time, you gain a little comfort and think well, I can [try something different] and it won't hurt my SOL scores.

Chris also mentioned that the time spent working on planning for SOLs diverted time from meaningful professional development that could improve his practice. He stated:

We have in-services a lot of times that involve sitting down with our curriculum, with what we teach, and tying it to specific SOLs. It's taken a lot of work and taken time away from effective learning from each other.

In general, these 10 teachers did not mind the standards, but they expressed important reservations. They believed that the SOL tests placed enormous time constraints on their planning, instruction, and assessment and encouraged a survey approach to history that did not allow for deep understanding or historical thinking.

DISCUSSION

This chapter began with two important questions: (1) How do secondary history teachers define "wise practice" within the context of standards and accountability in Virginia?, and (2) What are the influences of standards-based reform on the planning, instruction, and assessment of secondary history teachers in Virginia? Two contextual factors of this study hold implications for interpretation of the findings. First, the political context of the Commonwealth of Virginia serves as an important variable in understanding these teachers' responses to the standards and accountability reform measures. Virginia is a fairly conservative "right-to-work" state with relatively weak teachers' unions and a history of top-down mandated educational reforms. Thus, when teachers feel pressure from "the top" to improve test scores, they may feel as though they have little or no recourse but to comply. A second major contextual factor to consider is the nature of the sites and participants. These 10 exemplary history teachers were primarily middle- and upper-class and white. Six of the 10 teachers worked in a school district that has, with little effort, been able to produce test results deemed very successful by the state. Four of the teachers worked in a district that has struggled to meet the state mandates; however, while they taught at a diverse high school deemed "provisionally accredited/needs improvement," the history scores have met or exceeded the required 70% pass rate. If these highly regarded teachers were influenced by the state mandates, one can only speculate about the practices of the "average" secondary history teacher or those new to the profession.

Certainly, the findings of this qualitative study are transferable only to other samples of history teachers similar to the ones included in the study. It would be difficult to generalize the results to other history teachers deemed less highly rated or, for that matter, samples of teachers who are more racially and ethnically diverse than the 10 teachers included in this study. However, the findings of this study are useful for understanding the responses of other highly rated or experienced secondary history teachers to the accountability reforms occurring in this state.

Findings from the study clearly indicate that these 10 exemplary Virginia history teachers demonstrated components of wise practice as defined in the professional literature. Additionally, their meanings are congruent with the definitions put forth by professional organizations. Also clear, however, is that the high-stakes nature of the assessment component of the Virginia accountability initiative influences these teachers' planning, instruction, and assessment practices in ways contrary to professionally defined and teacher-held conceptions of wise practice. The pressure of the SOL tests and the demand for factual recall shaped the teachers' planning, instruction, and assessment practices in ways that reinforce findings from the literature on assessment: teachers teach what is tested (e.g., Corbett & Wilson, 1991; Grant, 2001; Grant et al., 2002; Smith, 1991).

These 10 Virginia teachers seemed to be forced to compromise their commitment to wise practice. As noted earlier, NCSS asserts that powerful social studies teaching and learning is meaningful, integrative, value-based, challenging, and active (*Expectations of Excellence: Curriculum Standards for Social Studies*, 1993). The types of practices described by NCSS (in-depth investigation of a few, significant topics, student engagement in learning, focus on "big ideas") had been eliminated or reduced by the teachers because of the state test's emphasis on factual recall, as had history instruction that included attention to historical thinking and "doing history" (Levstik & Baron, 2001; *National History Standards*, 1996; Wineburg, 2001).

Importantly, teachers in this study remarked on the dissonance created by the conflicting expectations of professional wise practice and politically mandated reform practice. Experienced clinical instructors reasonably might have continued to use a variety of wise practices in their planning, instruction, and assessment. They reasonably might have expected to employ a "teach to the ceiling" approach in which they continued to teach historical thinking and other higher-order historical concepts with the expectation that students would learn the factual knowledge along the way to prepare them for the SOL assessment. However, the experienced and highly regarded teachers in this study clearly had changed their instruction to represent their understandings of the state test, covering large amounts of content in a superficial "survey" manner. They appeared to be in the unenviable position of knowing what was best for their students to learn, but believing that if they taught the material in that manner, their students would not perform as well as they should on the state test. Thus, these 10 teachers engaged in compromise, adaptation, and rationalization.

The teachers in this study expressed both a defensive posture and a sense of relief about the transparency of performance objectives. They expressed acceptance of, and even some pleasure with, the specificity of the content standards proffered by the reforms. The teachers also observed that the standards and tests had settled the district- and schoolwide debates about what should be covered in the curriculum. Additionally, the teachers lauded these reforms for providing uniformity in curricula across the state, explaining that the SOLs had the salutary effect of expanding the list of historical topics to be covered and removing curricular decisions from teachers' parochial interests and discretion. On the other hand, they complained of a narrower conception of worthwhile historical content, in the form of a highly questionable focus on factual information.

On the whole, however, the teachers in the study did not appear to question the relationship between the SOLs and the impact of these standards and tests on their instruction. The teachers recognized that the reforms had compelled them to engage in some practices that were antithetical to their conceptions of wise practice. They admitted that they chose to compromise in order to raise their test scores and survive in this new political environment. In the absence of support for their conceptions of wise practice, they implemented the reforms as directed. An attitude of acquiescence and of compromises between professional expertise and political accountability pervaded this study. And there were few indications of teachers challenging a central premise of the accountability movement: that teachers' competence can be judged by student performance on one standardized test.

Under these conditions, it becomes increasingly difficult to implement wise practice. There has been little room at any level of the educational policy system for teachers to advocate for standards and assessments that reflect wise practice. Indeed, the teachers in this study appeared less able or willing to serve as a buffer between the shifting demands of the political system and the wisdom of professional and expert knowledge. In this kind of bargain, teachers can retain their jobs but lose some connection to their love of teaching certain topics, as well as the opportunity to focus on approaches that foster the "doing of history." Thus, the question remains:

Students may know the content to pass the state test, but do they really know history?

One teacher in this study expressed the belief that assessment-driven reform and wise practice are mutually exclusive:

> Just the other day we had our social studies coordinator for the county come to a department meeting, and she was talking about some of the goals for the county. She seemed to be talking to us about developing more along the lines of historical thinking, trying to structure our class and curriculum toward that. I think the problem with that is it's all within the structure of the SOLs. So when she talks about writing curriculum or methods and things like that, it's all framed by the SOLs and what she sees as historical thinking would be the big ideas, the essential understandings that you will find in the SOLs. I think it's a step away from where the SOLs have taken us in a lot of ways, but a lot of teachers who have only been teaching for 4, 5, or 6 years see the SOL model as what history is...I see most teachers looking at history as an exercise in trivia. (Chris, Interview)

And there are other unintended consequences; according to Larry:

> What you find happening, it happens in history, like with world geography.... People are doing lots of things to try to make SOL results look better, and...schools are now spending a lot of time to raise SOL scores without raising the quality of instruction.

This study holds implications for teaching and learning history in Virginia and, more specifically, for teacher education in Virginia. The teachers in this study reported that they now ensure that the content measured on the state test is covered in their classrooms. This situation impacts the content taught and the instructional and assessment methods used. It limits the time they might use to teach methods of historical inquiry and meaning making. Some teachers report that they teach what they need to teach in order to "get it out of the way" so that they can address content and processes that they feel are more important. They still, however, face severe time limits imposed by the test dates.

So what are the implications for continuing teacher education, professional development, and curriculum development? We can surmise from the opinions expressed by the 10 exemplary teachers featured in this study that teachers need help teaching *through the standards* rather than teaching *to the test*. We speculate that history teachers need guidance about how to use "wise practice," as professionally defined, within the context of high-stakes assessments and fact-oriented content standards. Perhaps these teachers need time and assistance in using the broad curricular goals to design process-oriented units that include the content reflected in the high-stakes assessments and that recognize the time limitations faced by teachers.

While not addressed in this study, student reactions to teachers' responses to the testing mandate should be investigated. It may well be that with many teachers sacrificing wise practice for political reality, students are becoming increasingly disengaged from the learning process. They may be scoring adequately on the tests, but they could be failing to develop a sense of agency in their own learning.

Also, because the 10 exemplary teachers in this study were drawn from the ranks of clinical instructors who serve as mentors for preservice teachers in a teacher education program, the results of our study raise some questions for teacher educators in Virginia. What does the experience of these 10 teachers imply for teacher education? Should teacher educators prepare teachers for the world of "wise practice," as professionally defined, or for practice that is politically defined? How should teachers be prepared to handle the dissonance between the two? Additionally, as current teacher education graduates become Virginia history teachers, how do they, who know no other context, interpret the influence of accountability on their practice?

REFERENCES

Barton, K. (1997). "Bossed around by the Queen": Elementary students' understanding of individuals and institutions in history. *Journal of Curriculum and Supervision, 12,* 290–314.

Corbett, H. D., & Wilson, B. (1991). *Testing, reform, and rebellion.* Norwood, NJ: Ablex.

Duke, D. L., & Reck, B. L. (2003). The evolution of educational accountability in the Old Dominion. In D. L. Duke, M. Grogan, P. D. Tucker, & W. F. Heinecke (Eds.), *Educational leadership in an age of accountability: The Virginia experience* (pp. 36–68). Albany: State University of New York Press.

Expectations of Excellence: Curriculum Standards for Social Studies. (1993). Washington, DC: National Council for the Social Studies.

Fordham Foundation. (2003). *Fordham Foundation Assessment of History Standards.* Retrieved June 9, 2003, from http://www.edexcellence.net/een/abouteen.html

Fore, L. C. (1995). *A case study of curriculum controversy: The Virginia Standards of Learning for History and the Social Sciences.* Unpublished doctoral dissertation, Virginia Polytechnic Institute and State University, Blacksburg.

Foster, S., Hoge, J., & Rosch, R. H. (1999). Thinking aloud about history: Children's and adolescent's responses to historical photographs. *Theory and Research in Social Education, 27,* 179–214.

Grant, S. G. (2001). An uncertain lever: The infuence of state-level testing in New York State on teaching social studies. *Teachers College Record, 103*(3), 398–426.

Grant, S. G., Gradwell, J., Lauricella, A., Derme-Insinna, A., Pullano, L., & Tzetzo, K. (2002). When increasing stakes need not mean increasing standards: The case of the New York State Global History and Geography Exam. *Theory and Research in Social Education, 30*(4), 488–515.

Grogan, M., & Roland, P. B. (2003). A study of successful teachers preparing high school students for the standards of learning tests in Virginia. In D. L. Duke, M. Grogan, P. D. Tucker, & W. F. Heinecke (Eds.), *Educational leadership in an age of accountability: The Virginia experience* (pp. 114–134). Albany: State University of New York Press.

Grogan, M., & Sherman, W. H. (2003). How superintendents in Virginia deal with issues surrounding the black–white test-score gap. In D. L. Duke, M. Grogan, P. D. Tucker, & W. F. Heinecke (Eds.), *Educational leadership in an age of accountability: The Virginia experience* (pp. 155–180). New York: State University of New York Press.

Heinecke, W. F., Curry-Cocoran, D. E., & Moon, T. R. (2003). U.S. schools and the new standards and accountability initiative. In D. L. Duke, M. Grogan, P. D. Tucker, & W. F. Heinecke (Eds.), *Educational leadership in an age of accountability: The Virginia experience*. New York: State University of New York Press.

How people learn: Brain, mind, experience, and school. (2000). Washington, DC: National Academy Press.

Levstik, L., & Barton, K. (2001). *Doing history: Investigating with children in elementary and middle schools* (2nd ed.). Mahwah, NJ: Erlbaum.

National History Standards. (1996). Los Angeles: National Center for History in the Schools.

Shulman, L. (1987). Knowledge and teaching: Foundations of the new reform. *Harvard Educational Review, 57*(1), 1–22.

Smith, M. L. (1991). Put to the test: The effects of external testing on teachers. *Educational Researcher, 20*(5), 8–11.

Tucker, P. D. (2003). The principalship: Renewed call for instructional leadership. In D. L. Duke, M. Grogan, P. D. Tucker, & W. F. Heinecke (Eds.), *Educational leadership in an age of accountability: The Virginia experience* (pp. 97–113). New York: State University of New York Press.

U.S. Department of Education, P. a. E. S. (2003). No Child Left Behind. Retrieved June 9, 2003

VanSledright, B. (1996). Closing the gap between school and disciplinary history? Historian as high school teacher. In J. Brophy (Ed.), *Advances in research on teaching: Teaching and learning history* (Vol. 6, pp. 257–289). Greenwich, CT: JAI Press.

VanSledright, B. (2002). *In search of America's past: Learning to read history in elementary school.* New York: Teachers College Press.

Virginia Board of Education. (2001). *History and social science standards of learning for Virginia Public Schools.* Richmond: Board of Education of the Commonwealth of Virginia.

Virginia Department of Education. (2003a). *State summary: Standards of learning assessments.* Retrieved June 11, 2003, from http://www.pen.k12.va.us/VDOE/

Virginia Department of Education. (2003b). *Virginia Department of Education.* Retrieved May 15, 2003, from http://www.pen.k12.va.us/VDOE

Wineburg, S. (1991). On the reading of historical texts: Notes on the breach between school and academy. *American Educational Research Journal, 28*(3), 495–519.

Wineburg, S. (2001). *Historical thinking and other unnatural acts: Charting the future of teaching the past.* Philadelphia: Temple University Press.

Winkler, A. (2002). Division in the ranks: Standardized testing draws lines between new and veteran teachers. *Phi Delta Kappan, 84*(3), 219–225.

Yeager, E. (2000). Thoughts on wise practice in the teaching of social studies. *Social Education, 64*(6), 352–353.

Yeager, E., & Davis, J., O.L. (1994). Understanding the "knowing how" of history: Elementary student teachers' thinking about historical texts. *Journal of Social Studies Research, 18*(2), 2–9.

Yeager, E., & Davis, O.L. (1995). Between campus and classroom: Secondary student teachers' thinking about historical texts. *Journal of Research and Development in Education, 29,* 1–8.

CHAPTER 7

MORE JOURNEY THAN END

A Case Study of Ambitious Teaching[1]

S.G. Grant

The construct of "wise practice" has much appeal. Researchers long have focused on "typical" classrooms, teachers, and students. As such, their reports are more valuable as a baseline than as an image of what is possible. Research that illustrates the practices of wise teachers broadens our sense of what classroom teaching truly can be and helps us imagine new and more robust roles for both teachers and their students.

Like every social interaction, powerful teaching develops in real and varied contexts. Broad characterizations of wise practice provide a useful conversational shorthand, but they are insufficient. Invaluable are rich, nuanced, and contextualized portraits of teachers working to enrich their practices. In my recent work (Grant, 2003), I have been using the language of *ambitious teaching* to represent the challenges that teachers face as they try to teach wisely in complex environs. Ambitious teaching develops (a) when teachers know their subject matter well and see within it the potential to enrich their students' lives; (b) when teachers know their students well, which includes understanding the kinds of lives their students lead, how these youngsters think about and perceive the world, and that they are far more capable than they and most others believe them to be; and (c) when teachers know how to create the necessary space for themselves and their students in environments in which others (e.g., administrators, other teachers) may not appreciate either of their efforts. Ambitious teachers deeply understand their subject matter and their students, and they are willing to push hard to create opportunities for powerful teaching and learning despite contextual factors (e.g., state curriculum, state tests, unsupportive administrators, and colleagues) that may be pushing them in different directions.

In this chapter, I develop the construct of ambitious teaching through the case of Paula, a 10th-grade Global History teacher in western New York State. From interview data collected before and after the first administration of a new, high-stakes state test, I argue that Paula constructs an ambitious classroom practice, albeit one that requires constant negotiation. The key conditions are her sense of history as a discipline and as a school subject, her sense of what her students know and need to know, and the school and policy environment in which she teaches. As subject matter, students, and context interact, Paula regularly negotiates a series of compromises with which she is variously satisfied. Thus Paula's story is less a model to follow than a case of what ambitious teaching can look like at the ground level. Ambitious teaching is no steady state to which one ascends and never leaves. Instead, the ambitiousness of Paula's practice represents a chain of complex, mutable, and pragmatic actions, always more journey than end.

THE NOTION OF AMBITIOUS TEACHING

The social studies literature is replete with talk about what constitutes good teaching practice. For example, the National Council for the Social Studies (1994) defines "ideal" teaching as meaningful, integrative, value-based, challenging, and active. Yeager (2000) adds a host of other criteria including content and pedagogical content knowledge, enthusiastic modeling of intellectual curiosity and engagement with others, critical thinking, drawing on a palette of teaching strategies, going beyond the textbook, and moving beyond reading, reciting, and writing facts.

Such characterizations are useful, especially when they develop alongside portraits that are nuanced and sensitive to the challenges that teachers face. Those challenges can be many—students with minimal English skills (Black, 2000), students with conservative and majoritarian views (Foster & Hoge, 2000; Romanowski, 1996), and students at risk of failure (Riley, Wilson, & Fogg, 2000). Students in real classes can prove formidable, but other challenges also arise. Many teachers confront insensitive administrators, apathetic colleagues, and weakly funded resources. In recent years, the challenges that teachers face increasingly include efforts by state governments to enrich the teaching and learning that goes on in classrooms

(Grant, 2003). Ostensibly designed to promote better teaching and learning, these efforts frequently offer mixed messages at best (e.g., Grant, 1997a, 1997b; Grant, Gradwell, et al., 2002).

This view of the multiple and interacting influences on teachers' work (see, e.g., Grant, 1996, 2003; Romanowski, 1996; Sturtevant, 1996) cautions the avoidance of separating teachers and their practices from the contexts in which they work. The conditions that teachers face reasonably vary from setting to setting, but all teachers face challenges of one sort or another.

Ambitious teaching is my attempt to express the complexity of teachers' worlds. Ambitious teachers know well the many conditions—subject matter, students, state policies, colleagues, and administrators—that confront their practices. They take seriously those conditions and the challenges they can impose, but they typically exhibit a willingness to carve out their own pedagogical path that aims toward more powerful teaching and learning. Ambitious teaching, then, does not focus on innovations or best practices alone. New teaching methods, alternative assessments, and flexible student groupings, for example, may appear in ambitious teachers' classrooms, but mere evidence of these practices—or reports that someone has so labeled them—apart from signs of robust learning opportunities is insufficient to demonstrate ambitious teaching.

DESIGN OF THE STUDY

Paula, a New York State high school teacher, was part of an initial sample of 16 urban, suburban, and rural teachers who were interviewed before and after the first administration of the new, state-mandated, high-stakes Regents test in Global History and Geography.[2]

Paula is a European American in her late 30s who came to teaching as a career change. Her undergraduate degree was in history with an art history minor; her master's degree had a social studies education emphasis. During her 3 years at Middletown High School, Paula has taught both years of the required 9th- and 10th-grade Global History and Geography course. Middletown High is in a first-ring suburb of Buffalo, New York.

As we analyzed the first-year interview data on all 16 teachers, my colleagues and I were struck by the complexity of Paula's story. In the ensuing paper (Grant, Derme-Insinna, et al., 2002), we argued that Paula represented a case of a teacher caught in the midst of a struggle regarding the use of historical documents to further her goals and those of the state test makers.[3]

This chapter draws primarily on the second round of interview data with Paula. My analysis began with many of the domains that emerged from the first data set. Those domains included Paula's interpretation of the new curriculum and test, the influence of these policies on her teaching, and other influences on her classroom practice. The emergent pattern from that first-level analysis suggested a teacher who chooses what she teaches and how she teaches it based on her sense of what students need, on her sense of what content matters (e.g., nationalism) and what content does not (e.g., 1848 revolutions, modern history of Latin America), and on other factors such as the state curriculum and the state test. The second-year data, then, present a teacher who senses tension between her desired practice and that which she perceives as evident in the state curriculum and test. It also reveals a teacher who is aware of the compromises she is making and who takes actions that generally attempt to promote more powerful teaching and learning opportunities. In these ways, we see that Paula's efforts as an ambitious teacher look more like a journey than a destination.

PAULA: A CASE OF AMBITIOUS TEACHING

"The map is not a substitute for a personal experience. The map does not take the place of the actual journey" (Dewey, 1902/1969, p. 20). John Dewey wrote these words to explain the relationship between collections of accumulated knowledge and the experiences of children as they encounter ideas. Dewey's point is simple: A *map* denotes an end, a static representation of an experience completed, a journey taken. By contrast, *traveling* involves continual negotiation as time, weather, route, and the like present challenges to be met. The success of those negotiations can be determined only at the journey's end. One last point: Although the knowledge gleaned from one voyage can be used for the next, conditions change such that each trip becomes its own journey.

I make these points because too often teaching is portrayed more as a map than as a journey. Lists of effective teaching characteristics, of successful classrooms, even of ideal practice represent fixed points, road maps to good teaching. Such representations may serve as signposts, but the journeys that teachers take as they construct their daily practices are far more complex, nuanced, and uncertain than such lists describe. Teachers like Paula constantly identify and respond to challenges, many of which are unforeseen. Ambitious teaching, then, is no steady state, no promised land to which one arrives and never departs. As a real case rather than an imagined model, Paula demonstrates that ambitious teaching is more journey than end.

What does Paula's journey look like? How does she negotiate the subject matter, her students, and the conditions under which she teaches? Earlier, my colleagues and I described how Paula juggled competing demands related to the use of historical documents (Grant, Derme-Insinna, et al., 2002). In this section, I examine the twists and turns, the conditions and challenges that Paula negotiates as she makes curriculum decisions.

NEGOTIATING THE CONDITIONS OF PRACTICE

The conditions that influence Paula's pedagogy are several—subject matter, students, the state curriculum, the state test—and strains of each can be detected across her classroom decisions:

On subject matter

> I haven't talked about Latin American History since we did the independence movements early in the year, when we were talking about the Enlightenment. And I won't talk about them again until we get to probably the late 20th century when I start talking about modern issues—environmental issues and economic issues. Then I'll back up a little bit and just talk a little bit about what happened in the 20th century in Latin America, but pretty much, you know, that's 150 years we just sort of erase.

On students

> I can't think of one good way to teach [the revolutions of 1848] that would have any kind of interest for the kids, unless you spend a lot of time on it and we're able to really read about it and read primary sources. But, you know, for that hour I have that I might be able to spend on it—it's more like a half an hour—there's just no way.

On the state curriculum

> I guess I fear treading too far from the scope and sequence at this point in my career.

On the state test

> I did some things [last year] that were time-consuming that frankly I just knew were not going to show up on the test. Things like, we did a little factory simulation, the difference between factory method and domestic production. That way it was very time-consuming in a classroom, and I just, you know, felt like we probably should go a little bit more quickly through it and get on to something else.

The interview data offer numerous examples of each of these four conditions. Teaching is a complex social activity, so it makes sense that teachers' decisions reflect multiple factors (e.g., Romanowski, 1996; Sturtevant,

1996). Less well understood, however, are the relationships among conditioning influences (Grant, 1998, 2003). Teachers, in some imagined sense, could respond to influences one at time; in real life, they must grapple with events as they occur. The conditions that affect teachers' practices are both several and interacting. Although references to single factors surface in Paula's talk, far more frequent are descriptions that show Paula negotiating several conditions at once. Consider this example:

> I really want to cruise through things a little bit more quickly so we get more time for current issues, which I spent almost no time on last year, especially economic issues. I think it's important and I also think kids are weak on it—showed some weakness on it. We did a thing over the summer with my department in which we analyzed the results of our kids' tests—the multiple-choice—and tried to figure out where the weaknesses were.

Here, Paula's decision to spend more time on economic topics by "cruis[ing] through" other curricular areas reflects the influence of several conditions. In terms of subject matter, Paula believes that economic issues constitute an "important" content area. Those issues, she noted later, include events such as the Industrial Revolution, concepts such as scarcity and surplus, and movements such as the globalization of national economies. Students' grasp of economics also figures into her decision making, as she perceives their understandings to be "weak." The key piece of evidence for her perception seems to be students' performance on the state test. Still, another matter influences her decision: her department colleagues. In their analysis of students' poor performance on economics questions, Paula's peers concluded that this area needed to be addressed.

In this brief example, we get a glimpse into Paula's negotiation of a complex interaction of content, learners, and state and local contexts. Key to our understanding of this negotiation is the realization that Paula cannot respond to these influences serially, for each has implications for the others. Ambitious teaching, then, means not only understanding the importance of individual influences, but also understanding that the interaction of these influences demands continual negotiation.

AMBITIOUS TEACHING: UNDERSTANDING AND ACTION

Ambitious teaching demands sophisticated understandings. It also demands action. Ambitious teachers are not pawns that react defensively to the winds that blow through their classrooms. Instead, they act as dynamic decision-makers or "gatekeepers" (Thornton, 1991). In that role, teachers "make day-to-day decisions concerning both the subject matter and the experiences to which students have access and the nature of that subject matter and those experiences" (p. 237). Such decision making is complicated, given the uncertainties of teaching and learning (Cohen, 1988; Lortie, 1975). Thus, all teachers must make decisions under less than ideal or completely autonomous circumstances. What separates ambitious teachers from others is their deep understanding of the subject matter, their students, and the contexts in which they teach and their willingness to construct powerful classroom environments in spite of conditions that seem ill-disposed to support such efforts.

The following example displays both Paula's understanding of the several and interacting influences on her practice and her negotiation of those influences in ways that promote an ambitious resolution.

Like every history teacher, Paula views time as her enemy. Even under the best circumstances, teachers find themselves with far more content to teach than the time to teach it. As Paula negotiates subject matter, student, and contextual factors, she does so with yet another condition in mind—the clock and the calendar. Asked if her awareness of time means that she has had to cut back on elements of the curriculum, Paula nodded and talked about changes she had made in the pace of her teaching: "I changed the pacing, I think, of my teaching through the course of the year. I've tried to go more quickly through the material that's in the scope and sequence. I spend less time on the Industrial Revolution, for example, than I did last year."

Time pressures provoke many teachers to adjust their instructional pace. As a relatively new teacher, Paula never is sure how long activities will last and, consequently, she recognizes the value of some year-to-year tinkering. Underscoring her uncertainty, however, is a tension Paula perceives between the state curriculum and the state test, and between those policies and the directions she would prefer to take. The curriculum gives sustained attention to topics like the Industrial Revolution, whereas the topic merits but a question or two on the state test:

> So there's that tension—you know—that tension between what the exam or what the scope and sequence emphasizes, and the things that I'd like to do. And there's some give and take, you know, so I drop something in the Industrial Revolution that I don't think that [the state curriculum developers] think is important, nor am I that interested in it, and I pick something up a little bit that I think is interesting.

Although some teachers might defer to the curriculum (and so spend more time on the Industrial Revolution) or to the test (and thus spend more time on tested material), Paula's sense of the subject leads her to drop some elements of the topic in favor of those she believes students will find more engaging. Paula understands the parameters of the curriculum and the test, and she does not ignore them. Neither, however, do they determine her resultant decision. She makes the decisions and she acts.

One of the things Paula picks up because she thinks it is more "interesting" is nationalism:

> As I look at it now, I may be spending more time on nationalism than I did last year, mostly because I just see that as a really important topic. I think it's very pertinent to today and will continue to be important in the world. And I think it's an extremely complicated topic, and I think that I myself still haven't gotten it all figured out.

Issues related to nationalism appear in both the state curriculum and test, but no more so than any other topic. The 2-year Global History and Geography curriculum is 27 single-spaced pages long and offers scant guidance as to which of the hundreds of topics are most worthy of study (Grant, 2001). The state test is no more prescriptive, although test designers clearly prefer items related to modern-era events (Grant, 2001).[4] Paula takes this mix of messages into account and sees it as an opportunity. Nationalism is a "very important topic" to her, albeit one that is "extremely complicated." With the autonomy to make classroom decisions and the willingness to explore an area out of her comfort zone, Paula makes an ambitious choice to highlight nationalism.

That choice is not the end of her teaching story, however, because ambitious teaching is no steady state. Her choice to emphasize nationalism translates automatically into neither thoughtful lessons nor assessments. Nor does it mean that the import of the curriculum and test diminish completely. In fact, the crush of content represented in these two policies seems more hindrance than help:

> I'm starting to sense that a lot of [content in the state curriculum] just jumbles their minds up when you try to really run through it all. So, I am trying to distill it as well through, partly through my own preference, and partly through what I think the exam will do, because I do think that's just a lot of crap [in the state curriculum] that seems to need a lot of editing. I mean, a lot of editing.

Ironically, some teachers perceive the push for higher standards through new curriculum and testing policies as antithetical to more powerful teaching and learning (Grant, Gradwell, & Cimbricz, in review). Paula's perception of a weak match between the curriculum and test is one example. Another is the one expressed just above: that the curriculum contains "a lot of crap here that seems to need a lot of editing."

In the end, Paula's approach to teaching nationalism negotiates several influences: the state curriculum, the test, her sense of her students, and her sense of the critical ideas, the "important strings":

> Nationalism, to me, is a very important string that I pull throughout, that I want to pull throughout. If there are things that don't connect to that string, then I'm not going to bother with them. I'm starting to see some really important concepts that I want to maintain, and I don't want to jumble [students'] minds up and confuse the issue. I want these concepts to be clear. I want their causes and effects and the events in them to be clear, so I am slowly starting to trim away a lot of the junk.

As she clears away the "junk" and constructs those "strings" that lead to a rich understanding of nationalism, Paula exercises judgment based on her understanding of historical content. An example of one content string that she develops is the link between imperialism and nationalism:

> I spent more time [this year] making the explicit connection between imperialism and nationalism. Rather than breaking it up by doing World War I in between the two [as the curriculum suggests], I did a more regional approach. I took imperialism, for example, in Africa straight through to independence in Africa, and then in India, and then in China, because I felt there was more continuity in doing that. And then I backed up and went to the nationalist elements of World War I.

Paula knows that her students struggle with broad concepts such as imperialism and nationalism, and that they typically perceive world events as isolated matters. If she were to strictly follow the state curriculum, she believes that she would reinforce these problems. Thus, Paula takes the initiative to construct a taught curriculum that reflects the key elements of ambitious teaching: a deep understanding of the conditions relevant to the situation and the willingness to craft opportunities for more powerful teaching and learning.

Whereas she acknowledges that nationalism remains an "extremely complicated topic," one that she has not gotten "all figured out," Paula is reasonably satisfied with her resolution. This conclusion is not always the case, however. Again, ambitious teaching is more journey than end; every curricular topic presents a new set of challenges and a new arrangement of contextual conditions. Paula's satisfaction with one curricular negotiation may mean little as she prepares for the next one. Consider this example of Paula's attempts to incorporate art and literature into her teaching:

> I do very little exploration of art and literature, which my first year of teaching I did a lot of, and it's something I really enjoy. I do very little art anymore. I still do some literature, poetry in particular. But, the art thing—it's not

there on the exam and it's not in the scope and sequence, and as much as I love teaching it, I just don't anymore. I'm afraid it would confuse the kids, get them too far away from—you know—the umbilical cord of the scope and sequence. I don't know. It just, it makes, I'm uncomfortable with it. I'm not really even sure why.

Paula has a strong background in art history; she knows and enjoys teaching it. She is less well versed in world literature, but she is no less committed to finding ways to use literary selections and interpretations in class. Her analysis of the state curriculum and the questions on the state exam, however, reinforces her belief that art and literature are undervalued: "It's not there on the exam and it's not in the scope and sequence." The subject-matter benefits of enriching historical study with art and literature are significant to Paula, but she worries that straying from explicit historical content may "confuse" her students on test day. She will not forsake all opportunities to use art and literature, but neither will she pursue all the opportunities that she recognizes.

In this example, ambitious inclinations go largely unfulfilled. Paula understands the conditions of subject matter, students, curriculum, and test, and she has negotiated a minor role for art and literature in her practice. Unlike her negotiations around the topic of nationalism, however, the success of her resolution seems unsettled and bitter. Her willingness to teach in ambitious ways guarantees no satisfaction. On the other hand, observers who are discouraged by Paula's decision miss a key point about ambitious teaching: Dissatisfaction with one compromise can breed the development of a new and more positive approach to teaching. Paula's current negotiation of the role for art and literature in her practice may not be her final one.

AMBITIOUS TEACHING: MORE JOURNEY THAN END

The "map" exemplified by cases like Paula's can be instructive to other teachers as they negotiate the conditions of their own ambitious teaching. Still, each teacher's journey is unique, and case studies, like maps, "are not a substitute for a personal experience" (Dewey, 1902/1956, p. 20). Just as Paula's practice is more journey than end, so will it be for each teacher inspired by her example.

What might teachers interested in ambitious teaching glean from this case? One implication centers on the powerful role teachers can play as gatekeepers of their classrooms. Conditions such as content, students, and state policies all matter, but they do not matter in the same ways or to the same extent. We detect the influence of the state curriculum and test on

Paula's decision to increase her instructional pace, to emphasize economic issues, and to reduce her use of art and literature. In each instance, however, we also recognize how Paula's sense of the subject matter and of her students plays out. One or another condition may seem to dominate her teaching at times. In most instances, however, Paula's decisions reflect a series of negotiations that sometimes result in resolutions both favorable (e.g., nationalism) and not so favorable (e.g., art and literature).

Like Paula, other perceptive teachers will appreciate the key role they play as pedagogical decision-makers. Although the influences on their teaching are many, they rarely coincide to promote a single direction. Teachers may choose to let a curriculum or a test or a textbook determine their practices, but note that they are *choosing* their route. Ambitious teachers like Paula know that they can choose otherwise.

Another implication is less obvious, but no less important: Ambitious teachers realize that they act within an uncertain world. As a pedagogical goal, ambitious teaching establishes no ultimate destination, nor does it prescribe a defined trail.

All metaphors break down at some point, and so does the notion of ambitious teaching as a journey. The biggest problem has to do with the notion of a destination, because explorers typically know when they have reached (or failed to reach) their goal. Lewis and Clark realized a good portion of their ambition once they set foot on the sands of the Pacific Ocean; Ponce de Leon's explorations ended less successfully.

Teaching is different. One of the endemic uncertainties of teaching that Lortie (1975) describes is teachers' uncertainty of knowing what constitutes classroom success. In Lortie's words, "Teaching demands, it seems, the capacity to work for protracted periods without the sure knowledge that one is having any positive effect on students" (p. 144). Additionally, Cohen (1988) observes that teachers and others in the human improvement fields face the uncertainty of complex practices: "The practitioner's assignment is thus to produce what they typically cannot define with any precision, and to do so in spite of their frequent inability to be sure how results are produced when they are or to know why things go awry, as they often do" (p. 56). In Paula's case, we see a teacher committed, for example, to constructing "strings" such as imperialism that pull nationalism throughout her curriculum. That said, nationalism is an "extremely complicated topic," and so Paula's sense of teaching this topic well is ill defined.

With an uncertain endpoint, it follows that an ambitious teacher can take no direct, predictable, or safe path. Teachers like Paula know only the vague outlines of their destinations and their routes, and they must negotiate an array of conditions and challenges that arise along the way. For example, Paula believes that nationalism is an important concept. She also knows that it gets some attention in the state curriculum and on the state test. These policies, however, lay out no clear pedagogical route. In order to help her students understand this complex topic, Paula must do a "lot of editing" of the curriculum to separate out the key ideas, and she must reconstruct the order in which the curriculum presents imperialism and nationalism. Her negotiation of the challenges posed by the state policies in this instance seems to be more satisfactory to her than the one at which she arrives in her use of art and literature. Yet in each situation, Paula finds that her ambitious goals put her on an unclear road.

Awareness of the uncertainties and the extra work inherent in Paula's classroom practice may discourage some teachers from pursuing an ambitious pedagogy. Still, many teachers construct similar practices, inspired largely by the impact that they recognize on their students, regardless of how their actions are perceived by others (Grant, 2003; Riley et al., 2000; Wineburg & Wilson, 1991). In the following quotation, Paula captures the promise and problems of ambitious teaching:

> We do other things in my room that other teachers don't do. I think if you put a box of crayons in front of somebody, I don't care who they are, they are going to have a good time. So we do a lot of drawing of historical concepts. And I know, I've actually had my colleagues tell me, "Oh I don't do that, I'm not comfortable with that." I'm sure they think it's a little odd, and I really think they think, "Well, are her kids going to pass the test doing this?"

Willing to try almost anything that might help her students understand the many complex concepts that she teaches, Paula does indeed break out boxes of crayons from time to time. She knows that the professional literature supports this action; alternative teaching approaches, on occasion, can effectively jump-start students' thinking. She also realizes that her willingness to teach this way will raise some eyebrows. Finally, she knows that those eyebrows may continue to rise regardless of the fact that her students performed satisfactorily on the first administration of the new state exam; in fact, her students had the second-highest passing rate in the school. Paula's colleagues, her administrators, and state education policymakers are not her primary concern, however; her students are. And so as an ambitious teacher, Paula pushes on.

CONCLUSION

If social studies teaching is to change in any real ways, then cases of ambitious teaching are needed now more than ever before. Descriptions of new curricular materials and new teaching strategies are useful. Nevertheless, case studies of teachers like Paula serve a powerful purpose because they demonstrate the complex and often uncertain worlds that ambitious teachers inhabit. Teaching in ambitious ways demands that teachers have a deep understanding of subject matter, of students, and of the many contextual factors that can influence their practices. Ambitious teaching also calls, however, for the willingness to make classroom decisions that may not be widely supported. Such teaching represents no endpoint, but rather a journey in which teachers face and negotiate challenges and conditions along the way. There can be satisfaction in reaching ends, but so too can satisfaction arise from the journey itself.

NOTES

1. Many thanks are due to Jill Gradwell, Cecil Robinson, and Diane Zigo for their careful and considered reading of earlier versions of this chapter.
2. The names and locations of participants are pseudonyms.
3. See Grant, Derme-Insinna, and colleagues (2001) for an overview of the new Regents exam for Global History and for more detail about the research methodology.
4. Interestingly enough, the 1-year U.S. History and Geography course of study consists of 33 single-spaced pages.

REFERENCES

Black, M. (2000). The geography of connection: Bringing the world to students. *Social Education, 64*(6), 354–358.

Cohen, D. (1988). Teaching practice: Plus que ca change... In P. Jackson (Ed.), *Contributing to educational change: Perspectives on research and practice* (pp. 27–84). Berkeley, CA: McCutchan.

Dewey, J. (1969). *The child and the curriculum.* Chicago: University of Chicago Press. (Original work published 1902)

Foster, S., & Hoge, J. (2000). "Dismantling the wall, one brick at a time": Overcoming barriers to parochialism in social studies classrooms. *Social Education, 64*(6), 368–370.

Grant, S. G. (1996). Locating authority over content and pedagogy: Cross-current influences on teachers' thinking and practice. *Theory and Research in Social Education, 24*(3), 237–272.

Grant, S. G. (1997a). Opportunities lost: Teachers learning about the New York state social studies framework. *Theory and Research in Social Education, 25*(3), 259–287.

Grant, S. G. (1997b). A policy at odds with itself: The tension between constructivist and traditional views in the New York state social studies framework. *Journal of Curriculum and Supervision, 13*(1), 92–113.

Grant, S. G. (1998). *Reforming reading, writing, and mathematics: Teachers' responses and the prospects for systemic reform.* Mahwah, NJ: Erlbaum.

Grant, S. G. (2001). When an "A" isn't enough: Analyzing the New York State global history exam. *Educational Policy Analysis Archives, 9*(39). Retrieved from http://www.epaa.asu.edu/epaa/v9n39.html

Grant, S. G. (2003). *History lessons: Teaching, learning, and testing in U. S. high school classrooms*. Mahwah, NJ: Erlbaum.

Grant, S. G., Derme-Insinna, A., Gradwell, J. M., Lauricella, A. M., Pullano, L., & Tzetzo, K. (2001). Teachers, tests, and tensions: Teachers respond to the New York state global history exam. *International Social Studies Forum, 1*(2), 107–125.

Grant, S. G., Derme-Insinna, A., Gradwell, J. M., Lauricella, A. M., Pullano, L., & Tzetzo, K. (2002). Juggling two sets of books: A teacher responds to the new global history exam. *Journal of Curriculum and Supervision, 17*(3), 232–255.

Grant, S.G., Gradwell, J.M., & Cimbricz, S. K. (2004). A question of authenticity: The document-based question as an assessment of students' knowledge of history. *Journal of Curriculum and Supervision, 19*(4), 309–337.

Grant, S. G., Gradwell, J. M., Lauricella, A. M., Derme-Insinna, A., Pullano, L., & Tzetzo, K. (2002). When increasing stakes need not mean increasing standards: The case of the New York State global history and geography exam. *Theory and Research in Social Education, 30*(4), 488–515.

Grant, S. G., Gradwell, J., & Cimbricz. (in review). A question of authenticity: Examining the document based question on the New York State global history and geography Regents exam. *Journal of Curriculum and Supervision*.

Lortie, D. (1975). *Schoolteacher*. Chicago: University of Chicago Press.

National Council for the Social Studies. (1994). *Expectations of excellence*. Washington, DC: Author.

Riley, K., Wilson, E., & Fogg, T. (2000). Transforming the spirit of teaching through wise practice: Observations of two Alabama social studies teachers. *Social Education, 64*(6), 361–363.

Romanowski, M. (1996). Issues and influences that shape the teaching of U.S. history. In J. Brophy (Ed.), *Advances in research on teaching* (Vol. 6, pp. 291–312). Greenwich, CT: JAI Press.

Sturtevant, E. (1996). Lifetime influences on the literacy-related instructional beliefs of experienced high school history teachers: Two comparative case studies. *Journal of Literacy Research, 28*(2), 227–257.

Thornton, S. (1991). Teacher as curricular-instructional gatekeeper in the social studies. In J. Shaver (Ed.), *Handbook of research on social studies teaching and learning* (pp. 237–248). New York: Macmillan.

Wineburg, S., & Wilson, S. (1991). Subject matter knowledge in the teaching of history. In J. Brophy (Ed.), *Advances in research on teaching* (Vol. 3, pp. 305–347). Greenwich, CT: JAI Press.

Yeager, E. (2000). Thoughts on wise practice in the teaching of social studies. *Social Education, 64*(6), 352–353.

CHAPTER 8

WISE PRACTICE IN AN INNOVATIVE PUBLIC SCHOOL

Diana Hess

Joe Park[1] has taught middle and high school social studies for 26 years, the last 10 at a small and innovative public high school that does not require students to follow a prescribed curriculum. Consequently, Park has the luxury of creating courses that reflect and instantiate his conceptions of "wise practice" in social studies teaching and learning. During the 2002–2003 school year he taught seven different 9-week courses on such diverse topics as *The History and Literature of the Holocaust, Protest and Reform in United States History, Important Supreme Court Decisions,* and *Street Law.* Park has taught the Supreme Court course for a number of years. I first encountered that course in 1998 when I was conducting a "models of wisdom study" of teachers who were particularly skillful at teaching their students to participate effectively in discussions of controversial public issues (Hess, 2002).

Since that time, Park and I have had numerous conversations about teaching and learning. In late 2002, I interviewed Park about how the standards, assessment, and public accountability trends in his state had affected his practices. I was curious about how an innovative teacher at a highly unusual school was dealing with what seemed to me to be a sea change in educational policy. More specifically, I wondered if the aspects of his practice that I had considered so unusually skillful were being supported or harmed by changes that had occurred since 1998.

This chapter focuses on Park's teaching as an example of wise practice in secondary social studies. I detail how Park teaches his students to participate in seminar discussions and briefly describe his emphasis on position paper writing, because I agree with Yeager (2000) that greatly needed is a much more extensive case literature that clearly articulates excellent practices. I explain why I consider Park's practice "wise" by assessing it against the standards embedded in *Powerful and Authentic Social Studies* (Harris & Yocum, 2000), before describing how Park's teaching has not been harmed appreciably by recent changes in his state's educational accountability policies. In fact, Park's descriptions of his teaching suggest that his practice has improved as a consequence of a state writing test. Looking into the future, I hypothesize about how testing policies common to many states, but not yet in place in Park's, could put his practice and the alternative setting in which he teaches at risk.

JOE PARK AT NEW HORIZONS HIGH SCHOOL

Joe Park's decision to become a teacher initially was motivated by his interest in social studies content, especially African studies. As an undergraduate student in one of the nation's premier universities, Park's preservice teacher education was "pretty phenomenal… I learned how to teach from people who really believed that social studies teaching was a special and very, very important trust." Park credits his superb preservice preparation as the reason he both likes teaching and feels successful as a teacher.

Since he graduated with a B.A. in history and a certificate to teach secondary social studies in 1975, Park has taught both middle and high school social studies at several schools, completed an M.A. degree in curriculum and instruction, and participated in a wide variety of professional development programs, in both the teacher and student roles. For example, early in his teaching career, he spent a year as a teacher associate for a social studies "think tank" at which he developed curriculum and led teacher in-service professional development programs. A few years later, he spent 2 years as a clinical professor in a university program; he supervised student teachers and facilitated staff development programs for teachers in his school district. Since that time, he has continued to participate in a number of professional development activities, including a national project to develop authentic assessments in civic education, and a locally based study group in which teachers share their curriculum and students' work as a way to improve their teaching. He also teaches democracy education programs in Eastern and Central Europe and a preservice course on secondary social studies for his state's flagship university.

The school in which Park currently teaches is located in a university community outside of a major western city in the United States. Park describes his community as a

> middle- to upper-middle-class college town, high expectations, high income, lots of scientists, privileged community that is obsessive about the success of its own children.... For the majority of the parents in this community, or a very vocal segment of the community, traditional schooling worked for them, they perceive that it will work for their children, and they don't want anything to get in the way of their children having the same privilege that they have. It is a community that prides itself on enlightened progressivism.

Not all the young people and parents in this community are attracted to schools that employ mainly traditional approaches. In fact, the school district has sponsored the development of several nontraditional schools, including New Horizons High School, which Park helped design and where he has taught for 10 years. Developed as a public high school of choice (similar to a magnet school) that opened as a "break the mold" high school in the fall of 1993, New Horizons High School became, from the outset, "a place to experiment... to do high school right. As we said, to take 25 years of research and try to implement it."

Founding principles of the new school included use of the community as a viable learning resource; valuing diversity, including not just race, gender, and ethnicity, but a vast spectrum of "other ways that kids are"; actively engaging students in their learning; teaching students to take responsibility for their learning; creating and fostering a climate of mutual respect; holding high expectations for all students; and personalizing education for students. Many of the original plans for the school did not work out in practice; after much trial and error, the teachers "came into a very strong understanding of what it means to teach from your passions, and that authentic curriculum is different than active learning."

New Horizons High School enrolls 350 students and is staffed by 20 teachers. Students choose to attend the school. As a school that serves students in grades 9 through 12, New Horizons uses a multiaged, mixed-ability, full-inclusion model. The school, by its very design, attracts students who want a nontraditional high school education. The promotional material for the school describes the kind of student well served by its unique approach:

> Based on our experience, New Horizons High School works really well for students who: are willing to be partners with teachers, parents and other adults; are willing to be partners with other students; work hard when they are treated with respect and given autonomy; believe a school should be a community of learners; advocate for themselves and negotiate with others to

solve problems; are ready for more responsibility for their own learning. (New Horizon promotional literature, 1997)

Undergirding the philosophy of the curriculum at New Horizons High School is student choice. In 1997–1998 it offered no required classes, although students had to complete units in areas such as science, language arts, and social studies. One consequence of the standards movement has been a new requirement of a small number of courses during the first 2 years in preparation for the state tests, which students take at the end of ninth and tenth grades. All courses are one quarter in length. Students also create their own "individual student paths," which culminate in major projects completed for graduation in their senior year.

Park's conception of his role as a teacher is explicitly focused on preparing young people for democratic participation: "It's my job to teach the concepts of citizenship and democracy.... In a democracy such as ours, it's my job to teach the concept of justice." Park distinguishes between working toward students' development of a general understanding of and appreciation for concepts such as justice, and specific views on controversial issues. When discussing controversial issues that involve democracy and justice, Park tells his students, "I don't have an answer, but it's my job to help you ask the questions." Park's interest in helping students ask questions is driven by his view that one of the purposes of social studies is to involve students in the "theory-making business." Drawing on constructivist learning theory, Park believes that knowledge is created, not transmitted. For example, when studying the First Amendment, Park encourages his students to create their own theories that respond to two central questions: Why do we have the First Amendment? How absolute ought it be?

Educating young people for citizen action is another goal embedded in Park's conception of teaching toward democracy. When asked what he would like to see one of his students doing 10 years in the future, Park told a story about a recent conversation with the mother of a former student. Since she graduated from college, this young woman has been a witness in Guatemala (accompanying indigenous people to protect them from government oppression) and is currently working as a political organizer. The mother attributed her daughter's citizen action to the influence of Park and his wife, also a social studies teacher. Upon hearing this, Park remembered that he "swelled up three sizes too big."

At the core of Park's conception of democratic citizenship is engagement that stems from personal agency. "Citizenship is about action... an effective citizen is someone who believes that he or she has agency of some sort." Park cites numerous examples of what political engagement might look like, such as standing up for the rights of others, running for office, and voting. He believes that each of these examples is indicative of two central beliefs held by effective citizens: They have a voice, and they have choices.

One way that Park thinks effective citizens should use their voice is by asking questions. Characterizing the ability to ask questions before acting as "the most important thing" that citizens should be able to do, Park defines effective citizens as people who substitute "ready, ask a question, think about it" for the more typical tendency of citizens to engage in "ready, fire, aim." The high premium Park places on thoughtful questioning is rooted in his belief that most of the decisions citizens need to make are very difficult.

The questions Park wants effective citizens to ask are built on content knowledge related to democracy, what he calls the fundamentals of democracy, defined as certain attitudes rooted in the Bill of Rights. For example, effective citizens should believe that "free speech is better than restricted speech, and the rights of the accused are more important than kangaroo courts." Knowledge of current events is another important facet of Park's conception of effective democratic citizenship because "citizenship is not just about history, but it's about the present and the future." In addition to becoming critical consumers of the news, citizens should use that knowledge to engage in voting and partisan politics because "that's the coin of the realm."

In all of Park's courses, he teaches students how to engage in discussions of controversial issues in order to provide the practice young people need to "become part of the great conversations that take place in our society, and are taking place increasingly poorly." Characterizing "great conversations" as exemplars of civic discourse, Park explicitly links controversial issues discussions to preparation for effective citizenship in a democracy. He does not intend such discussions to prepare students to participate in the kind of civic discourse that currently occurs in the United States:

> One of the things that drives me crazy is that what goes for political conversation in our society, on TV especially, and talk radio, is shouting matches. And it has absolutely nothing to do with thoughtful dialogue and the complexities of issues... and that, I think, is antidemocratic.

Park teaches his students to participate in discussions to counter this antidemocratic trend in the hope of creating an enriched democracy. Describing issues discussions as "one of the best ways to get kids to think critically," Park says that this goal is realized if three factors are present: (1) students are pushed to justify their thinking, (2) they are presented with alternatives, and (3) they interact with the ideas of other discussants. Issues discussions promote more complex thinking (i.e., more critical thinking) if the discussion is structured to help students become more comfortable "in their acceptance of a lack of closure regarding issues and questions."

Park also includes issues discussions as a way to help students develop process skills, such as the ability to both listen and talk well. Emphasizing the importance of practice to the development of these skills, Park states, "There has to be some sort of environment in society where kids practice doing that. They practice batting a baseball, for God's sakes, why can't they practice talking?"

A SEMINAR DISCUSSION IN JOE PARK'S COURSE

During the 1997–1998 school year, Park taught a 9-week course that focused on historically significant controversial public issues related to freedom of speech and press. Park designed the course to rely on Supreme Court cases because "you would be hard pressed to find a more authentic text than a Supreme Court decision." Although all nine of the cases read by the students were about the First Amendment's speech and press clauses, Park also hoped his students would gain a general understanding of content that extends beyond this amendment. On the first day of class, for example, he said to his students: "I want to grow old in a society that has many people understanding the way the Constitution and the Supreme Court works."

The 24 students enrolled in the course met three times per week for a weekly total of 4 hours. During most weeks, the grade 9 through 12 students read one First Amendment Supreme Court decision, prepared to participate in a seminar discussion on the case by completing a prediscussion assignment called a "ticket," worked in small groups to review the facts of the case, participated in a seminar, and wrote an issues-analysis paper.

The seminar model of discussion that Park used in the Supreme Court course is pervasive throughout New Horizons High School. He learned the model from the school's principal (who joins in the seminars as a model participant and, on occasion, as the facilitator) and used it for several years. The model, labeled simply "seminars" at the school, is a text-based, large-group discussion designed to help participants develop a deeper understanding of the issues, ideas, and values in the text (Gray, 1989). Park favors the model because of its potential to enhance critical thinking and to generate new ideas.

Preparing for the Seminar

This day's seminar focuses on the Supreme Court's decision in *New York Times Co. v. United States*, the famous "Pentagon Papers" case (1971), which highlights the tension between freedom of the press and national security. Beforehand, Park's students have read the 50 pages of the case and completed a "ticket" (a preseminar assignment) to participate in the seminar discussion. The ticket for this case required students to create and complete a data retrieval chart that identified the basic arguments made by each of the justices in the nine separate opinions issued in the case; in other words, Park's ticket assignments require students to read and interact with the text. Park does not expect, however, that the ticket will enable students to understand the text: That purpose will be pursued in the seminar discussion. The day before the Pentagon Papers seminar, students worked in small groups to determine the basic facts of the case and how it moved through various courts before it was granted certiorari by the United States Supreme Court.

An account of the proceedings on the day of the seminar follows. As students enter the classroom on seminar day, Park checks to see if their tickets are completed. Graded as a pass if completed and fail if not completed, the tickets also determine who might participate in the discussion. Students without a ticket are not permitted to sit in the circle, even if they report that they have completed the assigned reading. Instead, Park assigns them to be observers and to sit outside the circle and take notes about the participation of the seminar members. Park encourages students to complete their tickets by remarking, "It's preferable to sit in the circle and choose not to participate, rather than be on the outside and not be able to participate." Park's requirement that students complete their tickets is one way that he deals with the difficulties involved in talking across difference:

> The only thing that we know we have in common in a seminar is the text that we share in common. We've been raised differently. We have studied different materials in this class. We may have had U.S. history classes, others have not had U.S. history classes. All sorts of things. But what we do know is that we all have the text in common. A good discussion, a good seminar, begins from the premise that we are talking about a shared text.

As the 2-hour class period begins, 19 students, Park, and the school's principal (acting as a model seminar participant) are seated in the seminar circle. One student who did not complete the ticket is creating a list of participants, to be marked with checks each time an individual talks. Before the seminar begins, Park reminds the students to work hard and to "do the work of the seminar." By this, Park means adhering to the guidelines created by the students at the beginning of the course. These guidelines, written on butcher paper, are posted on the classroom wall and include: "Listen, respond to ideas out there, make the agenda yours, and refer to the text." Park explains what he means by this initial exhortation to his students: "I think it was a phrase they all understood ... that doing the work of the seminar is using the behaviors [required in seminars], is working hard with the text. It's living with ambiguity."

Park begins the discussion with a focus question: "What was the most compelling argument in the case?" He has developed this focus question using specific criteria: The question cannot be answered without using the text; it is open-ended in that there is no right or wrong answer; it is a question about which he, as the seminar facilitator, is genuinely curious.

A student immediately responds to Park's focus question by changing it: "Well, I can tell you the least compelling argument." The student then points the class to a part of Chief Justice Burger's dissenting opinion that laments the little time the Court has had to spend on the case, then he remarks, "He is just whining here." Later, I asked Park why he did not direct the student to stick with the question that was asked. He responded, "That's a no brainer. Just because I asked a question doesn't mean that I asked the right question.... Just because I was fishing for trout doesn't mean that I'm going to ignore the bass that bites." Moreover, he believes that the student's response accomplished the primary purpose of his focus question: It opened a door to the text in a way that prompted students to focus on the reasoning of the justices.

None of the other students comment on Burger's reasoning. After a short pause, several chime in and say that Justices Douglas and Black have particularly compelling reasons to support their opinions. Park asks the students to locate the beginning of Douglas's opinion, and they turn to a specific page in the text. He immediately poses a question to one of the students who likes the reasoning of Justice Douglas, "Betty, what was your sense of what Douglas was arguing?" She responds by paraphrasing the position Douglas took. Park follows up her comment by suggesting a label for Douglas's reasoning: "So he was a First Amendment absolutist?" Students agree and Park continues to probe: "Talk to us more about Douglas's arguments." Another student responds with a thorough explanation of why he finds the arguments compelling. This interchange continues for several minutes. Students refer to the text and talk about the basic tenets of the two First Amendment absolutists. During the opening several minutes of this seminar, Park asks a number of questions and continually reminds students to locate a specific portion of the text to which they are referring when they speak.

During the seminar, most of the students support the opinions of the court majority, which held that the First Amendment protected publication of the Pentagon Papers. One student, however, takes the opposing position. Park then comments, "There's our lone conservative, this time. We don't have to agree with Logan, but let's ... pretend to do so for a minute. Okay? Let's try to construct and give credence to the argument of the government in this case." For several minutes students identify parts of the dissenting opinions that represent the government's position in the dispute, and they explain what they think those arguments mean.

Later, Park explained to me why he refocused the seminar on the arguments that did not have the support of most of the students:

> I think a real important critical thinking skill is the ability to take a different position and to argue it with credence and credibility. I think it's an incredible skill for citizens, for enlightened citizens in a democracy, because it's rare that issues are completely black and white. It's important to give minority voices a really serious airing in a classroom. Because then people will give their true opinion. I think it's also real important to have kids take on different viewpoints as a way of better understanding their own viewpoints. So related, back to the earlier question, that's about doing the work of seminars. Doing the work of seminars is trying on ideas.

Several times in the seminar students do not understand the meanings of words in the text. The first time this occurs, Park states, "Let's look it up; here's the dictionary." A student then looks up the word and reads the definition to the class. Later, when several students do not understand another term in the text, a student reports, "I already looked this up last night; it means...." Throughout the seminar, students manifest their belief that meanings of words matter; they are willing to stop the seminar to make sure that everyone understands key terms.

The Pentagon Papers were stolen government documents, a fact that becomes the focus of conversation toward the end of the seminar. Park asks the students, "So, what should the *New York Times* have done when Daniel Ellsberg came to them with boxes of stolen government documents? If Logan steals a TV and gives it to me, and I know that he stole the TV, have I done something wrong?" Several students exclaim, "Yes!" Park follows up: "Is that the same thing as the *New York Times* did with the documents?" A student replies, "They didn't know." Another counters, "Oh yes, they knew." A third claims, "But they thought the public had a right to know." Park then refers students back to the text: "Doesn't one of the justices say something to the effect that there is this right to know right now and the *New York Times* feels a responsibility to provide that information? Who said that?" After a few seconds of looking, someone shouts, "page 749," and Park then reads an excerpt from this page. He comments, "You guys, most of you believe that what the Supreme Court did was right in this case." Several students say, "Yes." He continues, "Did the *New York Times* do the right thing?" A student responds, "In my opinion, it's just a matter of your opinion, more important that the public know—they did what they needed to do and I agree with them." Another student notes, "I agree, it's like this pull—they were publishing stolen documents, which was basically not the right thing to do, but yet it was important to let the public know what the government was doing. I have a question, did anything happen to the *New York Times* as a result of this?" Park replies, "The *New York Times* was fined, and Daniel Ellsberg was tried for taking the Pentagon Papers—do you want to know now or later what happened to Daniel Ellsberg?" One student pleads, "Now, right now, Joe." Another jokingly adds, "We have a right to know." This excerpt from the seminar discussion illustrates the moves that Park frequently makes to use the text to spark discussion of larger moral questions.

During the hour-long seminar, the student observer counts 150 different contributions: 104 (or 70%) made by seminar participants and 46 (or 30%) by Park. Of the 19 students in the seminar circle, 13 verbally participate. Compared to the eight other seminars in this course, the overall participation numbers have remained fairly constant. Most of Park's participation takes the form of questions to students; it is important to point out that this amount of teacher talk is remarkably lower than what has been routinely reported by other researchers.

Although students who prepared for the discussion by completing their tickets are not required to participate orally in the seminar discussion, they are required to share their critiques of the discussion during a debriefing period held immediately after the seminar ends. Park begins the debriefing session in a celebratory manner: "Give yourselves a round of applause, you guys got this thing." Following enthusiastic applause, one student exclaims, "I was terrified when I first saw it." Park then asks, "I would like to know what your sense of this seminar was as it compared to others and on its own merits." A student volunteers:

> I'll start.... I just thought this was a really comfortable seminar, not a lot of people talked, but those people who did really knew what their ideas were about the case, and that helped me, a person who didn't understand it a whole lot, to get a better sense of it all. I enjoyed the relaxed energy of it because it made it a lot more easy to get into.

Although many students agree that the seminar had a relaxed pace, their views about the text differ. Some students like the text, but a few believe that it was confusing or worse. One student asserts abruptly, "This text sucks." Another student critiques her own participation in the seminar:

> I finally completed my goal, which was to not talk during the seminar. I kept wanting to talk because I think this case was very confusing, but the seminar cleared it up. But I thought it was pretty good, but it is kind of weird trying

not to talk. I think I listen more when I am talking because I listen in order to respond.

Throughout the critique, Park says very little. However, when his turn arrives as the critique moves around the circle, he comments: "The coolest thing about this seminar was the opportunity to read this case because I have known about this case for a very long time. I found the ticket helped me a whole lot in terms of organizing nine separate opinions."

Later, Park describes the purpose of the seminar critique to me as "feedback loop for all of us," a way to enhance students' abilities to be reflective:

> It's a whole meta-cognitive process that I think is incredibly powerful for kids. It also, again, goes to that notion of power and voice and the politics of the classroom that I value by holding a space for them to reflect on what's going on, which says… whether or not it's my classroom or their classroom. My conversation or their conversation. And this is very, very concrete evidence that it's our conversation.

Park distinguishes between his informal assessment of the quality of students' participation in seminar discussions and his grading of their participation. He supports the former and is resolute about not doing the latter. Although he routinely provides each student with some oral and written feedback about their seminar discussion skills, he does not factor their participation in seminars into their course grades. He believes that the authenticity of the seminar would be diminished if students were graded on their verbal participation. The unique nature of seminars as discussions aimed collaboratively to create meaning makes his grading of an individual's verbal participation problematic:

> Seminars are about coming together in a public space to interact with people who are and are not like you. And that (comprises) different things, not less important, but different things than individual writing assignments [which Park does grade]. Not the least of which is the public performance aspect of it. And the fact that we're trying to make meaning together. If I want to make meaning together, I want only the contribution of authentic ingredients.

Another reason for his refusal to grade seminars is his conviction that students participate in seminars in various ways: "You see, I like it when kids speak in seminars. I've learned to get just as big a kick out of kids who say, 'I really, God I was there the whole time. I just didn't have anything to say because I was listening so intently and trying to figure stuff out.' So, I value being in seminars in a variety of ways." An assessment rubric for seminar participation that honors the various ways that students participate in the discussions seems to Park both impossible and undesirable.

To summarize, then, the seminar discussion about *New York Times Co. v. United States* portrays how this type of discussion occurs in Park's classes. Before a seminar, students read a text, complete a ticket, and work in small groups to become more familiar with the basic facts of the case. On seminar day, students review guidelines for seminar behavior prior to Park's launching of the seminar with a focus question. Although students often disagree about the text's meanings and implications, the conversation rarely is heated or adversarial. Instead, the pace is relaxed and the tone is civil. Frequent references to the meanings of specific words and to the text itself pepper the conversation, although both Park and the students employ nontext metaphors and analogies in their remarks. Each seminar concludes with a critique in which the verbal participation of all students is required. The critique focuses not on the issues or ideas in the text, but rather on participants' reactions to the text and their opinions about the quality of the seminar. Park informally assesses his students' participation in the seminars, but he does not assign grades. He believes that grading students' verbal participation would decrease the authenticity of the seminars. Following most seminars (although not this one because it occurs at the end of the course), he directs students to write an essay about the issues in the text.

CHANGES SINCE 1998

When I first studied Park's teaching, his state education agency had developed educational standards in academic areas (including history, civics, geography, and economics), but it had not instituted a testing system. Since that time, the agency has instituted a state testing system. At the secondary level, students take state-prepared tests at the end of ninth and tenth grades, and the ACT in the 11th grade.

Furthermore, in this state's comprehensive assessment system, public school students are tested at three points during their kindergarten through 12th-grade schooling in the areas of reading comprehension, mathematics, and writing. To date the state has not developed tests for the social studies. Schools schedule the writing examination over several days so that students have the opportunity to do prewriting and revision. Virtually all students are required to take the exams, and a school's overall score is lowered for each student who does not take the exam.[4] The state agency publishes specific information about how a school's students performed on the exams and ranks schools according to the results. As is the case in many states, a school's scores, and the extent to which they reveal improvement, are important public markers of the overall quality of the school.

For a school of choice, like Joe Park's New Horizons High School, the scores are especially important. Because students choose to enroll in the school, low scores by the school's students undoubtedly would make the school less appealing to prospective students and their parents. Moreover, given the fact that New Horizons High School provides its students a great deal of choice about which courses they take, and that the school has multiple forms of assessment that do not always include traditional multiple-choice tests, low scores on the state tests would reinforce the perception by some that the New Horizons brand of nontraditional curriculum fails to teach students how to do well on traditional forms of assessment. Park asserts that "these scores are going to mean something." Yet Park believes that because New Horizons students understand the consequences of the tests, they all show up to take them, and he believes that virtually all the students try to do their best. However, true to the ethos and philosophy undergirding the school, he points out that many students also participate in protests of the state testing requirement, organized by a student activist group ("Student Worker").

WRITING POSITION PAPERS

As a consequence of the state writing test, New Horizons social studies teachers work together to develop ways that their courses can help students become better writers. One of their decisions is to embed in each social studies course a certain amount of writing instruction and assignments designed to teach students how to take and defend a position on an issue. Park's opinion is that this form of writing is "at the heart of the social studies, because there is nothing more central to being a citizen than the ability to make and communicate decisions on challenging and important issues." Teachers clearly communicate this view to students in all of the school's social studies courses. For example, written instructions to students who are composing this kind of essay for the first time in a history course are as follows:

> Your new assignment, using your current research topic, is to learn how to take and defend a clear position. Taking a position involves more than just supporting your own viewpoint; it also includes finding out about opposing viewpoints. For the next several class periods, you will work on developing this important social studies skill. Keep in mind that most of what citizens do is "take positions" on important questions of public policy and other questions of life (e.g., What should we do about terrorism? Should unemployment benefits be extended to help the unemployed? Should the Olympics be held in Beijing? Should I purchase an SUV?).

With the extensive and ongoing assistance of a scholar at a nearby research university who specializes in assessment, the New Horizons social studies teachers have worked to develop a common understanding of what they mean by "position-taking essays" (see Figure 8.1), and how to incorporate their understandings into each course. For example, during the Supreme Court course in 1998, Park required students to write an expository essay about each case after the seminar discussion. Consequently, each student wrote eight formal essays during this 9-week course. Over time Park came to believe that students were just "chasing their tails" by writing a formal paper each week and that the quantity of work was getting in the way of his desire to focus more explicitly and thoroughly on the development of writing skills. By 2002, students in the course wrote informal papers the first 2 weeks, then three additional formal position papers on cases throughout the course. Typically, the position paper assignment now requires students to take a position on whether the majority decision is the "right decision" with the "right reasoning." Park believes that this more targeted and focused emphasis on a particular genre of writing, with more time between papers to work on revising, has resulted in fairly dramatic improvements in the quality of his students' writing.

WHAT MAKES PARK'S TEACHING WISE?

Two fundamental questions guide my assessment of teaching and learning. What is the nature of the intellectual work occurring in this course? Who is doing that work? I am most impressed when the intellectual work challenges students, is focused on important outcomes, and when all students engage in that work. Numerous conceptions of "wise practice" in teaching are reasonable, but I find that the ideas embedded in *Powerful and Authentic Social Studies* (PASS) are especially helpful in the determination of the quality of intellectual work occurring in a social studies lesson, unit, or course. PASS is a professional development program developed by educators in Michigan (Harris & Yocum, 2000) and published by the National Council for the Social Studies. PASS combines NCSS standards for powerful teaching (1994) with standards for authentic instruction derived from National Center on Organization and Restructuring of Schools research (Newmann, Secada, & Wehlage, 1995) to yield a set of expectations for social studies teachers' instruction, curriculum design, and assessment techniques. "Grounded in a vision of intellectual quality," PASS aims at "significant, meaningful" student achievement, which is made "evident in the mastery displayed by adults acting competently in their role as citizens (Harris & Yocum, 2000, pp. 15–16).

Name: _____ Topic: _____

Below are the criteria for your position paper and how to meet or exceed them. Revision of work is possible within stated dealines.

Criteria	Exceeds Criteria	Meets Criteria	Below Criteria
Position taken on the issue	• A paragraph of background "sets up" the identified issue • Second paragraph presents your position and the arguments to follow • A persuasive voice sets up position	• Introduction presents the identified issue and provides relevant background for it • A clear position on the issue is presented in the form of a thesis statement	• No identified position on the issue (no thesis) • No background for the issue provided • Factual errors
Arguments support the identified position	• Each argument demonstrates a deeper analysis of the position • More complex/ challenging arguments • Transitions between paragraphs link and weave the various arguments	• Each argument presented in separate paragraphs • Arguments are directly related to, and support, the identified position • Each argument is presented as the topic sentence of the paragraph	• Arguments in support of position either missing or confusing • Argument doesn't support position • Inaccurate information/ factual errors • Arguments not in separate paragraphs
Evidence supports each argument	• A mix of evidence; all of it clearly and directly connects to and supports each argument • Explanations are more extensive than "just" a single sentence	• Evidence, in the form of facts, data, ethical principles, or other forms of information, provided for each argument • Evidence is explained • Quotations from text used as evidence	• Evidence missing, unclear, or confusing • Explanations of how evidence supports arguments missing or unclear • Factual errors
Counter-argument(s) provided and explained (sometimes optional)	• One or more counter-arguments raised and given a "best case, fair hearing" • Response given to counterargument	• At least one credible counterargument is provided and responded to in a well-structured paragraph	• No counterargument provided • Unclear or inappropriate counterargument • Explanation and response to counterargument missing or unclear
Conclusion	• Includes call to action or other powerful closure	• Conclusion restates initial position and arguments • Paper has sense of closure	• Conclusion missing • No restatement of position or connection to position
Conventions	• Can only meet this expectation	• Error free • Where needed, arguments or evidence are cited	• Spelling errors, grammar mistakes • Disorganization in written form • No citations (if needed)

Overall Grade and Summary Comments:

Figure 8.1. Position paper rubric used at New Horizons High School.

> **Standard 1. Higher-Order Thinking:** Instruction involves students in manipulating information and ideas by synthesizing, generalizing, explaining, hypothesizing, or arriving at conclusions that produce new meaning and understandings for them.
>
> **Standard 2. Deep Knowledge:** Instruction addresses central ideas of a social studies discipline or topic with enough thoroughness to explore connections and relationships and to produce relatively complex understandings.
>
> **Standard 3. Substantive Conversation:** Students engage in extended conversational exchanges with the teacher and/or their peers about subject matter in a way that builds an improved and shared understanding of ideas or topics.
>
> **Standard 4. Connections to the World Beyond the Classroom:** Students make connections between substantive knowledge and personal experiences, social problems, or public policy.
>
> **Standard 5. Ethical Valuing:** Students consider core democratic values when making decisions on matters of public concern or when judging personal conduct.
>
> **Standard 6. Integration:** Instruction broadens the scope of learning by spanning social studies disciplines, linking social studies to other subject areas, bridging time or place, or blending knowledge with skills.

Figure 8.2. Standards for instruction from *Powerful and Authentic Social Studies* (Harris & Yocum, 2000, pp. 34–36).

Although the PASS program contains specific rubrics for determining the extent to which each standard is met in a lesson, I use them here more broadly to explain why I characterize Park's teaching as an example of wise practice. The two elements of Park's practice that I have described (seminar discussions and position paper writing) provide evidence that Park focuses his work on helping students learn to be better thinkers. He uses seminar discussions as a way to help students construct new and personal meanings and the position papers to help students focus on distinctions among positions, arguments, and evidence. Both of these tasks are bounded by Park's conception of the tight relationships between substantive knowledge, a particular kind of thinking, and effective citizenship. Thus, central to his practice is an emphasis on helping his students develop higher-order thinking skills. Moreover, this emphasis occurs within a context of substantive content that is unusually deep for a high school social studies course. For example, when I studied Park's Supreme Court course in 1998, all of the cases on which students worked involved the free speech/press clause of the First Amendment. By the end of the course, I became convinced that the students were highly conversant with many of the tensions and issues that permeate free speech/press in a democratic society. Although the question of whether such depth is necessary or even appropriate in a high school course may be challenged, the argument that free speech issues are outside the core of important social studies content would be difficult to support. Park's focus on helping students form "deep knowledge" of a specific body of intellectually rich content is at the heart of the educational philosophy of New Horizons High School.

The PASS standard about "substantive conversation" is also one that Park's classes frequently meet. Elsewhere I have analyzed the central elements of Park's discussion teaching practice (see Hess, 2002), but in this discussion, an important point is that Park holds the improvement of students' discussion abilities as a primary goal of his teaching. He approaches this goal systematically and methodically, scaffolding students' preparation for discussion to ensure that they *all* become more highly skilled discussants, not just those who have a natural affinity for public talk.

With respect to the PASS standard calling for connections to the world beyond school, Park frequently asks students to consider the connections between the Court's decision in a particular case and contemporary examples of the constitutional or legal issues and conflicts embedded in the case. Because he emphasizes the perennial nature of many of the issues and conflicts, he teaches students explicitly that connections exist between the historic cases they are studying and what is happening outside their classroom doors. Moreover, in all of his courses, Park emphasizes ethical decision making and core values such as justice and equality. He seeks to help his students understand that values often come into conflict and asks them to weigh which value should take precedence in a given situation. For example, in the Pentagon Papers seminar, is it more important not to steal than it is to inform the public of the government's actions?

As is the case with all teachers, Park's practice is not perfect. For example, at times during the discussions, I thought that he talked more than he should have, and I questioned whether he gave students as much feedback on their discussion skills as they needed. However, the general quality of the intellectual work Park demanded of his students was consistently high. I was particularly impressed by how well Park knew his students and how committed he was to their intellectual and civic development. Unlike some teachers who focus their attention on the most academically able students, Park seemed most interested in the students who needed the most assistance. His interest in students who often received little attention in school and the environment in which he taught seemed especially congruent. All of the courses at New Horizons were heterogeneously grouped, and students with special needs were not "pulled out" for special or separate instruction. Thus, I concluded that one of the factors supporting Park's "wise practice" was that he taught in a school that valued what he valued: He did not have "to buck" the administration or his colleagues.

In summary, Joe Park provides clear and explicit instruction on important social studies outcomes. Although his school is based on progressive ideas about education, he is not a romantic. That is, he does not believe that students' academic abilities will somehow magically flower if they are given freedom of choice about what they learn. Yet even though students at New Horizons have much more control over their learning than students in more traditional schools, I continually am struck by the high degree of structure and scaffolding in Park's approach to teaching core academic skills.

ADJUSTING TO THE TESTS

When New Horizons opened in 1992, it was part of a trend toward smaller high schools that were markedly different from traditional schools. Advocates promoted these "schools of choice" as a way to broaden educational options within the public school structure. School district administrators gave these schools waivers from various district rules (e.g., requirement of a certain sequence of courses) and permitted them to build unique approaches to the education of adolescents (see Crocco & Thornton, 2002; Meier, 1998). Although the vast majority of American students remained in more traditional public schools, magnet schools like New Horizons provided their students with a very different kind of education than they otherwise would receive. Moreover, magnet school advocates promoted them as models that should be replicated in whole or in part by other schools.

The next wave of school reform has moved in the opposite direction, focusing on common standards, testing, and various forms of public accountability. Whereas the alternative school movement valued experimentation, diversity of approaches, and choice, the standards movement clearly emphasizes the necessity of all students meeting common standards. In some states with especially rigid and precise testing systems (such as Virginia, Texas, and Florida), the new statewide tests have the potential to obviate the very essence of the alternative school models. However, the state in which Park teaches has not yet mandated state social studies tests for high school students, and its writing test is consistent with the emphasis traditionally placed on composition throughout New Horizons courses. This situation exists, in large part, because New Horizons does not use multiple-choice tests. All of its teachers in all subjects have used writing as an important means by which to assess students' learning. The advent of the state writing tests, to be sure, prompted the social studies teachers to change how they taught writing. Park, a staunch opponent of the way in which the current standards and testing movement has been put into practice, admits that writing instruction in social studies has improved at New

Horizons as a consequence of the increased attention to writing that has resulted from the tests.

The standards and testing movement in his state, I believe, have not harmed the strongest elements of Park's teaching. In fact, proponents of state tests could argue that Park's teaching is an example of how strong teachers can maintain (and even improve) their practice in the current era. Such a conclusion seems premature; certainly, the story of how state-level policy changes affect Park's practice remains unfinished.

To illustrate this situation, I argue that several possible consequences of standards and testing policies could create difficulties for Park and other teachers. Imagine, for example, that Park's students' social studies content knowledge declines as a consequence of a decreased emphasis on social studies in the elementary schools. As is the case in many states, elementary school teachers have come under increasing pressure to improve their students' performance on reading and mathematics tests. And because most state policies do not emphasize social studies to the same degree as reading and math, elementary teachers have little incentive to offer comprehensive social studies instruction. Indeed, these teachers likely teach what is on the mandated tests. Over time, as a result, students may enter New Horizons High School with an increasingly meager understanding of social studies content. The kinds of innovative and highly focused courses that Park teaches, such as the Supreme Court course, likely work better for students if they already possess solid social studies foundational knowledge gained in elementary and middle school. Retaining such innovative courses, therefore, may be difficult if state tests at the elementary level result in less attention to social studies knowledge.

On the other hand, another policy change that could wreak havoc on Park's teaching would be the implementation of mandatory, highly specific state social studies tests for high school students. For example, if Park's students had to take tests similar to the Virginia social studies exam, New Horizons High School might find it very difficult to continue permitting students to choose which social studies courses they want to take. Moreover, New Horizons High School probably would have to require more traditional survey courses to ensure that students "cover" the content on the state tests. Another scenario is also possible: Imagine that the state implements a number of content tests in other subject areas, such as science or literature, but not in social studies. Those subject areas probably would gain more emphasis in the curriculum. One likely result might be less attention to social studies in the curriculum than currently exists. Conversely, if social studies content is tested, the continued implementation of wise practice (Grant, 2002) may become difficult or impossible.

At this point, Joe Park is an example of a strong teacher whose practice has not been harmed by the increased emphasis on state standards, testing, and public accountability. However, as the scenarios sketched here illustrate, no guarantee exists that this situation will continue. Moreover, Park's teaching, as with all teachers, is influenced by the context in which he works. Because students at New Horizons currently score fairly well on the few state tests that are currently required, teachers there receive little pressure to make significant curricular or pedagogical changes. Teachers at New Horizons have been able to stay the course, albeit an unusual and innovative one. Many other schools in the state where Park teaches have not had this experience. In schools labeled by the state education agency as "low" or "unsatisfactory," administrators exert tremendous pressure on teachers to change their instruction. Thus, students in more privileged schools, like New Horizons, have teachers who are able to innovate. Students in high-poverty schools, on the other hand, are forced into the very kinds of traditional instruction that have not worked well in the past, but are often the fallback position as administrators and politicians seek a quick fix to improve test scores.

Pointing out the relative advantage that Park enjoys at New Horizons High School does not diminish my respect for Park's practice. I think he is an excellent teacher. That he teaches in a unique environment does not negate the high quality of his work. As Crocco and Thornton (2002) found in their study of restructured schools, social studies instruction in innovative schools is not always exemplary. Additionally, I remain impressed that Park has stayed in teaching for many years and continues to work as hard on his practice as he does. I worry, however, that policy changes could make it increasingly difficult for Park and other excellent teachers to put into practice their visions of what constitutes wise social studies instruction. If standards and testing policies, touted as avenues to higher educational achievement, result in constraints on the practice of especially wise and skillful teachers, then they are a bad bargain for the nation that policymakers should eschew.

NOTES

1. Joe Park is a pseudonym.
2. The description of this discussion was first published in *Theory and Research in Social Education* (Hess, 2002), pp. 10–44, and is reprinted here with permission.
3. See Goodlad (1984), McNeil (1986), and Nystrand, Gamoran, and Cabonara (1998) for evidence of the exceptionality of Park's discussion facilitation.
4. The state rules exempt students who do not speak English, special needs students who spend less than 45% of the school day in a regular classroom, or students who transferred to a school after February 1. Because all stu-

dents with special needs at New Horizons are only taking regular classes, none are exempt from the state tests.

REFERENCES

Crocco, M. S., & Thornton, S. T. (2002). Social studies in the New York City Public Schools: A descriptive study. *Journal of Curriculum and Supervision, 17*(3), 206–231.

Goodlad, J. I. (1984). *A place called school.* New York: McGraw-Hill.

Harris, D., & Yocum, M. (2000). *Powerful and authentic social studies: A professional development program for teachers.* Washington, DC: National Council for the Social Studies.

Hess, D. (2002, Winter). Discussing controversial public issues in secondary social studies classrooms: Learning from skilled teachers. *Theory and Research in Social Education, 30*(1), 10–44.

McNeil, L. M. (1986). *Contradictions of control: School structure and school knowledge.* Philadelphia: Metheun.

National Council for the Social Studies. (1994). *Expectations of excellence: Curriculum standards for social studies.* Washington, DC: Author.

Newmann, F. M., Secada, W.G., & Wehlage, G. G. (1995). *A guide to authentic instruction and assessment: Vision, standards, and scoring.* Madison: Wisconsin Center for Educational Research.

Nystrand, M., Gormoran, A., & Carbonara, W. (1998). *Towards an ecology of learning: The case of classroom discourse and its effects on writing in high school English and Social Studies.* Albany, NY: National Research Center on English Learning and Achievement.

Yeager, E. (2002). Thoughts on wise practice in the teaching of social studies. *Social Education, 64*(6), 353–353.

CHAPTER 9

WISE PRACTICE IN HIGH SCHOOL SOCIAL STUDIES

The Case of Joe Gotchy

Bruce Larson

Richly developed portrayals of expertise in teaching are rare. While many characterizations of effective teachers exist, most of these dwell on the teacher's management of the classroom. We find few descriptions or analyses of teachers that give careful attention not only to the management of students in classrooms, but also to the management of *ideas* within classroom discourse. Both kinds of emphasis will be needed if our portrayals of good practice are to serve as sufficient guides to the design of better education (Shulman, 1987, p. 1, original emphasis)

The call for portrayals of teaching that meet Shulman's request for research-refined examinations that proceed beyond simple descriptions of planning, organizing, and carrying out a lesson is impressive. Descriptions of the teachers' conceptual frameworks, decision-making processes, and strategies for engaging students in learning content, as well as embracing and utilizing student diversity, constitute mindful responses to Shulman's request. To that end, this chapter examines the practice of one high school social studies teacher who exemplifies wise practice by engaging his students in inquiry-based projects. He makes social studies compelling for his students. His work with students not only provides insight into the "look and feel" of how a teacher might have a positive impact on student learning, but it also provides an example of what Fred Newmann has called "authentic intellectual work" (Newmann & Wehlage, 1993; Scheurman & Newmann, 1998).

Newmann and others have identified three standards for the encouragement of authentic intellectual work by students: (1) construction of knowledge; (2) disciplined inquiry; and (3) value beyond school (Avery, 1999; Avery, Kouneski, & Odendahl, 2001; Newmann, 1996; Scheurman & Newmann, 1998). They may be understood simply.[1]

1. *Construction of knowledge* engages students in higher-order thinking skills such as interpretation, synthesis, and evaluation. In addition, students consider others' ideas, suspend judgment, and engage in the thoughtful work of understanding complex information. Students are not socially constructing knowledge, but they are looking closely at available sources and working to understand the content for future use.

2. *Disciplined inquiry requires* "students to present explanations and conclusions through extended forms of oral, written, and symbolic language" (Scheurman & Newmann, 1998, p. 24). Students engage in activities, thought processes, and methodologies similar to what social scientists do; they inquire into a problem in the ways, for example, that historians, geographers, or economists might. As a result, students develop a "deep knowledge" of the content and can discuss what they are learning as they engage in "substantive conversations" with one another and with experts (Newmann & Wehlage, 1993; Scheurman & Newmann, 1998).

3. *Value beyond school* seeks to make school knowledge applicable beyond the walls of the classroom. As a result of disciplined inquiry, students recognize the relational usefulness of academic content to public issues and policy. The teacher is not the only one to see student work, but others outside of the school engage in critique of the students' ideas.[2]

These three standards require a system of social support for achievement in which students are free to take intellectual risks, cooperate with classmates, and collaboratively inquire about public problems.

With these three categories of intellectual work in mind, I examined the work of Joe Gotchy, a teacher who engages students in the intellectual skills of inquiry, cooperative group processes, discussion, and policymaking. By having his students engage in these skills, he intends for students to learn course content deeply and to be able to make use of what they learn in school beyond the classroom. In addition, this teacher encourages students' use of computer technology to enhance their learning. Using computers is not necessarily meritorious, but his guidance of students as they use technology, his approach for using technology as a tool for instruction and curriculum development, and his assessments of student learning seem to portray the type of practice for which Shulman called.

INTRODUCING THE SETTING

Joe Gotchy teaches social studies at Thomas Jefferson High School in Auburn, Washington.[3] The school is typical in that it utilizes a modified, six-period block schedule in which all six classes meet on Monday and Friday, and four of the six classes meet on a rotating schedule Tuesday, Wednesday, and Thursday; the curriculum has both vocational and college-preparatory strands; and students take state- and district-mandated standardized tests. Yet this school is also unique because of an innovative program within the school in which an interdisciplinary team of teachers offers social studies, English, science, and information technology classes. Called "Raiderlinks" (after the school mascot, the "Raiders," and the idea of "linking" to each other and the world through computers and the Internet), the program includes the use of laptop computers so that students and teachers can enhance their learning of academic content. With a colleague who taught computer applications, Joe Gotchy initiated this program 8 years ago. They set out to help students learn social studies content, integrate content from other areas around social studies themes, and integrate appropriate uses of technology into their instruction. Of particular note is that three or four of the six classes Gotchy teaches are "Raiderlinks" classes; the other two classes are more "typical" in that they are not interdisciplinary and students do not have access to their own laptop computer. Although his teaching in each of these six social studies classes demonstrates many characteristics of "wise practice," his teaching in the Raiderlinks program especially provides useful illustrations of specific elements of this wisdom.

This special program, as well as the teaching of Joe Gotchy, differs from the "traditional curriculum" of most high schools. Raiderlinks is offered as an interdisciplinary curricular option to students of all abilities. At the heart of its curriculum is the teaching of skills and content knowledge while focusing the academic and personal needs of students on preparing to live, study, and work after high school.

Although not constrained by curricular pressure from Advanced Placement courses or achievement testing, students do continue the normal sequence of standardized testing for the state of Washington, college and/or vocational school entrance, and admission to military service. Students take the Washington Assessment of Student Learning, college-entrance exams, and AP tests in a traditional pattern if their individual learning plans call for these results.

Students and teachers at Thomas Jefferson High School certainly face the typical and continual challenges of decreasing budgets, accountability through testing, and the many social concerns facing today's adolescents. Raiderlinks is not a program that intends to solve these problems, nor does Joe Gotchy provide solutions to these persistent challenges to public education. However, his practice does offer examples of how a veteran social studies teacher utilizes computer technology to enhance his teaching and his students' learning. He asserts that his students develop deep knowledge, think at a high level, and engage in serious academic discussions about course content and public issues. The remainder of this chapter emphasizes one example of Gotchy's engagement with his students in authentic intellectual work.

INVESTIGATING MODERN CHINA

In his sophomore Global Studies course, Gotchy assigns a project designed to help his students understand the unique character and complexity of China. The tasks incorporate a variety of print, photographic, and electronic resources. The sequence of lessons emphasizes culture, education, government, and industry in present-day China, as well as how these conditions may transform in the future. In addition to print and photographic resources, he encourages students to access the Internet so that they can create a variety of products that demonstrate their understanding of the Chinese people, government, economy, society, and the nation's place in the world. This in-depth study of China does not occur in a vacuum, however. Students compare and contrast their findings with those from research into the infrastructure of other nations (e.g., United States, Japan, Germany, Saudi Arabia, Mexico). Through his own travels in China, Gotchy has created a photographic archive that contains 1,500 digital images of his experiences in visiting locations such as Beijing, Lanzhou, the Yangtze River, Three Gorges Dam, and many other sites of historic and/or cultural significance.[4] He uses these images to help his students take virtual field trips to these sites, and as sources of additional information about China.

Thus, Gotchy's China unit provides the setting for students' engagement of the three standards of authentic intellectual work. In the following sections, each of these standards is considered in light of the activities that Gotchy and his students undertake.

Construction of Knowledge

Gotchy provides opportunities for his students to think deeply about course content by providing an issue or problem for them to consider. In this China unit, his students consider recent changes in China's economy, political system, and culture. During his own travels in China, Gotchy was struck by the number of late-model luxury automobiles that he saw. He challenges his students to consider "who is driving that Audi" around the streets of such cities as Beijing, Xian, and Shanghai, and what phenomena have led to changes in the government's economic policy and to economic growth and increased trade. Gotchy's students examine photographs and analyze demographic data related to wealth distribution, education, government agencies, and industry. They also examine Chinese artifacts to determine if these sources of data support their existing preconceptions/ images of China and its people. Some of the artifacts Gotchy's students use include Chinese government documents and academic articles that have been translated into English; maps from various Asian or China studies centers around the United States; and "virtual visits" to online museums such as the Crow Asian Art Museum in Dallas, Texas. Data sets, photographs, media accounts, and policy statements can either highlight an individual topic related to culture, education, government, and industry, or provide a wide-ranging look at China and the diversity of Chinese society. Using the Internet, students locate information on sites such as the Central Intelligence Agency's homepage (http://www.cia.gov/) and its online version of *The World Factbook* (http://www.cia.gov/cia/publications/factbook/index.html) and from the website of the People's Republic of China's American Embassy (http://www.china-embassy.org/eng/index.html).

In observing Gotchy's teaching, I was immediately impressed by his enthusiasm for teaching history and culture, and by the obvious passion he has for challenging the assumptions students may bring to class. Gotchy models how to evaluate information, think critically about assumptions, and build a knowledge base about the topics he teaches; he requires that his students develop these intellectual skills as well. Gotchy does not merely encourage students to learn content; he challenges them to gain a sense of excitement and appreciation for the world and its events. Therefore, students are engaged in activities in which they need to apply the information they are learning and to build an increasingly flexible and robust understanding of this information. As students study about China, Gotchy expects them to access various media to gather more data with different points of view and different interpretations. They build on their fledgling understandings as they compare the values and ideals that have influenced the development of Chinese culture, education, government, and industry to influences that shape the China of today, and as they consider whether or not contemporary Chinese institutions address the needs of individual citizens and/or promote the common good.

Disciplined Inquiry

The China project is an example of the inquiry approach that Gotchy routinely employs. In the Raiderlinks program students use computers and networks as tools in order to communicate, solve problems, and gain access to varied sources of information. Students also develop the ability to use multimedia tools (e.g., PowerPoint, Front Page, Excel, and student-produced Web pages) to construct creative exhibitions of their work and thinking. These types of student activities require Gotchy to help students carry out their individual inquiry processes. Allowing students to engage in inquiry encourages students to personalize their individual learning. Deep knowledge is formed as students attempt to answer the difficult questions that they pose. Substantive conversations occur within the students' groups, during email communications, and as students engage in face-to-face classroom discussions. These interactions help students build a greater understanding of the issues. The following comment by Gotchy explains this clearly:

> You can spot the Raiderlinks students on campus because they are the ones who are sitting at a laptop during lunch sharing something from class.... But more importantly, we see the Raiderlinks kids developing a learning community that extends beyond the classroom and normal school day. Our students are using their machines at home via email and the Internet, but they are also sharing files, editing each other's papers, and using cell phones to continue their work. Raiderlinks was born with an "any time, anywhere" approach to learning. If you put [appropriate] tools in the hands of students and teach them the intellectual and social skills they need to be productive, they leave school with talents and skills that would be coveted by families, the workplace, and their fellow citizens.

This teaching approach can also create classroom management problems when students are either unmotivated to complete an assignment or unskilled in the process of inquiry. As Gotchy noted:

One of the challenges that teachers face is that their own definitions of "deep" and "substantive" are not always embraced by students who may not want to invest the time and intellectual capital that is required by such undertakings. Students need the teacher to serve as a mentor, or provide mentors, who can help students define excellence and...challenge [students' thinking] while not being so difficult that they stifle students' effort, creativity, or their willingness to participate.... While students work...the teacher creates and manages the learning environment, answers questions, gives cues, and acts as an intellectual mentor who helps decode scholarly writing, knowledge, and complex concepts. The teacher will also act as a conduit through which young scholars and their teammates...develop a deeper understanding of modern China.

Specifically with the China unit, Gotchy arranges students in task groups and informs the teammates that their inquiry will help them to become an "expert" on one of eight topic areas about China:

1. Culture in Modern China: A Contemporary Look at Continuity and Change among the Chinese People
2. Education in Modern China: Values, Ideals, and Current Trends in Chinese Schools and Universities
3. Government and Democracy in Modern China: Conformity, Continuity, Individuality, Change, and Public Policy Issues
4. Industry, Commerce, and the World Trade Organization in Modern China: Communist and Corporate Culture as a Reflection of the Values, Ideals, and Principles of Chinese Society
5. The Falun Gong and Religious Freedom: Can Buddha, Cults, Confucius, and Communism Coexist in Modern China?
6. Conflict and Accommodation in Hong Kong and Taiwan: What Are Their Past, Present, and Future Status in the People's Republic of China?
7. The Three Gorges Project: Must Modern China Submerge Its Past to Prepare for Its Future?
8. Chinese Foreign Policy: Past Is Prologue, or Brave New World? Chinese Foreign Policy As It Relates to the United States (combating terrorism, human rights, national security, and nuclear proliferation)

Gotchy then helps his students plan this phase of their research by asking each student to compose a document that builds on his or her acquired expertise to write about one of these topics. In addition to the main topical question, Gotchy has students examine the 10 themes of the National Council for the Social Studies (1994) to consider how these themes are reflected in their paper. For example, how might more insight be gained about Taiwan and its foreign policies when considering the impact of "Culture" (Theme I), or of the concepts represented by "Power, Authority, and Governance" (Theme VI)? The 10 themes are not new to students because Gotchy introduces them early in the year and returns to them in almost all of the units and topics the class studies.

Students receive academic support from peers in their cooperative groups (e.g., problem solving, peer editing). Gotchy also serves as a guide to help them pose questions, research hypothetical solutions, analyze available information, and compile evidence with which to answer the questions. Because the students are all "Internet ready" with their laptops, they have easy access to many online resources; they use basic search engines and interact through email; they also prepare and write their research papers on the computer. In addition, Gotchy serves as "cheerleader" not only for each student's progress during the inquiry, but also for encouraging the enjoyment that they can find in this kind of intellectual activity. Gotchy reports that his students

> revel in the research phase of these projects, looking for their own materials and sharing those that might be useful to a teammate.... It is not unusual for the classroom to mimic a beehive with the air filled with ideas and information zinging from one mind to another via discussion/debate/dialogue and from one computer to another via email packets.

One assumption that Gotchy makes is that every student has the capacity to be creative. Computer technology offers a platform from which every student can experiment, succeed, or fail and try again, and do it without the fear often associated with failure. Over the past 8 years, Gotchy has found that traditionally marginalized students and special needs students become much more involved in their learning activities because they "finally get a chance to show that they can compete and contribute" to the class.

Value Beyond School

Gotchy's learning assessments aim toward helping students to exhibit their work and to demonstrate their intellectual skills and mastery of knowledge. To move beyond the physical walls of the classroom, students in Gotchy's classes engage in activities such as exhibiting their work, publishing their opinions in newspapers, and becoming involved in the community about a pertinent problem or issue. The students can also access their laptop computers to compile electronic portfolios that provide additional evidence of what they have learned. However, even without the technology component that Raiderlinks provides, Gotchy assesses students daily through the conclusions they draw during research projects, classroom discussions, and daily performance expectations (e.g., group participation, use of class time for learning, preparedness for the day's activities).

For a final assessment of the China unit, Gotchy encourages students to "exhibit" their understanding in three primary activities: (1) a research paper and accompanying paper presentation to the class; (2) a classroom discussion and reflection paper; and (3) a formal presentation to members of the community. That is, after students have selected their inquiry question and have written their research papers, they present their "findings and conclusions" to the class; also, they make available on the Internet a summary of their presentation. In addition, students participate in a class discussion after the presentations, during which they talk about their initial perceptions of China and changes that may have occurred during their inquiries, as well as critique the use of the Internet as a research tool and the logistics of making formal presentations of research.

Furthermore, the day after the last student presentation and class discussion, Gotchy separates his students into two equal groups. He assigns one group to read "The Tiananmen Papers" (Nathan, 2001) and the second group to read "Crisis in the Taiwan Strait?" (Campbell & Mitchell, 2001). Both of these articles are lengthy, substantive essays originally published in the journal *Foreign Affairs*. After reading the articles, students discuss the authors' main points relative to their own inquiry project. As one group is discussing, the other group listens and takes notes (often referred to as a "fishbowl discussion" because the discussants are being watched by other peers). After students hear most of the points, Gotchy encourages those who have been listening to join the discussion and to share their ideas, even though they have not read the article. This process is then repeated with the student roles reversed for consideration of the second article. However, students are not assessed on their comments during the discussion. Gotchy assesses the paper that they write after the discussion in which they explain their thoughts on the Tiananmen Square and Taiwan crises.

Gotchy moves his students beyond the classroom to their community for the final phase of his assessment, giving students directions about their exhibition of knowledge, content understanding, thinking skills, and creativity. The assignment is as follows: He tells the class that the group presentations must focus on the current status and future of China's culture, schools, government, industry, religious freedom, the Three Gorges project, Hong Kong and Taiwan, or Chinese–U.S. foreign policy; that the presentations should reflect the research and papers written by team members; that each team member must participate in the development of the project as well as the actual presentation; that the presentations need to be 15–20 minutes in length, followed by 30 minutes of student-generated discussion; and that each presentation needs to highlight the common strands or themes that have been uncovered by the student research, reading, and discussion (e.g., What are the common values, ideals, patterns, or principles that seem to act as foundations for modern Chinese society? How do the concepts of continuity, change, conflict, and complexity permeate the Chinese experience? How do schools, government, industry, religion, public works projects, Taiwan, and foreign policy influence the people and culture of modern China?).

The student presentations are made to adults who live in the community (e.g., Chamber of Commerce, school board, professional groups, labor unions, teacher and/or parent groups, etc.). The final exhibitions must include a computer-generated multimedia presentation that is created with a software package such as PowerPoint; students are encouraged to use databases, spreadsheets, video clips, photographs, and other graphic organizers in their presentations.

Gotchy asks the adults who attend these presentations to evaluate them by providing brief narratives based on a rating scale that he has created. In addition, these "outside evaluators" write a brief description of what they perceive to be the strengths and weaknesses of each student and team. Thus, Gotchy's role at this point is to assist his students, not to assess their performance.

Following the final presentations, the class reconvenes to discuss the following questions:

- What have we learned about modern China, the Chinese people, and ourselves?
- What have the Chinese people done to create places that reflect their unique culture, human needs, government policy, current values, and ideals in terms of the society they have designed and built? How does this compare to the United States?
- What changes do you see in store for China in the next few decades?
- What have you learned that can be transferred to future lessons on different countries or regions?
- Do the United States and China seem to be headed in mutually compatible or mutually exclusive directions? What does the future hold for these two countries? How would you characterize future relations between the two countries?

CONCLUSION

Students who engage in study of the China unit need not take a formal test to demonstrate their understanding of course content. They have learned academic content about China, developed numerous intellectual thinking skills, and engaged in a system of social support through group activities. Gotchy tries to establish his classroom as a place in which students can take risks in how they think, consider their world and the issues that confront it, and work with others. He encourages students to debate and disagree with one another—as well as to form coalitions with peers who agree with them—because it puts them in a position to think deeply about course content.

Thomas Jefferson High School is not an elite or elitist high school. The students who attend it represent a wide range of socioeconomic status and ability that typifies many schools. Teachers like Gotchy and his colleagues in Raiderlinks engage "ordinary" students in extraordinary thinking and learning. Students learn "the basics" for the standardized tests, but also are prepared to take their knowledge into the future. By engaging in disciplined inquiry, these students become intellectual problem solvers. Gotchy states, "Rarely will you be faced with an identical set of challenges that confronted an earlier generation. You can *study* history and politics, but you can also *use* them to inform yourself. The knowledge [students] construct can be used by citizens who have to solve new problems." This use of knowledge and disciplined inquiry to solve problems is the essence of authentic intellectual work.

Finally, although Joe Gotchy is a well-informed history teacher, his connections to the field of political science are apparent in his teaching and in the kind of work he gives his students. He frequently reminds his students about James Madison's assertion that a large, complex republic is better able to protect individual liberty than a small, homogeneous society. Also, he emphasizes that because societal factions are inevitable, a government is needed to help people realize the freedoms afforded to them. Thus, he argues that citizens must be able and willing to participate in the governing process. Joe Gotchy attempts to help students not only learn social studies content, but learn *how* to *use* information, and his classroom provides a venue for preparing young people for the role of participatory citizen.

NOTES

1. These three standards for promoting authentic intellectual work incorporate Newmann and Wehlage's (1993) five standards of "authentic instruction": higher-order thinking; depth of knowledge; connectedness to the world; substantive conversation; and social support for student achievement.
2. Avery (1999) provides an excellent description of these three standards and adds insight into assessment of student learning.
3. Distribution of student ethnicity: white/Caucasian, 68%; Asian American, 15%; African American, 9%; Hispanic American, 7%; Native American, 1%.

4. The photos provide a wide range of images about aspects of China. They include portrayals of agriculture, architecture, art, ceramics, clothing, commerce, communications, culture, diet, fashion, historic sites, public works projects, religion, communities, schools, street life, tourism, and transportation.

REFERENCES

Avery, P. G. (1999). Authentic assessment and instruction. *Social Education, 63*(6), 368–373.

Avery, P. G., Kouneski, N. P., & Odendahl, T. (2001). Authentic pedagogy seminars: Renewing our commitment to teaching and learning. *The Social Studies, 92*(3), 97–101.

Campbell, K. M., & Mitchell, D. J. (2001). Crisis in the Taiwan Strait? *Foreign Affairs, 80*(4), 14–25.

National Council for the Social Studies. (1994). *Expectations for excellence: Curriculum standards for social studies*, Washington, DC: National Council for the Social Studies.

Nathan, A. J. (2001). The Tiananmen papers. *Foreign Affairs, 80*(1), 2–48.

Newmann, F. M. (1996). *Authentic achievement: Restructuring schools for intellectual quality.* Hoboken, NJ: Wiley.

Newmann, F. M., & Wehlage, G. C. (1993). Five standards of authentic instruction. *Educational Leadership, 50*(7), 8–12.

Scheurman, G., & Newmann, F. M. (1998). Authentic intellectual work in social studies: Putting performance before pedagogy. *Social Education, 62*(1), 23–25.

Shulman, L. S. (1987). Knowledge and teaching: Foundations for the new reform. *Harvard Educational Review, 57*, 1–22.

CHAPTER 10

ENGAGING PEDAGOGY IN AN ADVANCED PLACEMENT EUROPEAN HISTORY CLASSROOM

John K. Lee

> The AP European history examination plays a special role in the intellectual life of present day high schools.... In this day of standards and achievement testing, AP courses stand as practical and real measures of quality. (Hill, 1999, p. 1)

As much, if not more, than any other high school history course, Advanced Placement (AP) European history courses are driven by high achievement expectations (Rothschild, 1999). AP European history courses and exams also represent a unique opportunity for students to learn history in a standards-based, high-stakes testing context (Lurie, 2000). In this study, I examine the practice of Mike Nance, a veteran history teacher of an AP European history class in a Georgia high school. My focus is on how Mike teaches that course given the local constraints of the AP examination and standards.

Although a number of descriptions and anecdotes on teaching AP history have been published (e.g., Henry, 1994; Michael, 1991; Rothschild, 2000; Traill, 1998), only a few reports describe wise practice in AP history classrooms. Meckna (1999), for example, described his own practice of teaching AP European history in a multiethnic environment. Among a range of instructional strategies, he most prominently related content to his student's experiences. DiLorenzo (1999) also described his practice while teaching AP history; he emphasized discussion, small group work, practical strategies for synthesizing knowledge from secondary readings, and the making of inferences from primary source documents. Stovel (2000) described methods that teachers might use to prepare their students for writing responses to document-based questions (DBQs), focusing on changes in the scoring protocol for the DBQ response.

One consistent concern of teachers of AP European history courses (and all AP history courses, for that matter) is their tendency to focus their teaching too closely on AP expectations. As a Brown University undergraduate, Neutuch (1999) described his experience as a high school student in an AP history class as stifling. He remembered that his teacher suffered from examination-generated "tunnel vision." Chu (2000) has argued that teaching to the AP examination can be harmful, particularly when "teaching the text" includes the use of limited numbers of potential AP essay questions and/or teachers guessing about what questions will be on the examination. Such actions likely result in both narrow preparation for the examination and a tendency for students to use this narrowly prepared material regardless of the eventual questions on the examination. Although examination pressure often is viewed as dangerous, Lurie (2000) has suggested that standards in AP history courses may erode without the consistent application of rigorous examination grading, particularly on the test's free response portion of the examination.

Reports on teaching practice in history have been common over the last 15 years (e.g., Gudmundsdottir, 1991; McDiarmid, 1994; VanSledright, 1996; Wilson & Wineburg, 1988), but rarely have these reports considered testing, curriculum, or standards, either in AP or non-AP classes. In order to understand how teachers' practice takes form, local and authentic conditions must be considered (Davis, 1997). Given the current climate of educational reform, any consideration of teachers' knowledge and practice should be particularly focused on the role of curriculum standards and accompanying standardized testing.

Data for this study came from interviews with Mike Nance, multiple observations of his class, and an analysis of his instructional materials. This investigation sought to understand ways in which Mike demonstrates his knowledge of the substantive content of the course and transforms it into meaningful and creative pedagogical knowledge. In order to relate Mike's story, I visited his class on more than a dozen occasions and created audio recordings of all these observations. A graduate research assistant who worked with me on this project served as an intern in Mike's classroom during the semester of this study. She observed and recorded additional lessons. I also interviewed Mike on three occasions. Between my research assistant and me, someone associated with this research project was in Mike's class virtually every day of the semester.

TEACHING AP EUROPEAN HISTORY

A General Description of Mike's Teaching

Mike has taught history and social studies in a number of settings for 24 years. After receiving a degree in history and a state teaching certificate in social studies, he took his first job teaching state history to eighth-graders. Throughout his career he has taught a number of courses including U.S., world, and European history, as well as civics and government. Ten years ago, he received a master of arts in teaching with an emphasis in history. For the last 14 years, he has taught AP United States history and, 4 years ago, he began teaching the AP European history course at his school. Mike's substantive knowledge of history is wide ranging, although he has emphasized diplomatic and foreign policy history. During the semester of this study, Mike taught sections of U.S. and European AP history.

In the semester during which this study took place, Mike's second-period European history class, an energetic and dynamic group of young people, comprised 17 students: four African American and 13 white students (with a gender balance of eight females and nine males). Mike's school, in an urban area of a large southern city, was, during this academic year, 48% black, 36% white, 9% Asian, 4% Hispanic, and 3% multiracial. Thirty-three percent of the school's students were eligible to receive free and reduced-price lunch. Students' overall standardized test scores at this school were at the state average; roughly a fifth of the students exceeded the average by more than 20%, but the vast majority of students' test scores were 10–20% below the state average for students at this level.

Mike's teaching practice with this class incorporated several distinct methodological approaches. He often lectured, but he encouraged student questions and commentaries during these lectures. On occasion he organized students into discussion and seminar groups. Students spent considerable time writing in Mike's class. After in-class writing assessments and multiple-choice tests, he organized post-assessment feedback sessions. Mike also had his students present and defend formal theses. While he used most of these methods during his teaching, he did not follow a rigid daily procedure. From time to time, he used impressionistic approaches to account for idiosyncratic moments.

Below, I present a wide-ranging description and analysis of Mike's teaching practice, including this course's standardized testing expectations. I selected the two most common and descriptive forms of instruction that Mike uses, lecture and thesis presentation/defense, for special consideration.

Direct Instruction and Examination Preparation through Lecture

Mike uses a highly interactive didactic lecture format. On virtually all occasions, he plans detailed lectures; however, he does not script his lectures and does not strictly follow his notes or outline even though his plans correlate closely with the AP expectations. This approach allows Mike to meet the AP standards without limiting the flow of substantive content. Mike's lectures, in fact, take the form of a closely managed dialogue. Although the AP curriculum and examination serve as loose topical constraints, Mike does not limit the range of his lecture in order to conform rigidly to curriculum or examination expectations. Instead, he permits his lecture to flow in a way that adapts to the students' needs and interests.

An example of Mike's instructional style comes from a lecture on the causes of World War I.

Transcript of Teaching Episode—Time 3 Minutes and 45 Seconds, Student Names Omitted

1. Mike: So, _____ tell me about nationalism as a cause for World War I.
2. Student 1: Well, everyone wanted to… [*long pause*]
3. M: OK, while she is contemplating that, let's make sure we understand what the four
4. causes were that we discussed in class yesterday.
5. Students (several): We only got to 3 [*followed by several student comments regarding*
6. *the incompleteness of yesterday's work*].
7. M: Oh, I don't believe that—OK, there are four causes. What are they? [*pause*] We
8. already know what one of them is, right _____?
9. Students (several): Nationalism [a collective yet mostly unorganized series of
10. responses from the class results in three additional causes being named—militarism,
11. alliance system, and imperialism].
12. M: All right, now, what about nationalism, and this little package of maps I gave you?
13. [*Mike provides some directions for how to use the maps.*]
14. Student 2: Germany hopes to expand.
15. M: Such as?

Transcript of Teaching Episode—Time 3 Minutes and 45 Seconds, Student Names Omitted

16.	Student 2: Germany's desire for territory and influence in the east, at the expense of
17.	Russia [*read from a caption on the map*].
18.	M: And that is? [*pause*] That's what? [*Several incorrect answers are offered*] What do
19.	you call that? [*pause*] That's imperialism. OK, let's start at the top of the list. Let's
20.	start with nationalism. No offense _____. [*short pause*] _____ tell us about
21.	nationalism.
22.	Student 3: [*reads a description of nationalism*]
23.	M: That *is* nationalism and that's where what happens
24.	first?
25.	[Several students offer possible answers related to Serbia and the assassination of
26.	Archduke Ferdinand.]
27.	M: So that is nationalism [*Mike offers direction for students with regard to a map*
28.	*they are using*]. All right, that's where the assassination occurs. So, here's where
29.	the assassination occurs. If you can link up Sarajevo to Bosnia on the map you have
30.	there, you can see the various different national and ethnic groups that comprise all
31.	the countries. We have a very complicated situation there where basically the
32.	Austrians, a Germanic people, are the dominant governing power there and they want
33.	to hold on to that empire. Meanwhile, all these groups want—what? [*Mike points to*
34.	*Serbia on the map.*]
35.	Student 4: Territory.
36.	Mike: Or, I mean the Serbs who are not a part of Serbia probably want what?
37.	Student 4: Their own country.
38.	M: Or to be…?
39.	Student 4: Or to be part of Serbia?
40.	Student 5: But wait, isn't the French desire to win back Alsace–Lorraine imperialism?
41.	M: Alsace–Lorraine? That's really both, because France actually recovered those
42.	places that were, I'm trying to remember which German state they were part of or
43.	if in fact they were their own German state back in the 16th century, but anyway they
44.	had been part of France for a long time. So, you could call that imperialism, although
45.	I would really liken it more to nationalism because it was sort of a point of offended
46.	pride for the French that they had lost these territories, so to restore national honor
47.	they had to recover them.

Mike does several things in this portion of his lecture that demonstrate how he transforms his content knowledge into interactive explanatory pedagogy. First, he requires students to participate in the lecture, calling on nonvolunteers as well as the class in general and rarely limiting involvement from anyone. Five times in the transcript above (lines 3–4, 12, 15, 18–19, and 33), Mike poses questions to the class. On three occasions Mike poses questions to specific students (lines 1, 7–8, 20–21). In addition, Mike engages two students in brief exchanges (lines 14–17 and 35–39). These interrogatives and exchanges (10 in a 3-minute and 45-second period of time) demonstrate Mike's commitment to an interactive teaching style.

This type of interaction cannot occur without Mike's close attention to managing the classroom dynamic. In the process of delivering his presentation, Mike maintains a "leadership" position over the content. When one student raises the issue of imperialism before Mike is ready for the class to consider this concept, he shifts the class back to nationalism without ignoring this student's foray into imperialism (lines 40–47). Mike easily handles a range of content-related questions; for example, when the student asks about imperialism (line 40) and the French desire to "win back" Alsace–Lorraine, Mike demonstrates his knowledge of the topic (lines 41–47).

Mike also demonstrates his ability to weave content around a central theme. Leinhardt (1993) calls this *Ikat*, noting that it is an "explanation in which the teacher makes indirect or passing reference to a concept or idea that is later extended and used in an elaborate way" (p. 48). In the lecture, Mike weaves threads about nationalism and imperialism together in his response to the unsolicited student question/comment on Alsace–Lorraine (lines 40–47). By returning to previously mentioned content on nationalism and connecting it to new content on imperialism, Mike creates a narrative that encompasses a wide range of content. This technique allows Mike to emphasize the connectedness of otherwise discrete pieces of information and demonstrates for students how to construct the types of connected arguments that they will need to make in their AP examination essays.

Additional Direct Preparation for the AP Examination through Writing

Given the nature of the AP examination, the writing process is of critical importance in Mike's class. In fact, essay writing and multiple-choice questions are the primary means by which Mike's students formally demonstrate their understanding of course objectives. His two-part assessment format clearly matches the AP examination format (80 multiple-choice questions and two essays, including DBQs and free-response questions). Mike's tests serve as direct and deliberate preparation for students to take the AP test. Although he spends considerable time talking about the format of the test and what students should expect, Mike does not *teach* the AP test itself. His practice is consistent with Chu's (2000) assertion that AP history teachers should help students see the connections between facts, instead of focusing too closely on specific examination questions and expectations. In an interview, Mike emphasizes the importance of writing and the need to approximate the format of the AP examination: "Both the U.S. history and the European exams have gone to formats that I feel like I need to incorporate so that it's not a surprise when they get in there to take that test. I want them to know what they are going to have to do."

Yet Mike deliberately avoids trying to guess what will be on examinations, while still trying to prepare his students as completely as possible. Consequently, his students' learning experiences are focused on *depth of knowledge about substantive content through writing*, instead of *breadth of content coverage*. Mike knows that he cannot cover all the content that the semester's syllabus includes. As the examinations approach, he talks about this dilemma: "There are only so many days that we have and we've got to cover 150 years of history in a month. We just cannot do that without some sacrifice [of content coverage]."

He also discusses the importance of cooperative work in his class as a means of pressuring students into thorough preparation:

> If I give them the questions ahead of time, I expect preparation. They would rather get [essay questions] cold, most of them would, because then they don't have to bother. But, giving them the questions in advance encourages them to form study groups and divide the questions up.

Mike typically gives students five or six questions at the beginning of each unit and requires that they work in groups to answer those questions throughout the 2-week unit. Mike prepares his students by discussing test item possibilities in broad terms and providing students with lists of potential essay topics.

Indirect Instruction and Preparation for the AP Examination through Thesis Presentation and Defense

In his AP European class, Mike requires that students present and defend answers to potential essay test questions. Students work in groups to write a thesis paragraph on the question, then each group prepares an outline for their collective argument. Group members decide whose thesis is the best and present it along with more detailed content from their outline. This process allows Mike to assert his control over what he teaches, but limits his ability to control how the content is taught. Mike describes the relationship between the thesis presentation/defense and the manner in which he controls the flow of content in his class:

> (With the) essay questions, I may have addressed some more than others, but mostly what I do is pull out essays that are not directly about things I really hit heavy on in class, and then these guys have to prepare responses. So, the multiple choice ends up being the measure of what I directly taught, and the essay is [the students] being able to apply information from what I taught...and from what they learned from their classmates and be able to write well.

Moreover, for each unit, students use a variety of primary and secondary source materials to prepare their presentations. Mike wants their work with primary source documents to approximate the types of analytical activities required to answer DBQs on the AP test.

Below I present an account of a thesis presentation and defense to demonstrate Mike's style of facilitating this activity. The transcript begins with a student reading her group's thesis paragraph.

Transcript of Teaching Episode; Time Approximately 12 Minutes, Student Names Omitted. (All of the students who speak in this transcript are members of one cooperative group)

1. Student 1: The question is, analyze the theory of mercantilism on domestic and
2. foreign policy of France from 1589 to 1715. In the 16th century, precious metals
3. had become a universal means for acquiring goods. Much of the gold and silver
4. circulation came from Spanish mines in the New World and stayed in the hands of
5. the Spanish and Hapsburg financiers. France needed a way to finance its growing
6. bureaucracy and army, so its leaders turned to mercantilism. By applying
7. mercantilism to both domestic and foreign policy, French leaders were able to
8. bring Spanish gold into their country to clone their own Spanish government.
9. [After the thesis paragraph is presented, other students use their outline to offer
10. more detailed commentary on the theory of mercantilism, French domestic policy,
11. and French foreign policy during this time period. These comments are omitted.]
12. M: All right, I'm curious about foreign policy and its connection to—Are we saying
13. that because of a belief in mercantilism, Henry IV pursued these policies and
14. Richelieu and Mazarin involved France in the 30 Years War? Is that what
15. we're saying?
16. Student 2: Pretty much.
17. M: Then I want to know the connection between, I mean how does that expand
18. mercantile policy or how does mercantile policy suggest that they should, for

Transcript of Teaching Episode; Time Approximately 12 Minutes, Student Names Omitted. (All of the students who speak in this transcript are members of one cooperative group)

19. example, involve themselves in the 30 Years War?
20. Student 2: The spoils of war, they gained resources in areas that they were
21. able to control and were able to use that for trade.
22. M: OK, so what areas? [Mike is cut off by another student.]
23. Student 1: They were also able to expand their borders and to enhance their own
24. significant wealth and then also by weakening Spain and the Hapsburgs who
25. controlled a lot of the precious metals on the continent.
26. M: I am still somewhat troubled by foreign policy issues, especially with Henry
27. IV and Richelieu, and you can throw Mazarin in there as well, compared to Louis
28. XIV. I think we have omitted something that is very significant about French
29. foreign policy, especially under Louis XIV, but no less so than the others, and that
30. would be the colonial aspect of the conflict. In other words, their possessions in
31. Canada and the Caribbean, which obviously would have an important role. The
32. role of colonies needs to be addressed. I don't think that your classmates would
33. be able to talk about, for example, how Henry IV's waging war in Spain to
34. expand French influence connected to mercantilism.
35. Student 3: Hold on a second while I get this figured out in my head [Student 3
36. pauses, then attempts to answer Mike's rhetorical question about Henry IV's war
37. with Spain] . . . so that the Spanish wouldn't have so much influence over French
38. domestic trade and their industries and things like that. Again, having more
39. resources and being able to do want they want.
40. [Very long pause while Mike thinks about this answer]
41. M: I don't know. I think that's very tenuous. I'm not wanting to be too picky on
42. this, but I am concerned that, _____ [student name omitted], for example, if
43. number six comes up on the die, that he's going to start talking about how France
44. waged war on Spain because they wanted some little area in the Pyrenees, which
45. is what they got, and that was motivated by Henry's belief in mercantilism. I
46. don't think that's a very strong case. Various trade agreements and commercial
47. treaties obviously would be right on, but we didn't really say much about that.
48. Who did he make commercial treaties with?
49. Student 3: You mean Henry IV?
50. M: Yeah.
51. Student 3: Spain, England, and the Ottoman Empire.
52. M: All right, so what was the nature of those?

Transcript of Teaching Episode; Time Approximately 12 Minutes, Student Names Omitted. (All of the students who speak in this transcript are members of one cooperative group)

53. Student 3: I really wasn't able to find much information on that.
54. M: Then I would suggest that perhaps we should have left the foreign policy of
55. Henry IV out of this. OK, there is ample evidence that Henry's foreign policy was
56. not driven by mercantilism. It was mostly internal, coming out of the wars of
57. religion. That was the issue. He wanted to solidify his own authority. That was
58. really the issue as far as eliminating Spanish influence in France and the same
59. with the Hapsburgs. It was not about economic theory or anything of the sort. It
60. was about establishing the authority of the monarchy at a time when it had been,
61. what for a hundred years, in question. You know Richelieu perhaps, but again
62. [pause], I don't think you're going to be able to answer these questions. Basically,
63. _____ [Mike refers to the student who was responsible for the foreign policy
64. portion of the group's work] should say, What does the alliance with Sweden, for
65. example, have to do with mercantilism?
66. Student 1: Were there any [long pause while group members discuss how they
67. should respond] ... In France, were explorers funded by the government or were
68. they working for anyone?
69. M: They absolutely all were sponsored by the government.
70. Student 1: Well, is this in the right period for that?
71. M: Absolutely [pause] _____ [Mike calls on a member of the group.] Do you
72. know who some of those people are? [very long pause, while students confer]
73. M: Basically, the whole of the French colonial empire was established in this
74. period, mostly concentrated in Quebec and Canada, but extending even in this
75. period into the Mississippi Valley. What was the nature of that arrangement? I
76. mean, what was going on over there?
77. Student 1: Trading, fur trading.
78. M: OK, essentially the fur trade.
79. Student 4: [This student offers a long new argument about French foreign policy that Mike summarizes for the class.]
80. M: Anybody want to respond to that? If you didn't hear, he's saying that Louis'
81. minister of war Louvois was really the architect of French foreign policy in terms
82. of these wars of expansion under Louis XIV, and that it was more out of France's
83. interest in expanding its borders and becoming the dominant power in Europe,
84. more so than adherence to some economic philosophy that drove French
85. expansion.

Engaging Pedagogy in an Advanced Placement European History Classroom

Transcript of Teaching Episode; Time Approximately 12 Minutes, Student Names Omitted. (All of the students who speak in this transcript are members of one cooperative group)

86.	Student 1: Well I think that's true to a certain extent, but I think you can also say
87.	that it certainly doesn't hurt mercantilism, and it certainly went with the idea that
88.	if you have more resources than you have access to, the better off you are. I mean,
89.	why expand out to the natural borders? It makes it easier to consolidate your
90.	domestic resources, because you don't have to worry about, you know, well up in
91.	the mountains there is this little Spanish land that's causing problems for farmers or
92.	something like that.
93.	M: Anybody else have a view on that? [pause—no response] It could also be
94.	argued that Colbert had a greater influence on Louis in the early part of his
95.	reign up to the 1680s or maybe 1670s and Louvois held sway after that. And so
96.	France, especially with domestic policy, it's interesting that we keep coming back
97.	to that, but domestic policy was clearly motivated by mercantilist goals. In other
98.	words, Louis bought into Colbert's mercantile philosophy completely.

Mike's primary goal for this exchange is to challenge students to develop autonomous historical arguments and to defend them in a public forum. He does not hesitate to remind students if they are not holding their own in the discussion and points out flaws in their argument. The student defense transcribed above hinges on Mike's initial query about the relationship between Henry IV's foreign policy and his belief in mercantilism. Thus, Mike repeatedly focuses students' ideas about how mercantilism influenced French domestic policy, but not foreign policy, during this historical time period. Mike makes this point or hints at it on six separate occasions (lines 13–16, 18–20, 27–35, 42–49, 55–66, and 94–99), doing so without direct confrontation but permitting the discussion to proceed with student input. By continually returning to the same point, Mike essentially reconstructs the group's thesis to take shape around what he views to be the most viable historical interpretation.

In Wilson and Wineburg's (1988) analysis of the practice of two experienced teachers, they noted that one operated in the background as the course instruction unfolded, and the other dominated class discourse. Mike demonstrates both of these styles as he directs students' remarks during thesis presentation activities. At times, he moves to the background, particularly during the students' presentation of their thesis paragraphs and their outlines. Often, Mike dominates the class, and his approach allows him to accommodate the competing demands of teacher content authority and student knowledge autonomy. Mike requires students to continue to think for themselves, but he also goes to great lengths to corral the content in places where he thinks the students are inaccurate in their assumptions or conclusions.

Mike also demonstrates his knowledge of history and his defense of his thesis through his public construction of an argument in opposition to the student group's argument. For example, Mike lays out his argument that French foreign policy had a "colonial aspect" and that the group has ignored this point (lines 27–35). Also, he does not reject the group's position, but instead uses the language of scholarly discourse to assert his disagreement. He states at one point (line 27) that he is "troubled" by the group's argument. Again, in line 42, he refers to a student's response as "tenuous." In line 55, Mike takes more control of the argument but refrains from completely discounting the group's position. He states that he "would suggest that perhaps we should have left the foreign policy of Henry IV out of this [discussion]" (lines 55–56). The last exchange of the transcript (lines 87–99) is an example of Mike's attempt to integrate students' interpretations with his own. After a student argues that Louis XIV's foreign policy may have benefited from an aggressive mercantilist approach, Mike responds by laying his competing argument by saying "it could also be argued…" (lines 94–95).

Mike does not have the last word in the discussion and prompts the class to provide clarification or add information (see lines 15–16, 81, and 94). These requests are not so much questions as they are appeals for students to participate in the discourse. Mike asks almost emphatically, "Is that what we're saying?" in lines 15–16 in order to prompt student engagement. He asks for more input on a student-posed argument in line 81, "Anybody want to respond to that?" Mike also asks specific questions on numerous occasions (lines 18–20, 23, 49, 53, 65–66, 72–73, and 76–77), but these questions are much more specific than his general call for participation.

In addition to encouraging class participation and intellectual deliberation, Mike wants the whole class to focus on the goal of success on the AP examination. He opens his response to the group's thesis by asking, "Are we saying that because of a belief in mercantilism that Henry IV pursued these policies…" (lines 13–14)? Again, Mike refers to the plural "we" when responding to the group's arguments (lines 16 and 55). He is particularly obvious about the relationship between the test (and, by extension, the AP examination) and the group presentation when he expresses concern that students will have problems on the test if they follow the reasoning of the group on the issue of France's war with Spain (lines 42–46).

Additional Indirect Preparation for the AP Examination through Discussion Groups and Seminars

Mike conducts discussion groups approximately once every 2 weeks. Depending on the content he is covering at the time, he conducts two to four different discussions for each 2-week period on very similar topics. The activity usually requires at least an entire 90-minute class period. The discussion groups offer moderately structured opportunities for students to engage in academic conversations, facilitated by Mike, in a format that facilitates meaningful exchange and demands thoughtful participation. Mike reflects about his discussion group approach:

> At first I did it with four kids working in a group, not really debating, certainly not formally debating, but they would have one side of an issue, such as how has slavery been overemphasized as a cause for the Civil War? So, four kids would have one side of the issue and another four would have the other side. They would also have to prepare some written material.

He does not expect the discussion to flow from a script and hesitates to view discussion as debate. Instead, the discussion, as he guides it, becomes an exploration of a problem.

Mike's discussion group technique has evolved over time. For example, after observing that non–group members were not participating in the discussions, he thought of ways to better engage them. Now he assigns the textbook as well as outside readings from publications such as *Taking Sides* for students to use in developing their discussion topics. This additional reading, he believes, gives students more scholarly material to work with and limits the students' ability to copy arguments from each other and from the assigned reading.

Closely related to the discussion group is a seminar format that Mike adapted from another teacher who used the method to foster Socratic discussion. He describes the activity:

> The kind of discussion that I wanted to have was based on the idea that kids would read things that were, if not provocative, then at least historical controversies, something like the atomic bomb topic that we were talking about today. But I face the problem that I guess everyone does. If I give the kids something that comes from the textbook or something I make a copy of, and if I have 25 kids in the room, five of them will have read it in the way I wanted it done and will be ready to discuss, and the other 20 either will not have done it at all or will have read part of it. So, I have no discussion at all. Then I sat down and brainstormed ways to improve that [situation] and one [idea] was to make kids present it, not to have debates, which I still do, but to have other kinds of formats that require all students to get a grade. In the seminar all students get a grade and that's the way to do it.

Mike limits the seminar to 10 students at a time. While one group is participating in a seminar, the other completes a self-guided activity (e.g., document analysis, reading). Seminars are conducted at a large, round table, and Mike makes every effort to formalize the experience. Ideally, Mike would like to have five students in a group and more seminars. However, he believes that the amount of content and testing in the AP European history course limits the time he can spend on seminars, so he conducts them only a couple of times each semester.

Beyond the Test: Post-Assessment Feedback Sessions

Another meaningful teaching method that Mike uses is a post-assessment feedback session. These activities are open-ended reconsiderations of students' test answers, conducted immediately after he has graded and returned tests. Mike looks for multiple-choice questions that were missed by more than 66% of the class. He also identifies essay questions on which large numbers of students scored poorly. Then, these questions become the subjects of an open debate about the students' responses or interpretations. Mike ordinarily dominates these post-assessment feedback sessions because he uses them also to carefully reteach the content with regard to specific weaknesses in his students' test answers.

During one feedback session, Mike talks with students about what they would have needed to do in order to receive the highest score possible on an essay about how gender issues affected any two women rulers or regents of the Enlightenment. Mike describes to his students what they should have included and mentions two weaknesses he has noticed in the papers:

> Actually, there are two big problems with these essays, the reasons we don't have higher scores than this. One was the tendency to talk an awful lot about one person, mostly Elizabeth, and very little about other people, whoever else it was you picked. Or, the other big problem was the issue of gender. So, if you talked about the accomplishments of Elizabeth or Isabella or Catherine, very little of it was made relevant to gender.

Mike also talks about specific problems students had in making analytical arguments, modeling how one grounds such arguments in substantive content. Mike balances what he sees as a dual responsibility: to help students develop specific knowledge of facts, associations, and interpretations such as those prioritized on the multiple-choice section of the AP test, and to prepare them to synthesize knowledge as they must do on the writing portion of the AP examination. For example, although he views Queen Elizabeth's reign as rich content that is valuable on its own merits, he also knows that students must understand how to construct an argument, and he uses information about Elizabeth's reign to emphasis this point.

Mike describes feedback sessions as "argument sessions, when the kids argue that their answers were as good as mine, hopefully using historical facts to support what they say." He understands that these meetings are going to be highly charged and sometimes emotional because grades and test points are involved. But he argues: "You can't turn high school students loose and say I'm going to let you argue with me for points and not expect them to say, 'well, the wording of this question made me think that....'"

CONCLUSION

Mike employs a mix of pedagogical approaches that involve writing, discussion groups, seminars, feedback sessions, lecture, thesis presentation/defense, and post-assessment feedback sessions that he believes engages students productively while also preparing them appropriately for the AP test. Lecture and thesis presentation/defense perhaps best illustrate Mike's direct approach to AP test preparation and to the development of his students' historical understandings.

With an engaging style, Mike tries to integrate didactic instruction with challenging questions. Through his discussion formats, Mike creates a negotiated space in the classroom that allows all students to address vital historical content. Although he closely manages the epistemological terrain of knowledge in the class, Mike is at times willing to cede his authority in order to encourage a contest over interpretations. Through successive units of study, he moves students in and out of meaningful and intense considerations of historical systems, events, themes, and structures. Although Mike's teaching practices primarily focus on helping his students to construct narrative understandings of the past, they also indirectly help students to "breach" the gap that Wineburg (2001) described between the school and the academy. That is, Mike requires students to engage primary source documents and scholarly writings, and he facilitates students' development of their historical reasoning skills.

The approaches Mike uses could be considered a mix of what Seixas (2000) has termed "enhanced collective memory" and "disciplinary" approaches to history. Seixas described the enhanced collective memory approach to teaching as a "best story" culled from people's collective memory about the past. He equated it with a "heritage" approach to history, which relies on lecture and discussion as the best methods of transmission for inculcating a commonly agreed-upon story about the past that is usually uplifting or progressive. Seixas characterized a disciplinary approach as more akin to the work of historians, in which students take tentative epistemological stances and interrogate conflicting versions of the past through document analysis. Mike combines these styles by controlling the flow of content and the topical ground from which interpretations are launched. Still, he allows students a certain amount of freedom to explore various interpretations.

Clearly, all of Mike's teaching in his AP European history class, of necessity, relates in some way to preparation of students for the AP examination. Mike focuses his instruction in practical ways to address what he knows will be useful on the exam. Yet he does not feel the need to take students on a "forced march" through a mass of content, lecturing day after day to ensure that students learn the factual material for the exam. Though he tends to come down more often on the side of "teacher-centered" approaches because of his own sense of pressure and responsibility to see that his students pass the AP test, he serves as a good example of an AP teacher who seems to have struck something of a balance between lecture and discussion, didacticism and engagement, and teacher authority and student intellectual responsibility.

REFERENCES

Chu, J. M. (2000). Preparing for the AP exam: The dangers of teaching to the test. *The History Teacher, 33*(4), 511–520.

Davis, O. L. (1997). Editorial: Beyond "Best practices" toward wise practices. *Journal of Curriculum and Supervision, 13*(1), 1–5.

DiLorenzo, R. (1999). Teaching Advanced Placement United States History in the urban, minority high school: Successful strategies. *The History Teacher, 32*(2), 207–221.

Gudmundsdottir, S. (1991). Ways of seeing are ways of knowing: The pedagogical content knowledge of an expert teacher. *Journal of Curriculum Studies, 23*(5), 409–421.

Henry, M. S. (1994). The AP United States history exam: Have free response essays changed in the last thirty years? *Social Education, 58*(3), 145–148.

Hill, J. (1999). The special role of the AP European history course. *The History Teacher, 32*(2), 269–275.

Leinhardt, G. (1993). Weaving instructional explanations in history. *British Journal of Educational Psychology, 63*, 46–74.

Lurie, M. N. (2000). AP U.S. History: Beneficial or problematic? *The History Teacher, 33*(4), 521–525.

McDiarmid, G. W. (1994). Understanding history for teaching: A study of the historical thinking of prospective teachers. In M. Carretero & J. F. Voss (Eds.), *Cognitive and instructional processes in history and the social sciences* (pp. 159–185). Hillside, NJ: Erlbaum.

Meckna, S. H. (1999). Teaching AP European history in a multiethnic setting. *The College Board Review, 188*, 18–25, 30–31.

Michael, H. (1991). Advanced placement U.S. history: What happens after the examination? *Social Studies, 82*(3), 94–96.

Neutuch, E. (1999). Advanced Placement United States history: A student's perspective. *The History Teacher, 32*(2), 245–248.

Rothschild, E. (1999). Four decades of the Advanced Placement program. *The History Teacher, 32*(2), 175–206.

Rothschild, E. (2000). The impact of the document-based question on the teaching of United States history. *The History Teacher, 33*(4), 495–500.

Seixas, P. (2000). Scweigen! Die kinder! or Does postmodern history have a place in the schools? In P. N. Stearns, P Seixas, & S. Wineburg (Eds.), *Knowing, teaching, and learning history* (pp. 19–37). New York: New York University Press.

Stoval, J. E. (2000). Document analysis as a tool to strengthen student writing. *The History Teacher, 33*(4), 501–509.

Traill, D. (1998). Team-teaching AP history and English. *Social Education, 62*(2), 77–79.

Vansledright, B. A. (1996). Closing the gap between school and disciplinary history? Historian as high school history teacher. *Advances in Research on Teaching, 6*, 257–289.

Wilson S. M., & Wineburg S. S. (1988). Peering through different lenses: The role of disciplinary perspectives in teaching history. *Teachers College Record, 89*(4), 525–539.

Wineburg, S. (2001). *Historical thinking and other unnatural acts: Charting the future of teaching the past.* Philadelphia: Temple University Press.

CHAPTER 11

A JOURNEY TOWARD WISER PRACTICE IN THE TEACHING OF AMERICAN HISTORY

Timothy Kelly
Bruce VanSledright

Good history, like good literature, beckons those who read it to understand the world. In the end, if deeply engaged, it asks that they more fully understand themselves. How do they arrive at that sort of deep self-understanding? Clearly, one way would be to engage school students in learning history through the exercise of wise teaching practice (Shulman, 1987). But what might that look like?

Common practice in teaching American history in U.S. schools consists of attempts to invite students to commit the story of the birth and development of the United States as a nation to memory (e.g., Cuban, 1991; Shaver, Davis, & Helburn, 1978). This story is typically revealed on the pages of standard U.S. history textbooks used in almost every classroom in the country. Teaching practice frequently entails asking students to read the textbook account. Teachers then reinforce the textbook account by pressing students with lectures and spoken-word reiterations of its contents. Assessments follow at various intervals in which students are required to recount what they ostensibly have learned by occasionally writing essays and more often by selecting the correct answers from a list supplied in multiple-choice format.

The goal of these practices appears to be tied up in imbuing students with knowledge of their common heritage, as participants in a collective memory that fills them with pride in their distinct (some would say exceptional) identities as Americans. Nations all over the world employ similar strategies in order to teach collective memory. U.S. schools, though, seem especially committed to the practice, if evidence from classrooms and assessment approaches is any indication (see reviews by Voss, 1998; Wineburg, 2001).

Those interested might ask, however, if these kinds of efforts engaged in by many history teachers constitute wise teaching practice in the domain of American history, if they indeed promote deep self-understanding. In response, some would argue that, by the shear breadth and history of the practice (see, e.g., Cuban, 1991, and Wineburg, 2001, on its resiliency across the 20th century), a "wisdom of resilient pedagogy" must be prevailing. And others would argue that the nation's children must be socialized into understanding "our" collective memory if they are to be knowledgeable citizens of the country (e.g., Schlesinger, 1992). As Schlesinger noted, without an insistence that children commit that collective understanding, that common heritage, to memory, we truly would be a disunited cluster of feuding tribes.

It is difficult to disagree with such claims. However, in this chapter, we ask if such common practice is enough for the nation's children and youth; if it is wiser than choosing from among other alternatives; and if teachers relying on typical and resilient pedagogies actually succeed in enticing learners to fully engage collective memory, to adequately appropriate their heritage, and to understand themselves. Also, we ask if there is truly a collective memory at all, or if collective memory is simply one group's effort to define it for everyone else.

In this chapter, the first author tells a story about changes in his history teaching practices over 8 years. We believe this story documents a journey toward wiser practice. We see it as an account that diverges from what typically occurs in history classrooms precisely because the first author was predisposed to question the existence of a common collective memory and, therefore, compelled to seek alternative ways of assisting his students in understanding their differing experiences with the American past. Before laying out this story (with interspersed analytic commentary by the second author), we briefly note some arguments about why efforts to employ typical teaching practices—and the curriculum coverage demands that underpin them—lack little wisdom of practice after all. These arguments form the centerpiece of our claim that wiser practice lies beyond the scope of efforts to teach collective memory alone.

LIMITATIONS OF COLLECTIVE MEMORY PRACTICES IN THE CLASSROOM

In 1987, Ravitch and Finn vigorously complained that U.S. high school students did not know their American history. After the authors had completed a secondary analysis of the first National Assessment of Education Progress (NAEP) in history and the humanities, they concluded that what students did not know about the story of their nation was categorically appalling. However, they were hardly the first to be so chagrined. Almost three-quarters of a century before, Bell and McCollum (1917) reached the same conclusion, following their survey of what U.S. grade school and college students could recall about their nation's story. In 1923, Eikenberry, replicating the Bell and McCollum study, echoed their concerns. In the early 1940s, the *New York Times* undertook a massive survey of U.S. students' capacity to recall ostensible facts about American history and found largely the same picture: Students were woefully ignorant. All told, such periodic surveys appeared to arrive at the same conclusions (see Wineburg, 2001, for a more thorough review).

Now, considering what research says about common teaching practice in the United States with respect to what these periodic surveys point out about students' knowledge, or in this case lack of knowledge, readers could reach at least one conclusion: The common practice of narrating the nation-building story in the hope of urging students to commit it to memory appears to fall considerably short of achieving its goal. Students simply do not emerge from the experience with detailed knowledge about the narrative, and therefore fail to acquire the hoped-for collective remembrance. Those who decry such failings seem to suggest that American history teachers simply are not working hard enough at their jobs and must be chastened into doing so. Still, as the quaint aphorism goes, more of the wrong medicine surely will not cure the patient.

Another way of thinking about the research on history teaching is that common practice turns out not to be very wise. Simply put, students of history apparently do not learn about their nation's past via a combination of curriculum-coverage demands, textbooks, teacher talk, and recall assessments. As Holt (1990) once ruefully observed, students under this regime categorize what they hear and read as other people's historical facts, ones that they do not need to take seriously because the talking heads in the classrooms and the textbook accounts fail to connect the nation's story to their lives in any meaningful way. In this sense, *wise practice* and *common practice* seem far from isomorphic.

What are students to think of the rendition of collective memory served up on the plate of classroom lectures and textbook accounts? Epstein's (1998, 2000) work is instructive in this regard. Her research with American students of European and African descent indicated that individuals in each group built different collective memories, much of them constructed from the same fabric many Americans think of as United States history. White and black students' heroes and choices about the most significant historical events actually were quite different, each harbored differing stories of national development prefigured by trust in sources that varied considerably. White students placed more credence in the stories told by their teachers and textbooks (despite the fact that they did not remember the details of these stories), whereas black students distrusted those very stories, and preferred instead the more personal (hi)stories narrated by their families and sources within their communities. Research by Seixas (1993) and Wertsch (1998) bear out similar results within other diverse populations and contexts.

Conclusions from this line of research into students' historical thinking and assessments of significance in American history suggest that, at least among those studied, a singular collective memory does not exist. Instead, collective *memories* abound. They vary from one cultural group to another and are influenced by family, community, genealogical tracings, and conceptions of identity. As Bodnar (1992) noted, an "official story" of, say, the nation state and its history may exist, but a host of competing "vernacular histories" ("collective memory" and "popular memory," according to Kammen, 1991) also compete with it. The students, then, to whom Holt (1990) referred may well be saying that they are deeply skeptical of the (hi)story advertised in the classroom because they are well aware of other equally credible competing (hi)stories that are not narrated there. In the presence of multiple memories, students wonder which they are to learn and which should be discarded. The poor NAEP results appear to be *prima facie* evidence about the choices students make. Here again, common practice and wise practice seem to diverge.

Given these limitations of common practice, what might be some wiser ways to proceed? By wiser, we are thinking of those practices that succeed at cultivating deeper historical and self-understandings among students who study this school subject. We are thinking about practices that nuance and texture students' historical consciousness in ways that make them likely to speak in cognitively sophisticated ways about the American past, prompt them routinely to relate details of narratives and counternarratives that convey both official and vernacular versions of events (Bodnar, 1992), and lead them to construct understandings that display the distinction that Lowenthal (1998) observed between celebratory *heritage* accounts and evidence-based *historical* ones.

Seixas's (2000) distinctions also are helpful here. Seixas maintains that there are at least three ways of engaging the past in history classrooms. The first is a stress on collective memory. By collective memory, Seixas refers to what we described as the substance of common practice: in the case of American history, the repeated telling of the univocal nation-building narrative. Second, Seixas describes the disciplinary approach that entails teaching students about how historical accounts are constructed; it is an investigative practice in which students are invited to learn the craft of building historical narratives drawn from the careful, systematic, critical analysis of the shards and traces of the past. Seixas also offers a third practice, the postmodern approach, through which students learn to ask why certain narratives are created, who benefits from their telling, and how the telling empowers some individuals and disempowers others.

In the portrayal that follows, the collective memory and disciplinary approaches are our primary concerns. This dual emphasis stemmed from the first author's journey from an understanding of the power of collective memory, to his dissatisfaction with it because of his growing conviction that a univocal collective memory is a myth, to his pursuit of the disciplinary approach as a means of developing wiser practices in teaching history by providing more depth and texture to his students' understanding of the American past and themselves. These changes in his teaching also involved navigating some structural and institutional constraints, what VanSledright and James (2002) called "external forces." In other words, he modified his practice as he faced these constraints.

At this point in the chapter, we shift to the first author's voice as he narrates the early days of his development as a history teacher.

TIMOTHY KELLY

The Journey Begins

My journey as a social studies educator began during my initial teaching internship in an urban public high school. As a beginning teacher, one of my biggest concerns was whether I knew enough about history, the so-called "litany of facts," to teach secondary students and to field their questions about the past. My worries about my own knowledge deficits subsided when I became aware of how little my students knew. I also discovered that my tenth-graders needed to work on basic skills (e.g., critical reading and organized writing), which I could teach using American history as the medium for learning. Students would need these skills, transferable to other areas of learning, for a thoughtful and productive life after high school.

In the course of experimenting with a basic-skills approach, I still hoped to introduce my students to some important ideas about American history and to help them connect with the past in meaningful ways. Rather than focus on covering material, however, I believed I could teach the subject matter and stimulate student interest by having them "do history," or at least begin to think and work like historians. I had a reasonably good grasp of the discipline, but my social studies methods professor showed me what history teaching might be if young people actually "did history" in the classroom.

I framed my first unit on the American Revolution and Founding Period around the concept of "competing visions" and organized the historical content around the essential question, "Were all people in America included in the founders' vision?" I introduced students to the founders' vision through a reading of the Declaration of Independence. The students decoded the Declaration by rewriting the document in language that was easier for them to understand. Although this exercise in translation would have been useful for even the most proficient readers, my students faced language barriers that demanded such scaffolding; many of them were recent immigrants whose families spoke a language other than English at home. After the students acquired a basic grasp of the language of natural rights and examined social and political aspects of the founding period, I introduced them to alternative accounts of American "freedom" and "liberty" contained in primary sources written by slaves, free blacks, women, and Native Americans.

Leading students to understand the diversity of experiences and divergent perspectives that emerge from a careful reading of historical documents from the founding period was one of my major goals for the unit. However, if I expected students to comprehend the historical meanings embedded in competing narratives, it was essential that I first explain what primary sources were and prepare the students to read them thoughtfully. "It is helpful to keep two big questions in mind in order to better understand a primary source document," I noted in a handout I created for the class. "What is the writer's point of view; who is s/he and why might s/he be writing this account?" *and* "What is the writer's main idea; what does s/he want to tell readers?" In addition to reading primary documents and understanding a range of historical narratives, students were responsible for learning the major concepts and facts central to this period. For example, they read about federalism in their textbook and took notes during presentations on the Great Compromise and the Three-Fifths Compromise.

In the second unit, I sought to capture the students' interest with a dramatic guiding question: "Was a growing America a nation with a glorious destiny, or was it a vicious, hungry monster?" Again, students examined multiple viewpoints through a variety of texts—primary sources by Native Americans and government officials, portraits and sketches, and scenes from the movie *Dances with Wolves*. I devoted a significant amount of time during the unit to guided writing-skills exercises. Utilizing a writing process rubric I created, students practiced developing thesis sentences with well-supported details and examples. I stressed the importance of organization, but also the inclusion of accurate historical concepts and well-reasoned arguments. I did not require students to quote specific documents, but I did expect them to draw from the sources in order to generalize about the multiple perspectives they examined.

The final unit involved a student-centered project that encouraged students to reflect on their own lived experiences in the context of U.S. immigration, both voluntary and forced. I introduced the five-chapter "Personal and Family History Project" using a quotation from Jesse Jackson (1992), "We all came on different boats. Some were captured for our labor; some were captivated by a vision of opportunity. We all have different histories, different dates to mourn and celebrate" (p. 148). The students' personally constructed (hi)stories were richer and more representative of their individual and collective experiences than any narrative recited by their teacher or textbook. By engaging students in personal research and interpretive writing, I hoped that the project would enable them to work "like" historians and produce narratives that were meaningful to them. I believed the project had the potential to foster self-understanding among the young people in my class, but also to encourage them to connect with something larger than themselves.

Having attended college in the early 1990s, I was influenced heavily by debates over multiculturalism and historical revisionism. I did not believe I had a political ax to grind, but I wanted to present another side to the traditional nation-building story, to give voice to alternative perspectives on the past found in the experiences of indigenous peoples, slaves, industrial laborers, and those in lost utopian movements. In this sense, my outlook reflected the moral framework of multiculturalism and revisionism. I also drew from my own experience as a secondary student. I remember my high school history teacher framing history as a struggle between the "haves" and the "have-nots." I learned early to champion the underdog and the downtrodden, even if I was not yet consciously aware of the political purposes of history.

Confronting Practice Constraints in the Early Teaching Years

In the early years of my professional experience, I continued to utilize a liberal, even neo-Marxist framework to conceptualize the past and to facilitate historical understanding among my students. This approach must have impressed some of them. At my first parent–teacher conference, one father asked, "You're not teaching that political correctness crap, are you?" He was referring to my unit on the Encounter of Two Worlds, in which I supplemented the textbook readings with excerpts from Columbus's log and native accounts of the conquest of the Americas. I was attempting to expose my students to a variety of perspectives in order to paint a more nuanced picture of the Columbian encounter. I reminded my students that, like the conflict between Cortes's band of conquistadores and the Aztecs of Tenochtitlan, history could be understood as a battleground of competing stories, images, and ideas. I was much more concerned that my students understand this concept than for them to memorize the names of European explorers and their New World exploits. That some parents did not agree with my position was evidence of the different interests vying for control of the past in my classroom.

During my first year as a full-time teacher, my anxieties about not knowing enough historical knowledge returned. I now had my own classroom and could no longer use my mentor teacher as a crutch. Also, unlike my situation in the internship experience, I would now be responsible for six classes and three preparations. Teaching at a parochial school meant that the curriculum guidelines likely were less constraining than what I imagined to be the case in some public institutions. Still, I accepted the tacit expectation that I should cover American history from its beginning to the present day. My department head encouraged me to get through my first year with my head above water. I relied on my undergraduate education, but I lost some of its disciplinary focus as I struggled to keep ahead of the students in the textbook, to learn new material, to write lesson plans, and to grade quizzes and tests. I was still very much a novice.

Teacher-directed lessons consumed a large part of typical weeks in my early years. For every unit, I provided students with an outline of the material (at first on the board and then, increasingly, as a photocopied set as I gained a firmer grasp of the material). My presentations usually were spirited and dramatic. I tried to tell good stories. Still, I stopped occasionally to stress key points or to ask students to make sense of the big picture. Each year, as time permitted, I added to those outlines, supplying anecdotes and a few primary sources I obtained from supplementary texts.

I used primary sources to enhance both the textual narrative and the one I provided: a soldier's account of a battle, a song or poem that memorialized an event, a famous speech. I hoped that these historical accounts would transport my students back in time, highlight the thoughts and actions of different people, and expose them to competing perspectives. Because many of my students did not rank history among their favorite subjects, I believed that my challenge was to provide them with a compelling story. I also believed that primary sources helped to serve that purpose—that they helped transform history into something real.

As much as I tried to make my courses interesting and exciting, my 11th-grade American history students predictably grew tired of listening to my lectures and taking notes. In fact, I often grew tired of hearing myself talk and, sometimes, I was not prepared to plow through another Roman numeral on the outline. At these moments, I might take more time to examine primary documents in detail. Of course, finding sources and making photocopies required an investment in time. Each year I added to my collection of documents. The more I read, and the more sources I accessed, the deeper my understanding of an event or period became. My units grew longer. However, less obtainable was that quixotic goal of covering the entirety of American history in a year.

By my third or fourth year of teaching, primary sources became more central to the learning experiences and assessments that I created. On unit tests I regularly gave students an excerpt (most often from a document we had read in class), asked them to identify who wrote it, and asked a series of questions about the meaning or historical relevance of the quotation. During our unit on the Civil War, I used songs of the Union and Confederacy to illustrate the opposing sides' rationales for fighting the war. On the test, students analyzed a line from Dixie or *Battle Hymn of the Republic*. They also identified the Emancipation Proclamation and determined why it was "an act of military necessity." Other sources included the Gettysburg Address, as a means by which students could analyze Lincoln's moral imperatives, and excerpts from Elisha Hunt Rhodes's diary (Rhodes, Rhodes, & Hunt, 1992), as a way for them to understand the changing nature of warfare and weapons technology.

This kind of work with primary sources was enhanced when I added *Ordinary Americans* (Monk, 1994) to the course syllabus. I also included historical fiction and short stories, such as Ambrose Bierce's (1994) *Chickamauga*, in order to discern historical meanings through literature and metaphor. I incorporated pictorial evidence offered by the advent of daguerreotypes and later photography. My students examined Matthew Brady's Civil War photographs and the muckraking photojournalism of Jacob Riis. I hoped these sources would bring history to life and enable my students not only to reason about the past, but to "feel" it as well.

In my early teaching years, history was not simply a neatly packaged product to be delivered to students during class sessions, but students played a limited role nonetheless. When I added the initial unit of study, "What is History?", my students were forced to wrestle a bit with some of the complex issues surrounding the production of historical knowledge. Still, I carried out (with the aid of the textbook) much of the interpretive work that is so central to history. Certainly, the students were part of this guided process, but most of the important questions already had been interpreted for them. Students simply needed to read assignments, take good notes, and remember the ideas for the test. My hope of leading students to do the analytic work of historians remained in the recesses of my mind, but as a secondary concern. Instead, my students and I studied history with a hammer; we pounded our way through each textbook chapter and unit outline.

As I reviewed the tests I wrote for those units, I noticed that they progressively became more objective in nature—long lists of names of Progressive reformers, New Deal acts, and World War II battles. My choices resulted from the pressure I perceived to get through more material more quickly as the end of the year approached. Still, I found time to immerse my students in what I considered particularly meaningful encounters with historical knowledge. For example, during the Great Depression and New Deal unit (in my third year), students took on the persona of someone living in the United States (e.g., a farmer in the Midwest, a New York stock broker, a black sharecropper in the South) and wrote a series of letters to FDR both before and after relevant New Deal acts were passed. I asked them to integrate their understanding of the context and results of the Depression, their knowledge of New Deal measures, and their readings of some primary source accounts in order to craft both human and historically accurate letters.

In other units I required that students "solve" hypothetical problems from the past and wrestle with contemporary issues. For example, they compared and contrasted the approaches taken by Booker T. Washington, W.E.B. DuBois, and Marcus Garvey to combat racism and improve the condition of African Americans in the United States. Afterward, they reasoned about which approach or combination of approaches they thought would be most effective for today's problems. Similarly, after reading a series of primary sources by Native Americans and mainstream white Americans and learning about the stages of federal government Indian policy, I asked students to create an ideal policy solution to the so-called "Indian problem." Increasingly, I demanded that they use specific examples from class discussions and their assigned readings to support their arguments.

Indeed, engaging students in disciplinary exercises and critical problem-solving projects required a heavy investment in time. I learned to drop entire chapters in the textbook from my teaching, choosing instead to go into more depth with less material. As a result, each year I covered less of the chronological scope of American history. My practice became a departmental and then a faculty-room joke when it became known that I never got beyond World War II. I learned to hold my tongue in the same way that I did when my internship mentor regularly mocked me: "Come on, do you really believe *less is more*?" As I gained valuable classroom experience and became more knowledgeable about history and my teaching craft, I became increasingly determined to emphasize depth and complexity of understanding over the lures of breadth of coverage, despite the pressure that I felt to cover the vast span of U.S. history.

BRUCE VANSLEDRIGHT RESPONDS

Analyzing the Early Teaching Years

In Timothy Kelly's account of his early teaching experience, readers can recognize a teacher who is conscious of the constraints of singular collective memory. He observed that, due to the influence of multicultural and revisionist histories he read and heard about as an undergraduate, he was interested in showing his students that different stories could be told about the American past, that these stories were sometimes in conflict, and that they could be construed as contested terrain between the "haves" and the "have-nots." In this sense, he already appeared to possess a more finely textured and nuanced sense of American history than many history teachers who rely on common practice. He also carried with him a rudimentary understanding of history's disciplinary practice, with which he had worked in his internship under the tutelage of his methods-course professor. His different types of knowledge about the past and about disciplinary practice shaped his early classroom efforts, but they did so unevenly.

Part of the reason for this, he noted, was the pressure he perceived to make his practice more consistent with what typically went on in his first teaching assignment. There, a parent once chided him for engaging in what he thought was history in the political–correctness vein. Also, his colleagues conveyed to him the need to cover adequately the span of history he was charged to teach. Telling contested stories and engaging students in learning experiences around answering the question "What is history?" variously caused some parents to question his efforts and resulted in jovial criticism from colleagues, both of whom served as significant socialization agents with respect to his pedagogical practice. He experimented with approaches to get around these constraints, but in many ways, he was forced to return to what is common practice: retell the textbook narrative, do it quickly, assess accordingly, and move on.

However, Kelly's disposition to and conviction about the importance of helping his students understand the contested nature of collective memory, and his interest in providing some opportunities to illustrate disciplinary practice to his students, made his teaching unlike what is commonly seen. Nonetheless, the constraints on his efforts were real. He felt the influence of those who would socialize him into the profession. He found general support for his practice but little specific encouragement from within his immediate teaching culture to engage fully his convictions and interests. As a result, the latter languished, at least until he reached beyond that culture to the accumulating research on teaching and learning history. There he found support and a vocabulary with which to enhance his practice in ways consistent with what he was attempting to accomplish in the history classroom. In the next section, we return to his journey and again to his voice.

TIMOTHY KELLY

Evolution in Knowledge and Pedagogy

My teaching practice over the first 5 years developed as I worked to resolve the puzzles and problems arising from my use of a variety of approaches to teaching history. Informal conversations with colleagues also contributed to my professional growth; however, the schedule of the school day allowed neither the time nor the occasion for the kind of collaborative inquiry or extended dialogue that might have facilitated reflective practice. On the other hand, I took graduate classes on a part-time basis in order to explore some of the questions prompted by my years of experience and experimentation in teaching history. In particular, I sought to gain a deeper understanding of history's disciplinary practice and to translate that knowledge into more meaningful learning experiences for students. In that sense, I was traveling a path designed to overcome constraints in my teaching and to make my practice wiser.

I had explored history's disciplinary landscape in varying degrees since my initial teaching internship. However, not until I took a graduate course entitled "Recent Research in Social Studies Education with Implications for Teaching" did I begin to traverse the complicated terrain associated with historical thinking. This course challenged me to extend my thinking and to reflect on my teaching practice in light of recent scholarship in the field. The seminar comprised masters and doctoral students, most of whom were current or former history and social studies teachers. The course readings, class discussions, and writing assignments prompted me to think even more critically about my teaching and my students' learning of history. The experience that semester both enlightened and unsettled me. On the one hand, the disciplinary understandings I gained from my study of history education research afforded me the conceptual tools to foster the development of historical thinking in my students; at the same time, the challenges I faced in my efforts to develop a disciplinary approach made me realize that my practice remained a work in progress.

Two of the particular benefits of the seminar experience were that it stimulated me to clarify my purposes for implementing my initial "What is

History?" unit, and to refine those lessons aimed at awakening my students' understanding of the nature of historical knowledge. For example, when I asked my 11th-grade U.S. history classes to define history, the students typically responded that it was "what happened in the past." Their comments seldom reflected an understanding of the difference between history as a past event and history as an interpretative and socially constructed account. Students' descriptions of their experiences with conventional school history revealed the origins of their rudimentary epistemology. History classes, they remarked, usually were "boring"; teachers demanded "too much memorization" of facts, names, and dates. They seldom ranked history among their favorite school subjects.

After completing the assigned readings on the seminar syllabus and talking with the other history teachers in the class, I discovered that my students' responses reflected prevalent, although naive, conceptions about the structure of the discipline of history. Especially, VanSledright's (1997) study expanded my thinking. In it, he explored young people's beliefs about why they study history in American schools. He explained that "students understand history as a fixed tale, a body of inert facts" (p. 550). Similarly, researcher-practitioner Bain (2000) related the kinds of assumptions and beliefs his students expressed about history in series of journal entries. He noted that their responses revealed a "static, formulaic vision of history. The past is filled with facts; historians retrieve those facts; students memorize the facts; and all this somehow improves the present" (p. 237). My thinking about the results of these kinds of studies reinforced for me the importance of gauging students' understanding of the discipline and locating the source of their misconceptions.

I also discovered that Bain and VanSledright had created mental models of the discipline with their students in the course of conducting their research projects. Bain (2000) guided his students to "develop a graphic record of their understanding of the discipline" and led them to use this concept map to locate classroom activities within a disciplinary frame (p. 339). Before engaging his fifth-graders in a historical investigation of Jamestown's Starving Time, VanSledright (2002) took his students through a step-by-step process for being what he called "good historical detectives" (p. 6). These examples helped me to refine a "four-step process of discovering and recreating the past" that I had developed a few years earlier.

Prior to my experience in this research seminar, I had taken my students through the process by which historians work with evidence to piece together an account that is "as close to the truth as possible." The seminar encouraged me to develop this component of the "What is History?" unit even further. For example, in a follow-up exercise, I asked my students, "What prevents us from arriving at the absolute truth about the past?" Answers to this question touched on the following issues: the significance of lost, missing, altered, or destroyed evidence; the particular biases and perspectives contained in primary sources; the beliefs and interpretive license historians bring to the act of reconstructing the past; and, finally, the idea that history is always being changed, rewritten, or better yet, reevaluated as a result of new findings and interpretations.

As I continued this line of instruction, my students and I discussed the ways we might overcome several issues or problems: learning to critically read primary sources in order to detect biases and subtexts; to gather evidence from a variety of viewpoints and perspectives; and to be aware of the biases that influence both historians and students as they attempt to reconstruct and interpret the past. As a result of my seminar experience, I renewed my commitment to guide students toward a more complex and dynamic view of history, or to borrow from Bain (2000) to engage them in epistemic acts. I became convinced that the creation of mental models of the discipline was an effective tool for problematizing the idea of history and for leading students to "disturb" their comfortable notions of history as a ready-made product, and thus, a completed process.

I ended the "What is History?" unit by marshalling my students to act like historians, explaining that I was responsible for engaging them in disciplinary exercises and learning projects. Looking back at the units that followed, however, I now notice that I made only sporadic references to the mental model of the discipline that we developed together. The research seminar continued to challenge me to better integrate disciplinary methods with the teaching and learning of history's substantive knowledge. Thus, I began to post the concept maps in plain view and to encourage students to place their efforts within that disciplinary framework. I became more conscious of treating the initial unit not as an end in itself, but as a first step toward the development of the cognitive processes that characterize historical thinking.

Although some recent research supported the kind of teaching and learning that was occurring in my classroom, it did not remove the pressure that I felt to cover the vast span of American history. In fact, that constraint never fully disappeared. However, the readings and discussions I had been using provided me with a broader context in which to think about that faculty room joke concerning my coverage of American history. I was able to place my own struggles with breadth versus depth within a larger debate taking place in the research community and the much larger national political arena. I became familiar with the arguments of Ravitch and Finn (1987), who lamented the factual knowledge deficits of U.S. history students. I also studied the contemporary movement toward tighter state-level bureaucratic control over curricula and new, stricter testing standards, and examined how these external forces impact what is being taught in classrooms (Cornbleth, 2002).

I was encouraged professionally by the research of Kobrin (1996), Segall (1999), and Seixas (1996), who critiqued the collective memory approach to learning history and argued, instead, for the development of students' disciplinary understandings and historical thinking. At one point, I introduced sourcing, corroboration, and contextualization to my students prior to my enrollment in the research course. Still, I did not possess a rich, technical vocabulary until I read Wineburg (1991, 2001) and Stahl, Hynd, Britton, McNish, and Bosquet (1996). After studying the implications of this scholarship, I began to direct my students to examine every documentary source with an eye toward determining its reliability. If they made a statement about a historical fact or generalized about an event or period, I asked them to support their arguments with evidence. This mode of questioning and evidence gathering made an impact on several students. For example, after I gave a brief presentation, one student asked me where I got my information and wanted to know on what grounds I was making my claims. His reaction was exactly what I wanted: critical analysis and healthy skepticism. Still, I also identified with the concerns of researchers who did not want students to develop an unwavering cynicism or to blindly deny the veracity of everything they heard or read.

Toward the end of the university semester and in the middle of the teaching year, I developed a unit project that I hoped would help my 11th-grade U.S. history students to move beyond the familiar practices of recitation common to previous papers and tests. I asked them to construct an interpretive essay of the period between 1830 and 1850 in U.S. history. The essay prompt read, "The history of the United States from 1830 to 1850 may best be described as a story of positive growth and steady progress for American civilization." The assignment called upon students to discuss/defend/refute this statement in the context of at least two or three historical developments or concepts we had studied previously: U.S. territorial expansion and the doctrine of Manifest Destiny; the growth of the U.S. economy, transportation, industry, and population; federal government Indian policy; and the Mexican–American War.

What was different about this essay prompt was how I instructed my students to respond. I asked them to "utilize [their] textbook, class notes, *Ordinary Americans* (Monk, 1994), the *Us and Them* (Bullard, 1995) articles, and any primary sources I had provided in class when crafting [an] argument." I encouraged them to rely mostly on primary source materials in order to interpret this period in American history and the variety of perspectives that exist. I also directed them to introduce, cite, and analyze all quoted materials. Here, I thought, was history: the building of interpretations from the remnants of the past. Finally, I was asking my students to continue the historical work I had introduced in my initial "What is History?" unit.

I shared the essay prompt with my department head and explained my goal of leading students to develop a personal interpretation using source documents. He thought that the idea was "great," but wondered if the students would be able to accomplish the task. I explained that I had worked with my students on critically reading primary sources, but had not given them extensive practice in the construction of written arguments from documentary evidence. I left the conversation worried about my department head's response and even more bothered that I had not prepared my students to craft written interpretations of the past that go beyond simple narration. Frustrated, I cancelled the assignment (which I believe delighted my students) and replaced it with a test, mostly objective and short answer in nature.

My experience in the research seminar had influenced my decision to assign interpretive essays in the first place. That experience also helped me to make sense of the subsequent disappointment associated with my decision not to follow through with it. My frustrations no longer stemmed from my inability to master historical knowledge or cover American history in its entirety. I now faced new challenges, mainly the application of a disciplinary approach to history instruction and the preparation of my students to investigate and construct interpretations of the past. I learned that presenting students with multiple texts was an insufficient change in my practice. Clearly, disciplinary knowledge must be taught and practiced in the classroom. VanSledright's (2002) study also provided substantial evidence of what is involved in leading a classroom of student historians to investigate and interpret historical events. I continued to utilize the research I had read in the seminar to critique my teaching practice and to improve the disciplinary exercises that I crafted for my students.

My interest in having adolescents "do history" stretches back to my initial internship. In the 9 years since that experience, I have deepened my understanding of the discipline and intensified my resolve to engage students in historical investigation and interpretation. Furthermore, I now can articulate the value of a disciplinary approach for history education, because I have become increasingly clear about its goals and have integrated these with my larger purposes for teaching social studies. In the research seminar I learned that conventional school history promotes consensus accounts of American history that imply a unified national heritage that universally links all Americans together (see Epstein, 1998; Levstik & Barton, 1998). However, I also came to believe that a disciplinary approach to learning history does not preclude all notions of shared national identity and experience. Nonetheless, it does open the door for alternative accounts of the past that are located in the personal experiences and vernacular histories of the students themselves. I have discovered that this approach, reflectively employed, may also cultivate respect for diversity and democratic principles by providing students the tools to critique their culture and society. A disciplinary approach to teaching history, as I envision it, accomplishes a central goal so often associated with social studies education: the development of an independent, thoughtful citizenry. In this sense, I believe that my practice did become "wiser," despite the constraints that I continued to face.

BRUCE VANSLEDRIGHT RESPONDS

Assessing the Journey to Date

Teaching about contested collective memories by narrating them and providing opportunities for students to *do* history while simultaneously achieving curriculum coverage objectives proved to be a daunting challenge in Timothy Kelly's continuing journey as a teacher. Curriculum coverage constraints often worked at cross-purposes with his other goals. He sought ways to resolve those tensions as best he could. His strategy appeared to turn on his strong embrace of what Seixas (2000) calls the disciplinary approach, one for which he found support in the research literature. He seemed to reason that wiser practice would encourage his students' development of their own capacity to analyze and critique the stories told about the American past. When students are armed with disciplinary tools and historical thinking strategies, they can learn to ferret out contested collective memories, to read them for what they are, and to understand more deeply the nature of a contested past.

In traversing this path, however, Kelly encountered additional constraints on his practice. As he has observed, he needed time and concerted energy to teach students how to think historically because many of them had never been asked to do so (something Bain [2000] and VanSledright [2002] also encountered in their researcher-practitioner studies). To understand history, as we have noted, beckons teachers and students to understand themselves. But such self-understanding is difficult; it demands serious thinking, analysis, and reflection, and it entails, as Wineburg (2001) claims, a host of cognitive activities that are "unnatural acts." The disciplinary approach has the potential to teach students how to navigate these unnatural acts and to approach self-understanding in ways that sole reliance on common practice and collective memory cannot provide. In this sense, we would argue, the disciplinary approach that Kelly has begun to employ is a form of wiser practice.

The constraints of common practice and of curricular obsessions with collective memory no doubt will remain. What distinguishes Kelly's case is his disposition and commitment to offer his students more than a singular collective memory rendition of the American past. Certainly, his disposition and commitment likely have their roots in his undergraduate experiences in both history and pre-service teacher education. What Kelly still lacked after college—which also functioned as a constraint—was additional knowledge of the discipline, a vocabulary for expressing it, and some type of support structure for embracing it in the classroom. In the research literature and in the graduate seminar room, he found the beginnings of all three of these, and was thus able to experiment further with his practice. He moved toward overcoming the knowledge constraint. And, in turn, he began to recognize pathways for navigating the structural and institutional constraints that he encountered.

Wiser practice in Kelly's case appears to turn on a combination of factors: deeper knowledge of subject matter, immersion in a rich research literature, and a conviction and disposition to improving practice. It also implies a commitment to use the subject and its disciplinary *accoutrements* to cultivate a deeper self-understanding in students. Through this understanding, Kelly hopes, his students can fully participate in the world rather than merely be passive spectators of it.

REFERENCES

Bain, R. (2000). Into the breach: Using theory and research to shape history instruction. In P. Stearns, P. Seixas, & S. Wineburg (Eds.), *Knowing, teaching, and learning history National and international perspectives* (pp. 331–352). New York: New York University Press.

Barton, K., & Levstik, L. (1998). "It wasn't a good part of history": National identity and students' explanations of historical significance. *Teachers College Record, 90*, 478–513.

Bell, J. C., & McCollum, D. (1917). A study of the attainments of pupils in United States history. *Journal of Educational Psychology, 8*, 257–274.

Bierce, A. (1994). Chickamauga. In C. Ward (Ed.), *Civil War stories* (pp. 41–46). New York: Dover Publications.

Bodnar, J. (1992). *Remaking America: Public memory, commemoration, and patriotism in the twentieth century.* Princeton, NJ: Princeton University Press.

Bullard, S. (Ed.). (1995). *Us and them: A history of intolerance in America.* Montgomery, AL: Southern Poverty Law Center.

Cornbleth, C. (2002). What constrains meaningful social studies teaching? *Social Education, 66*(3), 186–190.

Cuban, L. (1991). History of teaching in social studies. In J. Shaver (Ed.), *Handbook of research on social studies teaching and learning* (pp. 197–209). New York: Macmillan.

Eikenberry, D. H. (1923). Permanence of high school learning. *Journal of Educational Psychology, 14*, 463–481.

Epstein, T. (1998). Deconstructing differences in African American and European American adolescents' perspectives on United States history. *Curriculum Inquiry, 28*(4), 397–423.

Epstein, T. (2000). Adolescent perspectives on racial diversity in U.S. history: Case studies from an urban classroom. *American Educational Research Journal, 37*(1), 185–214.

Holt, T. (1990). *Thinking historically: Narrative, imagination, and understanding.* New York: College Entrance Examination Board.

Jackson, J. (1992). A call to bold action. In D. Hazen (Ed.). *Inside the L.A. riots: What really happened—and why it will happen again* (pp. 148–150). Los Angeles: Institute for Alternative Journalism.

Kammen, M. (1991). *Mystic chords of memory: The transformation of tradition in American culture.* New York: Vintage.

Kobrin, D. (1996). *Beyond the textbook: Teaching history using documents and primary sources.* Portsmouth, NH: Heinemann.

Lowenthal, D. (1998). *The heritage crusade and the spoils of history.* Cambridge, UK: Cambridge University Press.

Monk, L. R. (Ed.). (1994). *Ordinary Americans: U.S. history through the eyes of everyday people.* Washington, DC: Close Up Publishing.

Ravitch, D., & Finn, C., Jr. (1987). *What do our 17-year-olds know? A report on the first national assessment of history and literature.* New York: Harper & Row.

Rhodes, E. H., Rhodes, R. H., & Ward, G. C. (Eds.). (1992). *All for the union: The Civil War diary and letters of Elisha Hunt Rhodes.* New York: Vintage Books.

Schlesinger, A., Jr. (1992). *The dis-uniting of America: Reflections on a multicultural society.* New York: W.W. Norton.

Segall, A. (1999). Critical history: Implications for history/social studies education. *Theory and Research in Social Education, 27*(4), 358–374.

Seixas, P. (1993). Historical understanding among adolescents in a multicultural setting. *Curriculum Inquiry, 23*(3), 301–327.

Seixas, P. (1996). Conceptualizing the growth of historical understanding. In D. Olson & N. Torrance, (Eds.), *The handbook of psychology in education.* Oxford, UK: Blackwell.

Seixas, P. (2000). Schweigen! die kinder! or, does postmodern history have a place in the schools? In P. Stearns, P. Seixas, & S. Wineburg, (Eds.), *Knowing, teaching, and learning history National and international perspectives* (pp. 15–37). New York: New York University Press.

Shaver, J., Davis, O.L., & Helburn, S. (1978). *An interpretive report on pre-college social studies education based on three NSF-funded studies.* Washington, DC: National Council for the Social Studies.

Shulman, L. (1987). Knowledge and teaching: Foundations of a new reform. *Harvard Educational Review, 57,* 1–22.

Stahl, S., Hynd, C., Britton, B., McNish, M., & Bosquet, D. (1996). What happens when students read multiple source documents in history? *Reading Research Quarterly, 31*(4), 430–456.

VanSledright, B. (1997). And Santayana lives on: Students' views on the purposes for studying American history. *Journal of Curriculum Studies, 29*(5), 529–557.

VanSledright, B. (2002). *In search of America's past: Learning to read history in elementary school.* New York: Teachers College Press.

VanSledright, B., & James, J.H. (2002). Constructing ideas about history in the classroom: The influence of competing forces on pedagogical decision making. In J. Brophy (Ed.), *Advances in Research on Teaching* (Vol. 9, pp. 263–299). Stamford, CT: JAI Press.

Voss, J. (1998). Issues in the learning of history. *Issues in Education, 4*(2), 163–210.

Wertsch, J. V. (1998). *Mind as action.* New York: Oxford University Press.

Wineburg, S. (1991). On the reading of historical texts: Notes on the breach between school and academy. *American Educational Research Journal, 28*(3), 495–519.

Wineburg, S. (2001). *Historical thinking and other unnatural acts: Charting the future of teaching the past.* Philadelphia: Temple University Press.

ABOUT THE AUTHORS

Elizabeth Anne Yeager is Associate Professor of Social Studies Education at the University of Florida. She is also editor of *Theory and Research in Social Education*. Her research interests focus on the teaching and learning of history and on civic education.

O. L. Davis, Jr., is Catherine Mae Parker Centennial Professor of Curriculum and Instruction at The University of Texas at Austin and a Kappa Delta Pi Laureate. His research and writing focus on curriculum history (England and United States); social studies in schools; research studies in the teaching of school history; curriculum development, practice, and theory; educational policy analysis; and social studies education. He is the former editor of the *Journal of Curriculum and Supervision*.

Keith C. Barton, a former elementary and middle school teacher, is Professor in the Division of Teacher Education at the University of Cincinnati. His research focuses on the history curriculum and on children's understanding of the past.

Andrea S. Libresco is Special Assistant Professor in the Department of Curriculum and Teaching at Hofstra University, where she teaches social studies methods. Her positions in the public schools have included social studies department chair, lead teacher for elementary social studies, and classroom teacher of social studies for fifteen years. She was named Long Island Secondary Social Studies Teacher of the Year in 1997.

Diane Yendol Hoppey is Assistant Professor in the School of Teaching and Learning at the University of Florida. Her research focuses on teacher professional development within a context of high stakes testing.

ABOUT THE AUTHORS

Jennifer Jacobs is a doctoral student in the School of Teaching and Learning at the University of Florida. Her research interests focus on professional development, teacher education, and critical pedagogy.

Keith Tilford is a doctoral student in the Department of Educational Administration at the University of Florida. His research focuses on the development of professional learning communities, middle school, and social studies education.

Mary Lee Webeck is Assistant Professor of Curriculum and Instruction (Social Studies Education) in the Department of Curriculum and Instruction at The University of Texas at Austin. She conducts research on civic learning, teacher development, Holocaust education, philanthropy and education, and arts-based approaches to learning.

Cinthia Salinas is an Assistant Professor of Curriculum and Instruction (Social Studies Education) at The University of Texas at Austin in Curriculum and Instruction. She conducts research on high school migrant students, social studies and high stakes testing, and citizenship.

Sherry L. Field is Professor of Curriculum and Instruction (Social Studies Education) at The University of Texas at Austin. Her current research interests focus on elementary social studies curriculum and instruction, young children's thinking about social studies, and civic learning.

Stephanie van Hover is Assistant Professor of Social Studies Education in the Curry School of Education at the University of Virginia. Her research interests include the teaching of history, beginning teachers, and the influence of standards and accountability on instructional decision-making.

Walter Heinecke is Associate Professor of Educational Evaluation and Policy Studies in the Curry School of Education of the University of Virginia. His research interests include the relation between policy and educational practice, educational accountability, standards and testing, and the evaluation of educational technology.

S. G. Grant is Associate Professor of Social Studies Education at the University at Buffalo. His research interests lie at the intersection of curriculum and assessment policy and teachers' classroom practice.

Diana Hess is Assistant Professor of Curriculum and Instruction at the University of Wisconsin-Madison. She researches how young people learn how to deliberate highly controversial political and legal issues.

About the Authors

Bruce E. Larson is Associate Professor of Secondary Education and Social Studies at Western Washington University. His research interests follow three integrated strands: teacher education, social studies education, and computer technology related to curriculum development and classroom instruction. He has also conducted research on classroom discussion.

John K. Lee is currently Assistant Professor and Coordinator of the social studies teacher education program at Georgia State University. His teaching and research interests include social studies pedagogical content knowledge and digital history.

Timothy Kelly is a doctoral candidate in the Department of Curriculum and Instruction at the University of Maryland, College Park. A former secondary social studies teacher, he is now a research assistant on a Teaching American History Grant Project, *The Corps of Historical Discovery*, funded by the U.S. Department of Education.

Bruce VanSledright is Associate Professor of Curriculum and Instruction at the University of Maryland, College Park. He is Evaluation Project Director for *The Corps of Historical Discovery*. Also a former social studies teacher, he studies and writes about the teaching and learning of American history.

Printed in the United States
69859LV00001B/104